D1245733

Cervantes' *Don Quixote*

A CASEBOOK

CERVANTES'
Don Quixote

◆ ◆ ◆

A CASEBOOK

Edited by
Roberto González Echevarría

OXFORD
UNIVERSITY PRESS

2005

OXFORD
UNIVERSITY PRESS

Oxford University Press, Inc., publishes works that further
Oxford University's objective of excellence
in research, scholarship, and education.

Oxford   New York
Auckland   Cape Town   Dar es Salaam   Hong Kong   Karachi
Kuala Lumpur   Madrid   Melbourne   Mexico City   Nairobi
New Delhi   Shanghai   Taipei   Toronto

With offices in
Argentina   Austria   Brazil   Chile   Czech Republic   France   Greece
Guatemala   Hungary   Italy   Japan   Poland   Portugal   Singapore
South Korea   Switzerland   Thailand   Turkey   Ukraine   Vietnam

Published by Oxford University Press, Inc.
198 Madison Avenue, New York, New York, 10016

www.oup.com

Oxford is a registered trademark of Oxford University Press

Library of Congress Cataloging-in-Publication Data
Cervantes' Don Quixote : a casebook / edited by Roberto González Echevarría.
p. cm. —(Casebooks in criticism)
Includes bibliographical references and index.
Contents: Cervantes' harassed and vagabond life / Manuel Durán—The enchanted
Dulcinea / Erich Auerbach—The genesis of Don Quixote / Ramón Menéndez Pidal —
Canons afire : libraries, books, and bodies in Don Quixote's Spain / Georgina Dopico Black
—Literature and life in Don Quixote / E. C. Riley—Don Quixote: story or history? / Bruce
W. Wardropper—Linguistic perspectivism in the Don Quijote / Leo Spitzer—Don
Quixote : crossed eyes and vision / Roberto González Echevarría—The narrator in Don
Quijote : Maese Pedro's puppet show / George Haley—Self-portraits / Miguel de Cervantes.

ISBN-13 978-0-19-516938-6

1. Cervantes Saavedra, Miguel de, 1547–1616. Don Quixote I. González Echevarría,
Roberto. II. Series.

PQ6352.C37 2005
863'.3   dc22   2004063569

Printed in the United States of America
on acid-free paper

To the cherished memory of Turan Onat:
gentle soul, true friend, fellow aviator

Credits

Acknowledgments

I want to thank first of all Claude Rawson, my distinguished colleague from the English department at Yale, who recommended to Oxford University Press that I prepare one of its new series of "casebooks." His suggestion was heeded by Elissa Morris, editor at the Press, who saw me through the elaboration and completion of the project. She and I were ably supported first by Jeremy Lewis and later by Eve Bachrach.

This collection is derived from the reading assignments for two of my courses at Yale University: first, the DeVane Lectures, which I delivered in the spring of 2002, and my undergraduate class on *Don Quixote*, particularly the one given in the fall of 2003. My superb teaching assistants, Anke Birkenmaier and Isabel Jaén Portillo for the first course and Antonio Carreño Rodríguez for the second, were of invaluable help in assessing the value of each of the pieces included as coursework. This book closely resembles the packet of readings the students used in both instances. The feedback from all of them was extremely useful to me. My colleagues Vera Kutzinski, now of Vanderbilt University, but earlier at Yale, and Rolena Adorno, of our Spanish and Portuguese department, performed the most arduous tasks. Vera provided me with an English version of my own piece, written and published originally in Spanish. Rolena helped me "fix" the extant translation of Ramón Menéndez Pidal's essay. This was a labor-intensive job that I and all who benefit from reading that piece should be grateful to her for. Lourdes Sabé, also a colleague in Spanish, and above all, Sandra Guardo, always my guide and savior, helped me prepare the manuscript of the introduction. Charlotte W. Rogers provided great help in the final stages of the manuscript. I thank them all and, of course, assume responsibility for all the errors and shortcomings the reader may find.

The Cervantes portrait that was chosen for the paperback edition was done by Gregorio Ferro, a Spanish artist born in Santa María de Lamas (La Coruña) in 1742. He died in Madrid in 1812. In addition to this portrait of Cervantes, he produced several illustrations for the 1780 edition of *Don Quixote* published by the Spanish Academy. Ferro's style was neoclassical, noticeable in the idealized, abstract figure of Cervantes, which does not even depict his maimed left arm. The engraver of this print was Fernando Selma, also a Spaniard from Valencia (1752–1810). The print is courtesy of Rolena Adorno's collection.

Contents

A Note on the Title of *Don Quixote*

A misunderstanding about the sound the *x* represented in the Spanish of Cervantes' time led to the pronunciation of his hero's name in English as kwiksət, and its derivation "quixotic" as "kwik sotik." Throughout the sixteenth century the "sh" sound of words spelled with an *x*, such as "xabon," which led to the modern "jabón," "soap," evolved toward the aspirated sound which would be represented by a *j* in today's Spanish. Whether Cervantes pronounced the name of his hero "Quishote" or "Quihote" is a matter of some dispute. The English, seeing that *x*, pronounced it the way that tradition has established in their language. In Spanish, however, it is always pronounced "kihote." (The French, who heard a sound like *sh* came up with Quichotte, which is how they still say it and write it.) I will always write *Don Quixote* when referring to the book and Don Quijote when mentioning the character, but the authors of the articles included in this book vary in their usage.

Another variation stems from the abbreviated forms of the novel's title, which some authors may render as "the *Quijote*," others "the *Don Quijote*," and so forth. These titles normally refer to the book as one work, but the reader may keep in mind that, in the original, there were two parts with slightly different titles. Part I (1605) was called *El ingenioso hidalgo don Qvixote de la Mancha*, or *The Witty Hidalgo Don Quixote of La Mancha*. "Ingenioso" meant "witty" in the sense of inventive to an almost pathological degree. "Hidalgo" (son of something) was a member of the low nobility. "Don" was a deferential form of address to which our hero really had no right because of his social station. "La Mancha" was a region of Spain of no particular distinction—plain in the literal and figurative sense—meant to contrast with the more dignified areas famous knights hailed from. Amadís was from Wales and Palmerín from England. Next to them La Mancha is supposed to look and sound ridiculous. Ironically, the success of Cervantes' book has given La Mancha a poetic aura that it did not have. Part II (1615) is called *Segvnda Parte del ingenioso cavallero Don Quixote de La Mancha*, to which it is added "Por Miguel de Cervantes, autor de su primera parte" ("By Miguel de Cervantes, author of its first part") to make clear that this is the legitimate sequel, not the one published in 1614 by Alonso Fernández de Avellaneda. Don Quijote has now been elevated to "knight." Unless the authors whose work is included in this book make it explicit that they refer to part I or part II, they mean the whole ensemble comprising both parts.

—R.G.E.

Cervantes' *Don Quixote*

A CASEBOOK

Introduction

ROBERTO GONZÁLEZ ECHEVARRÍA

❖ ❖ ❖

IN THE EARLY DAYS of 1605, Miguel de Cervantes, a minor author, former soldier, and tax collector published in Madrid a book titled *El ingenioso hidalgo don Quixote de la Mancha*, or, *The Witty Hidalgo Don Quixote of la Mancha* (an hidalgo being a member of the low aristocracy). Fifty-eight years old at the time and largely unsuccessful in his previous literary ventures, Cervantes seems to have decided to gamble it all with this bold and original book: the story of a middle-aged, sedentary man who suddenly decides to become a knight-errant and sets out in search of adventures. Don Quijote and his creator both invent themselves in a quest for freedom that their advanced age makes urgent, breaking on the one hand with literary tradition and on the other with social expectations.

Cervantes' triumph was immediate and enduring. The book went through various printings, was translated into other languages very soon, publishers became interested in other works of his, and an apocryphal sequel to *Don Quixote* appeared in 1614. Cervantes, who was already at work on his own second part,

3

rushed to finish and published it in 1615, a year before his death. This book was also a major success, completing a narrative sequence of as much consequence as the combined *Iliad* and *Odyssey*. Some critics consider part II an even better novel than the original. Both are traditionally read as one work, thus increasing the book's overall value. This is possible because of the profound unity given the entire ensemble by the protagonist, who became the most famous literary character of the modern era, whose likeness has been represented more than any other.

Cervantes' protagonist has had such lasting appeal because he embodies a modern yearning to shape one's life according to one's desires, together with the confidence that such a thing is possible by an act of will undeterred by natural or man-made obstacles. It is perhaps the universal desire to become another closer to one's dreams and aspirations. Because he is old and single, Don Quixote is, in contrast to other modern heroes, beyond the pull of family determinations, be they real or imagined. He is clear of Hamlet's kind of debt to his father or his hatred for a usurping uncle, free from the burning jealousy of Othello, and, having no children, not beset by a litigious brood such as Lear's. Unlike Dante's pilgrim in *The Divine Comedy*, Don Quijote's quest is not to invest erotic passion with transcendental, theological meaning. Although grounded on desire for a nearby young peasant woman (Aldonza Lorenzo), Don Quijote's beloved, Dulcinea, is, like himself, his own invention. Much of the book's greatness derives from Cervantes having placed his protagonist's idealizations in a very concrete and tangible context and allowed the clash between the two to play itself out. The result of this is his book's sublime mixture of pathos and humor, an unresolved combination that reads like an accurate enough assessment of the human condition.

Much of *Don Quixote*'s originality is due to the way in which Cervantes recycles narrative traditions and incorporates discourses that lie outside the literary. Being ostensibly and avowedly a parody of chivalric romances, the book takes some of its shape from them, particularly the sequence of adventures in which the protagonist engages while on the road. But Cervantes also wrote during the heyday of picaresque novels, a new genre that emerged in Spain during the sixteenth century, specifically after 1554 when *The Life of Lazarillo de Tormes* was published. These novels told the life of a youngster from an impoverished background who narrates his story in the first person, as if, as an accused criminal, he were giving a deposition before judicial authorities. The lasting novelty of this kind of fiction was the detailed description of the pícaro's tawdry environment, the representation of low life in towns, roads, and inns. It is a decisive step in the evolution of what we now know as realism. In 1599, a short six years before the publication of *Don Quixote*, Mateo Alemán brought out his *The Life of the Pícaro Guzmán de Alfarache*, with a substantial second part that appeared precisely in 1605, when part I of Cervantes' masterpiece was published. This work developed substantially the new Picaresque genre, particularly the depiction of criminal life. Cervantes learned much from the Picaresque, and *Don Quixote's* narrative structure owes a great deal to it, not only in its episodic plot, which derived too from chivalric romances, but also in all the scenes in inns and roads, with their colorful gallery of rogues. More important, *Don Quixote* tells the life of the hero until his death; life is the narrative unit and that which gives the book its shape. Moreover, the tension that propels the plot in part I is provided by the persecution and eventual capture of Don Quijote by the officers of the Holy Brotherhood, who turn him over to the priest and the barber (one in charge of souls, the other of the body). The hero is, like the pícaro, a fugitive from justice. Chivalric romances and picaresque novels do not clash in *Don Quixote*; they both live within the mad hidalgo.

The flow of a life is a narrative pattern that everyone can understand, and this is also one of *Don Quixote's* many appealing features. Cervantes appreciated and adapted other narrative schemes drawn from bookish traditions—for instance, the Byzantine romance—which he used in his posthumously published *The Trials of Persiles and Sigismunda* (1617). He also experiments with several others in the stories interpolated in *Don Quixote* and those he included in his *Exemplary Stories* (1613). The results were often brilliant. But in his masterpiece it is the life of the hero that, like those of the knight and the pícaro, frames the action, with one major deviation. Cervantes begins Don Quijote's life not when he is born as Alonso Quijano but when he invents himself as Don Quijote. The same is true of his esquire, Sancho Panza, closer to the Picaresque because of his class extraction, whose early life is filled out retrospectively throughout the book but whose life in the novel begins when he joins Don Quijote. Cervantes learned from the Picaresque but rejected two of its crucial elements: the deterministic quality of a life deeply scarred by a painful youth and the first-person narrative. He uses the latter within *Don Quixote* when a character like the captive tells his life's story, but always within the overarching fiction of the knight's life as told in the manuscripts found by the narrator. Cervantes probably considered the Picaresque first-person narrative to be too confining and lacking the possibility of presenting simultaneously several points of view.

The device of the manuscript discovered under unusual circumstances is one that Cervantes borrowed from chivalric romances, but he embroidered upon it to such a degree that the novel's self-reflexiveness has become its hallmark for many—particularly for contemporary writers and critics. Cervantes' most radical creation is the character of the narrator of *Don Quixote*, who styles himself a sort of editor of the story, presumably first written by Arabic historian Cide Hamete Benengeli and translated into Spanish by several translators. The first translation available is incomplete, however, and when the narrator-editor finds the balance of the manuscript by chance he has to hire someone to translate it for him. Both that translator and the narrator offer comments about the work that are included in the "final" text. In the famous prologue to part I, Cervantes states, in the spirit of this game of multiple attributions, that he is not the father but the stepfather of the work. Without pursuing to an ever elusive resolution all of the implications of this play of mirrors, one can more or less safely conclude that the two most important ones are these: (1) that Cervantes, as creator, wishes to remain within the fiction, not outside like an all-knowing god in total control of the product of his will, and (2) that this leads to an ironic perspective because his limited powers put him at risk of erring with comic results, as does his hapless hero on more than one occasion. The fact that Cervantes did make several mistakes in part I (at one point he forgets that Sancho's ass had been stolen) give *Don Quixote* a work-in-progress quality very much in keeping with the ironic effect generated by the novel's self-consciousness.

That irony, very reminiscent of Michel de Montaigne's elegant self-deprecations, underlines a major idea present in *Don Quixote*: that the world is man-made, with all the failings inherent to the human and independent from God (in fact, Hungarian critic Georg Lukacs once wrote that *Don Quixote* was the first work to portray a world abandoned by the gods). The literary work is the product of human labor, such as that performed by the various agents who generate the texts. This is a very humble, Christian position, and Cervantes was a profoundly Christian writer. But, at the same time, it draws attention to his debt to renaissance ideas, particularly Italian humanism and the scientific advances of the likes of Copernicus and Galileo. Cervantes and the humanists had developed a system of parallel truths whose uneasy if not impossible convergence was prudently left untested. Church dogma and human knowledge as that achieved by the new thinkers coexisted in his writings. Cervantes' ironic stance in *Don Quixote*, a book in which God is never involved (there were no pious books in the knight's library), is not so much a personal defense (he had no trouble with the Inquisition) as a program for living under new, rapidly evolving ideological conditions. It was also an ethics and aesthetics for the genre he virtually created single-handedly: the modern novel.

Perhaps the deepest irony is embodied in the mad hero. Don Quijote's insanity sets him radically apart from the world that he inhabits, both physically and morally. In the physical sense this is evident in all the violence, in all the blows and injuries he sustains as he clashes with the real world. In the moral it is revealed in the disagreements and ensuing beatings he suffers at the hands of uncomprehending characters, baffled and annoyed by Don Quijote's bizarre behavior, particularly his outrageous demands. These are made in the name of a higher kind of moral than the one prevailing in the fallen world through which he travels. The ambiguous outcome of many adventures, however, can lead the reader to question who is right: the deranged hero or those who pummel the hero? In short, could Don Quijote's grasp on reality be deeper and truer than that of ordinary people like us? Could this tale "told by an idiot" be a higher kind of understanding? Because Don Quijote's views and actions are sharply contrasted by those of his squire, who may be a rustic but is certainly not a simpleton, Sancho may represent our own kind of common sense. The contrast and ambiguity are often put squarely before the reader, asking him to make a judgment and in the process have a hard look at himself and his own sanity. Dostoyevsky in *The Idiot*, Faulkner in *The Sound and the Fury*, and not a few other writers have found Cervantes' formula compelling.

Sancho's presence in the book—which does not begin until the second sally—helped anchor the novel in reality, as if the plump peasant's body mass served as ballast to anchor down the thin knight's fancy. The disparity between the two could not be sharper. Don Quijote belongs to the low nobility, the squire to the peasant class; the hidalgo is a voracious reader, Sancho is illiterate; Don Quijote's mind is cluttered with bookish knowledge reaching back to the dawn of the West in the Bible and the Greeks, Sancho's knowledge is of the present, yet also timeless, reaching down to the emergence of mankind and stored in the oral tradition, particularly in all those proverbs he strings along to Don Quijote's irritation. It is a practical knowledge that often saves them from further trouble and that is sufficient to get by in the real world. One of the most moving qualities of *Don Quixote* is that Sancho is not portrayed with condescension or reduced to his gluttony, as Falstaff sometimes is in Shakespeare. The squire is endowed with natural reason, a medieval concept of unsuspecting revolutionary repercussions. Sancho's allotment of spiritual light serves him well enough in challenging predicaments, for instance, when he is finally made governor of an island (a prank by the Duke and Duchess in part II), he foils everyone's expectations by being a prudent, shrewd, and just ruler. Sancho embodies the common man who will eventually begin to be the master of his destiny after the Enlightenment.

If the narrator, the knight, and his squire are memorable and enduring creations, Dulcinea is the most remarkable character in the novel, one who seems to touch the very limits of the literary imagination. She is a "meta-character" in that she is the creation of other characters—first Don Quijote's—in the novel. She has no lines in the book. The hidalgo invents her and gives her a name as he is preparing to set out the first time, for a knight-errant would be incomplete without a lady love. Hence, Dulcinea is a projection of his quest to be a knight like those he has read about in romances of chivalry: She is to be an incomparable beauty, cruel in her aloofness. Dulcinea will be the one to whom he will dedicate all of his efforts without much hope of ever deserving her love. But she has a basis in reality, as the reader finds out from the conversations between Don Quijote and Sancho: The hidalgo has for years been infatuated with a peasant lass from his village named Aldonza Lorenzo. Don Quijote's and Sancho's descriptions of Dulcinea and Aldonza respectively reveal that the knight's desire for the stout, somewhat manly, wench, had a perverse dimension that the sublimated figure of Dulcinea still bears. In part II the Duke's steward organizes a pageant in the forest in which the character of Dulcinea is played by a page, a young man who manages to appear like a beautiful young woman but who cannot disguise his masculine voice. This transvestite Dulcinea is like a phantom from Don Quijote's subconscious, an image of desire unbound thinly covered with a veil of decency, but made even more alluring precisely because of its ambiguous, multivalent shape.

Because *Don Quixote* is commonly thought of as one book, rarely is it taken into account that it is two novels. Parts I and II share the principal characters, of course, but the ten years separating them have not elapsed in vain. Most important, the Cervantes who wrote part II had the experience of having written part I and now had to try to top it, not to mention a sequel published by one Alfonso Fernández de Avellaneda in 1614. Part I saw the birth of Don Quijote, established the pattern of adventures that the hero would have, and developed the main themes of the work. Sancho also made his appearance and the interplay between the two characters was set in motion. Part I also included a number of interpolated stories, some intertwined with the actions of the two protagonists, others not. They are all connected by the common themes of love and its legal complications, as young people are led from desire to marriage and its attendant issues involving financial and social transactions. The end comes when the hero is nabbed by the authorities and turned over to his neighbors who return him home. There are many memorable adventures, including the one with the windmills, that have become emblematic of the book. Most of these take place on the road, under the relentless Castilian sun.

Much of part II takes place indoors. The book begins in Alonso Quijano's house with a wide-ranging discussion among the characters about the political situation of Spain. This sets the tone. Part II is very much a political novel, no doubt the first, that deals with many contemporary issues, some as recent and polemical as the expulsion of the *moriscos* from the Peninsula (they were Muslim populations remaining from the time when much of Spain was in the hands of the Arabs). While some adventures still take place outdoors, in the open road, many develop in the plush homes of the well-to-do, and the action leads the protagonists to a major urban center, Barcelona, where Don Quijote meets his final defeat and heads back home, to die peacefully in his own bed. The self-reflexive complications of part I increase exponentially in part II. Here the protagonists meet other characters who know about them because they have read part I, others have read or are even characters in the spurious *Don Quixote* (they are asked to attest, from within Cervantes' fiction, to the falsity of Avellaneda's!). Because characters like the Duke and Duchess know Don Quijote and Sancho as protagonists of the novel, they stage pranks to have them act accordingly. Many adventures in their house and later at Antonio Moreno's in Barcelona are charades, elaborate jokes, like the episodes in which Sancho performs as governor of his "island." The world is a stage in part II, with roles and plots scripted for the protagonists by other characters. There is no solid ground outside fiction; everything is caught in an infinitely receding sequence of fictions. Because of all this, part II is extremely complicated (though, responding to criticisms of part I, Cervantes eliminated the interpolated stories). It is baroque.

A biting critique of Spanish society, part II portrays the upper classes as idle, frivolous, and even cruel. They use Don Quijote and Sancho for their entertainment and spend money in pleasures beyond what they can afford. The Duke, for instance, is often bailed out of debt by loans from a rich peasant within his domain. The wealthy and powerful in Barcelona are on friendly terms with brigand Roque Guinart. The ecclesiastic who chastises Don Quijote at the Duke's dinner table is reprimanded by the knight for living off the aristocracy. Meanwhile, Ricote, an honest morisco from Don Quijote's village and a friend of Sancho's, has been forced to leave Spain. His daughter, born and raised a Christian, has been sent to Morocco with her mother, where they are treated as foreigners by their presumed Muslim brethren. She is betrothed to an aristocrat from their village, a *mayorazgo* (first-born male in line to inherit a substantial estate), but their marriage is postponed beyond the end of the novel because, by returning to Spain she has violated the edict of expulsion and could be sentenced to death. An exemption is requested from the authorities in Madrid but there is little hope that it will be granted, certainly not expeditiously. Her forestalled marriage stands in contrast to those that are eventually arranged in part I, which are comedy-like happy endings to the amorous conflicts. Part II is pessimistic with regard to the future of Spain, painting a black picture of the country under the latter Hapsburgs. Like the aristocrats in the novel, the monarchy was living frivolously beyond the country's means, in hock to German bankers.

The shift in focus to these historical contingencies in part II does not detract from *Don Quixote*'s broader, more universal concerns; on the contrary, it gives them sharper relief. Don Quijote's penchant to play-act, his self as invention, the clash between desire and what the real allows, the bafflements provoked by a shifting reality, the errors that ensue, and the constant friction between humans and the world into which they have been thrown now appear as an integral part of social and political life, not just as the aberrations of a solitary madman. The "world is out of kilter" in part II, and the mad hero, his lofty ideals untouched, is its victim. The novel does not end with his arrest but with his death, not as Don Quijote but as Alonso Quijano. With all illusions gone, Don Quijote reverts back to his old self, renounces his life of folly and dies a Christian death, hoping for salvation in an after world.

Don Quixote's impact on narrative prose was immediate. Thomas Shelton translated the book into English before part II appeared, and French translations and adaptations soon followed. At first Cervantes' disciples were struck mainly by the comic possibilities inherent in the two main characters, a trend that continued until the eighteenth century, when English novelists like Henry Fielding and Thomas Sterne began to exploit some of the novel's more technical innovations. The Romantics made Don Quijote into a more pathetic figure than Cervantes probably intended. By then the book had won a prominent position both in Spain and throughout Europe and the Americas. In the United States Herman Melville and Mark Twain became Cervantes' avowed followers, and in Latin America the Brazilian Machado de Assis, the Cuban Cirilo Villaverde, the Argentine Domingo Faustino Sarmiento, and nearly all writers of note incorporated Cervantes into their narrative projects. *Don Quixote* was by then and until now has been at the core of programs of study in schools and universities. In Spain the figure of the mad knight became a central component in all meditations about the essence of Spanishness, particularly in the writings of Miguel de Unamuno, Ramiro de Maeztu and Azorín, members all of the so-called Generation of '98.

The avant gardes, both in Europe and the New World, found in Cervantes' masterpiece a work that anticipated their wildest rebellions against artistic conventions. The fact that Don Quijote and Sancho are present in Joyce's *Ulysses* (1922), and Franz Kafka's *Metamorphosis* (1915) owes much to the hidalgo's self-transformation into a knight. The Argentine Jorge Luis Borges made Cervantes and his hero a key to his meditations on authorship in his influential narrative experiments. The Mexican Carlos Fuentes made Cervantes a character in his ambitious novel *Terra Nostra* (1978), and Colombian Nobel Prize winner, Gabriel García Márquez has expressed with both admiration and despair that "everything is already in Cervantes." The book that minor author Miguel de Cervantes published in 1605, when he should have been past his prime, turned out to be a classic among classics.

MANUEL DURÁN's "CERVANTES' Harassed and Vagabond Life" is a succinct, yet sufficient biography of the writer. It provides a reliable portrait of Cervantes and his times as well as the social and literary context in which his works were created. Durán's view of the author of *Don Quixote* as an ironist who could look at Spain simultaneously from the outside and the inside while maintaining a positive, even joyful outlook on the human condition is one that I and most critics share. How Cervantes struggled to keep himself and his family economically afloat and how his appeals for favors from the Court went unheard reveal a man who had to have (and his work shows it) a grip on the harsh realities of life. Durán's puzzlement as to how Cervantes came to acquire such a vast literary culture is one that besets all his biographers. It is futile to attempt to fully understand genius. I am not convinced by the hypothesis, timidly advanced by Durán, that his teacher Américo Castro and other students of his proposed on very flimsy evidence, of a *converso* Cervantes—one, that is, whose purportedly Jewish background would have made him marginal. Social advancement, financial stability, and success at Court were rewards denied to many—to most, in fact—in the Spain of the period. A sense of not belonging and its ensuing ironic posture were not necessarily the dubious privilege of a single social group. Castro's theories are, to my mind, too dependent on the racial hatreds and atrocities of the twentieth century to be applicable with little proof to the sixteenth and seventeenth centuries.

Mimesis is one of the greatest works of literary criticism ever. It is as persuasive an analysis of the development of realism as there is, being based on a philologist's broad understanding of the development of the Romance languages and supported by the textual analyses that such knowledge allows. Auerbach moves from the minute to the general with ease and elegance. He was able to trace how the representation of reality in literature advanced from the Bible and the Greeks through the Middle Ages and shows how the advent and growth of Christianity, with its need to adapt rhetoric to reach the humble, fostered the creation of a literary medium to represent everyday life. The clash of rhetorical styles, the high and the low, provides the heat in which the vernacular literatures in the various romance languages are forged. "The Enchanted Dulcinea" was not a part of the original (German) edition of *Mimesis*. It was included in the English at the request of friends and editors who persuaded Auerbach that the absence of *Don Quixote* from his book was a flaw. The new chapter was not well received by Cervantes scholars, particularly Hispanists, who objected to Auerbach's apparent reduction of the novel to its comic elements. There is some validity to this criticism. But "The Enchanted Dulcinea" should be read in the context of the whole of *Mimesis*, not in isolation. Auerbach's reading of Cervantes' masterpiece through his theory of styles sheds considerable light on the book at the most basic textual level, and his overall appraisal of *Don Quixote* in the context of European literary history is of enormous value. His struggle to define the "Cervantean" at the close of his essay is priceless to help us grasp the meaning of the whole book.

Ramón Menéndez Pidal (1869–1968) was the most distinguished philologist, historian, and literary historian that Spain and the Spanish language have known. His monumental contributions to understanding how Spanish developed as a language and how this evolution is inscribed in its literature are beyond dispute. His greatest work in the field of literature concerns the epic poems about Castilian heroes like the Cid, Fernán González, and others, and their derivations and dissemination as ballads from the Middle Ages through the Renaissance and beyond—the so-called Romancero, or the accumulation of *romances*, as the ballads are known in Spanish. In this literary tradition, which he took as the product of the collective popular imagination, Menéndez Pidal saw reflected the essence of Spain. So it is not surprising that he would seek the genesis of Spain's greatest literary work within that tradition, given that he and other intellectuals of his generation saw Cervantes' hero as the finest representation of the nation. (Menéndez Pidal shared many nationalistic concerns with members of the Generation of '98, the group of writers and thinkers whose anxieties were aroused by Spain's humiliating defeat in the Spanish-American War.)

Menéndez Pidal, or Don Ramón as he was reverentially known, being by training and conviction a philologist, needed a text on which to ground his case and he found it in the anonymous "Entremés de los romances," a comic one-act play first published in 1611, six years after *Don Quixote* but performed earlier. Whether this did happen before or after Cervantes' masterpiece was conceived soon became a matter of dispute, with Don Ramón in favor of before. In the play, Bartolo, a rustic, goes insane from reading too many ballads, believes himself to be one of their heroes, is beaten up with his own lance, and is carried to bed to be cared for. The action bears a close resemblance to Don Quijote's clash with the Toledan merchants in chapters 4 and 5 of part I when he is similarly pummeled and begins to recite lines from the ballads, also believing himself to be one of their paladins. The "Entremés" is a very minor work and Don Ramón knows it well. He is very much aware that as a source—if it be that—it is dwarfed by what flowed from it. Menéndez Pidal was neither a fool nor a hopelessly obsolete critic. We can never fully ascertain the genesis of a work of genius, but trying to do so is always a valuable exercise with many side benefits.

And there are many to "The Genesis of Don Quixote," which in the original (1920) Spanish had the much more modest title of "Un aspecto en la elaboración del *Quijote*" ("A Factor in the Production of *Don Quixote*"). (The essay was only available in English in a very poor translation that I have completely recast and refreshed for this volume with the help of my learned colleague Rolena Adorno.) The first benefit is to be able to observe closely Don Ramón's struggle with his own ambivalences. He downgrades the "Entremés" for being merely a comical piece and because Bartolo wishes to relinquish his own being to become one of the epic heroes, something he seems to have bequeathed to the Don Quijote of the early chapters, when Cervantes had yet to hit upon a more profound kind of madness, one in which his protagonist attempted to imitate chivalric heroes while remaining himself. Thus, in order to make a plausible cause for the play as source, Menéndez Pidal has to disparage both it and its first impression on Cervantes, postponing or displacing the actual spark of genius beyond it. But there are many other benefits to be derived from this piece. For instance, Menéndez Pidal's careful genealogy of the romances of chivalry up to the *Amadís*, Don Quijote's most important model, teasing out their heroic and amorous elements and debt to French romances and Spanish epic poems. This is the background of Don Quijote's obsession, which is quite foreign to the modern reader, who has probably a very vague idea about chivalry. There are also fine pages on other topics related to the presence of the ballads in *Don Quixote*, such as the ones devoted to the Cave of Montesinos episode. Finally, "The Genesis of *Don Quixote*" is an excellent example of how Spanish intellectuals and artists turned Cervantes' masterpiece into a crucial element in the development of a sense of nationhood.

Menéndez Pidal's hypothesis leads to another even more suggestive idea about the genesis of *Don Quixote* that does not really depend on his being right about the "Entremés": that the book was originally intended to be a nouvelle like those he collected in *Exemplary Stories* which would end after the knight is returned home for the first time in chapter 5. If this was so—and I am inclined to believe it—the rest of the novel is something that imposed itself on Cervantes and carried him along much like his hero's obsession launches him on his adventures. Such a serendipitous beginning, a self-determined start and principle of creation, would account for the work-in-progress quality of the novel, including all the self-reflexive games of authorship. The novel is making itself as it goes and telling the reader in the process how this is happening because Cervantes himself is following along, driven by the work's own internal drive. The much bandied about Cervantean irony would also issue from this: The author does not have total control over his creation. In the modern era, and Cervantes may well be its herald in literature, the more the creative self seeks self-knowledge through artistic work and he realizes that such knowledge is becoming ever more elusive, as is the knowledge of a universe made larger and difficult to grasp by the methods and instruments of the new science (such as the telescope). I believe that it is because his invention got away from him that Cervantes—mockingly and earnestly at once—does not want to claim authorship.

Those who have criticized Menéndez Pidal have done so from within his own assumptions and premises, arguing that the "Entremés" came after *Don Quixote*, which was its source (if so, why is Cervantes' hero not even mentioned?). But a critique from outside them is, it seems to me, more fruitful, even without diminishing the value of his essay. What Don Ramón is attempting to do by linking the creation of *Don Quixote* to the collective invention of ballads is to find a traditional myth (if the redundancy be allowed) behind the figure of the mad hidalgo that would make the work more the product of Spain than of Cervantes. This is consonant with his view about the creative spirit of nations, at the core of his critical ideology. It is also something that is true of other masterpieces. It can be argued, for instance, that *The Divine Comedy* originates in an Easter liturgical tradition, and the genesis of literary myths such as Don Juan and Faust from popular sources is undeniable and well known. In fact, it was Menéndez Pidal himself who demonstrated that Don Juan was the result of the happy convergence of the figure of the serial seducer (derived, of course, from ballads) and the traditional story of the dinner invitation to a cemetery, thus forever joining Eros and Thanatos in the story that was first told by Tirso de Molina. But Don Quijote is a truly modern hero who emerges from and makes an issue of the development of printing and the dissemination of books. Don Quijote emerges from the print, not the oral tradition. This is what sets him apart and renders Don Ramón's quest a misguided one, even if still fruitful.

It is precisely on the proliferation of books in Spain and its reflection in *Don Quixote* that Georgina Dopico Black writes about in her essay. She deftly traces the history of libraries in the Peninsula in relation to the emergence of the Spanish state and the associated process of including and excluding books and bodies— connected as they are by a common terminology to name them (*cuerpos de libros*). Dopico Black shows the many resonances of these sociopolitical developments in the episode when the priest, the barber, the housekeeper, and the niece expurgate the mad hero's library and burn the condemned books. The whole conflict among cultures and faiths at the core of the Spain of the sixteenth century (which Américo Castro called "conflictive Spain") is dramatized in that episode and others, such as the one involving the translation from the Arabic of Cide Hamete Benengeli, the alleged author of the original *Don Quixote* within the novel's fiction. Proceeding from historical generalization to specific philological analysis and by means of a stunning associative method, her essay is the product of some of the most advanced current critical trends without being the slave to any.

The recently deceased E. C. Riley published in 1962 *Cervantes's Theory of the Novel*, which became a classic, and from which the essay included here is extracted. Riley's book finally focused on a topic that had long been bandied about by critics, Cervantes' debt to renaissance poetics, and produced what is likely to remain the definitive statement on the subject. His "Literature and Life in *Don Quixote*" goes beyond the constraints of poetics to consider how Cervantes incorporates daily life and his own life into the novel, and how the inclusion of all the bookish material highlights by contrast the reality and vividness of his characters. He also considers how, by his own appearance in the book in various guises, Cervantes anticipates questions about the relationship between art and reality and between artistic creation and creator that would vex and become a major theme in the works of modern writers such as Unamuno and Pirandello. I would add to this what I said earlier, that the self-reflexiveness of *Don Quixote* underlines its being a product of human work, or better of humans at work. A required complement to Riley's essay (and book) is Jorge Luis Borges "Pierre Menard, author of the Quijote," and other writings by the Argentine that he regretfully did not take into account.

Cervantes' frequent use of the term "history" to refer to *Don Quixote* is Bruce W. Wardropper's point of departure. His essay, going beyond Riley's reliance on renaissance poetics, places Cervantes' book in the context of the inherent difficulties in telling the truth in historical writing and compares these to those of ordinary mortals in distinguishing between the true and the false. *Don Quixote* dramatizes, according to Wardropper, this very human predicament: It is the book's main theme. But he adds to this somewhat abstract insight a historical background: the existence, during Cervantes' life, of deliberately false histories, veritable forgeries that nevertheless enjoyed royal legitimacy. One of these, Miguel de Luna's *Historia verdadera del rey don Rodrigo, compuesta por Albucácim Tárif*, was offered by its author as a translation of the work of an eighth-century Moorish historian. The parallel with Cervantes' Cide Hamete Benenjeli is compelling, but Wardropper is prudent in not making de Luna's book the immediate source of *Don Quixote*.

If Menéndez Pidal suggested that the "Entremés de los romances" was what triggered Cervantes' imagination, Wardropper claims that role for history and the apocryphal chronicles mentioned. In the end this seems like a more plausible hypothesis, given that we are in the realm of books. But, as I have argued in my *Love and the Law in Cervantes*, I would add yet another element to the mix: legal discourse, which proliferated in Spain beginning with the reign of the Catholic Kings, peaking during that of Philip II. As Richard L. Kagan has amply demonstrated, the Spain of the sixteenth and seventeenth centuries was a very litigious nation. The individual was enmeshed in a web of legal writing that both enfranchised him and constrained him. Out of the archive housing all those documents emerged the picaresque novel, which mimicked a legal document (a deposition given by a criminal) and made available a discourse capable of assimilating into literature the transactions of everyday life, particularly those among the members of the lower classes, criminals specially. That underworld is present throughout Cervantes' work, and the knight and his squire are, throughout part I, fugitives from justice. As we already saw, the plot is closed when the officers of the Holy

Brotherhood finally nab the pair and turn them over to the priest and barber.

Leo Spitzer's "Linguistic Perspectivism in the *Don Quijote*" is, to my mind, the most insightful essay ever written on Cervantes' masterpiece. Only Américo Castro's 1925 book *El pensamiento de Cervantes* surpasses it as a contribution to the criticism of the Spanish author. Spitzer demonstrates, through detailed linguistic analysis, that the idea advanced by José Ortega y Gasset and Castro about perspectivism in the novel is correct, but not just in a thematic or dramatic way (as when two characters see or say different things) but woven into the very fabric of its text. He is also able to link Cervantes' various devices (polyethymology, for instance) to the evolution of linguistic thought from the Middle Ages to the Baroque. His article is full of rich commentary on matters as diverse and interesting as the shifting names of characters and their use of dialect. Spitzer was also able to propose a general interpretation of the book that issues convincingly from his analyses: *Don Quixote* is about the freedom of the individual to choose and to create according to what he perceives and feels as being the true and the real. In spite of the differences that he himself expresses between his take on *Don Quixote* and that of Auerbach, both agree on the question of freedom and its ironic manifestation. It is an irony filled with Christian humility but which, at the same time, asserts the existence of a self who is self-created, much as Descartes would propose three decades later in abstract fashion. The perspectivism that Spitzer argues for belies his own idiosyncratically belligerent attitude toward other critics, expressed in his pungent, extensive, and polyphonic footnotes.

My own "*Don Quixote*: Crossed Eyes and Vision" attempts to take the issue of perspectivism one step further by deconstructing, as it were, that concept, using elements drawn from the novel itself. I concentrate on the issue of seeing in the most concrete fashion possible by focusing on the eyes of characters, particularly Ginés de Pasamonte's, whom I take as the representation of the modern author and obliquely of Cervantes himself. Ginés is crossed-eyed and in part II appears posing as one-eyed by covering one side of his face. I argue that his real and feigned defects of vision speak to his skewed perception and representation of reality, one that does not constitute a unified point of view anchored on a harmonious self but, on the contrary, one that is multiple and conflictive within itself. Perspectivism is not the result of different characters seeing things differently but of each being split within himself or herself. Perpectivism begins within the individual self before it can occur elsewhere. *Don Quixote* is about freedom, as Spitzer and Auerbach argue, but that freedom is housed in a self that is limited by defects of vision that reflect or reproduce those that beset its very constitution and foundation: It is a freedom that allows and even promotes not just doubt about the world, but more radically self-doubt. It is the insecurity, the dissatisfaction, the yearning to be another that propels the mad hidalgo out of his own house to face the ambiguous possibilities of the void, the Montiel plain in which, under the relentless light of the Castilian sun, he will be confused by the aspects of things and confuse and astonish others by his own strange appearance.

George Haley's "The Narrator in *Don Quijote*: Maese Pedro's Puppet Show" is a masterful reading of that significant episode in part II, proposing that it is a kind of synecdoche of the entire novel, a part that reflects the whole. Haley's reading begins with a scrupulous discrimination of the various narrators present in *Don Quixote*. He shows how this device allows Cervantes to present his work as a self-sufficient fiction that, by displaying the functioning of its artistic machinery, establishes a Brechtian kind of distancing from both creator and spectator. Haley then goes on to demonstrate how the same process is at work in the miniature world of the puppet show, with Ginés de Pasamonte disguised as Master Pedro and his assistant or barker who tells the story to the audience at the inn, the latter playing our role as reader-spectators. This whole construct is contained within the novel's own elaborate self-staging. To Haley the episode is like an allegory of *Don Quixote*'s own games of illusion, one of several in the book, that further the distancing effect mentioned and that also serve the practical purpose of training readers to be aware of fiction's tricks, so as not to be deceived like Don Quijote before the puppet show or as a reader of romances of chivalry. He emphasizes in closing that by doing this Cervantes is not rejecting the romances but proposing a method of reading them that can be instructive and pleasurable at the same time.

Haley's insights can be applied to our own reading of *Don Quixote* and to the readings performed by criticism, including those in this book. I believe that they lead to the following generalization: that Cervantes' masterpiece anticipates and exhausts all interpretations because all possible approaches are already contained within its fictive world. This is achieved by including so much commentary about its own creation as part of the process of writing and storytelling. But more radically because, by focusing on the longings and limitations of the modern mind—bound by its sense of self-sufficiency with all its inherent lacks and trapped in an infinite universe beyond its grasp—it does not allow us to truly stand outside fiction to gauge its truth or assess its value. We are forever unsure if we inhabit the whole or the part as spectators or actors, or as spectator-actors like those at Master Pedro's performance. In this we are all potential Don Quijotes.

Cervantes' Harassed and Vagabond Life

MANUEL DURÁN

◆ ◆ ◆

WE CAN THINK of many great writers whose lives have left only a few traces upon their work. This is not so with Cervantes: his biography sheds light upon his masterpieces. He was seldom a cold and distant observer of his world: His presence as a witness and occasionally as a judge of what he saw is discreet yet undeniable. He made good use of his experience: he went so far as to include himself, as a minor character, in several of his works—much in the same way as one of our contemporary film directors, Alfred Hitchcock, appears fleetingly in his own movies. His presence is discreet yet insistent: he will not deny or betray his own personality; he begs us to take it into account when reading his texts. Pride and humility go hand in hand in him, helping him to become a good witness of his time—and of the human condition of all time.

Cervantes was born in Alcalá de Henares, a small university city not far from Madrid, in 1547, probably on September 29, St. Michael's day, since it was often the custom to bestow the name of the saint in the calendar upon a child born on that day. He was baptized in the church of Santa María la Mayor on Sunday, October 9.

His father, Rodrigo de Cervantes, was an impecunious hidalgo. He had become a practical surgeon after a few months of hurried studies at the University of Alcalá, where he had excellent friends among the medical faculty; not too long after acquiring his degree, Rodrigo married (in 1543) Leonor de Cortinas, a young girl born in Barajas, near Madrid, also a member of the gentry, also impecunious. They had seven children, all but the last two born in Alcalá de Henares.

Nothing is known about the first years of Miguel de Cervantes' life except that his family moved often. Miguel was only three and a half years old when his family moved away from Alcalá de Henares. The family was going through a period of hardship. Rodrigo's income was meager. With nine mouths to feed and little or no income, the family moved to Valladolid. Debts accumulated. Miguel's father went to jail for a few months. We find the family in Córdoba (where they settled in 1553); Córdoba was but a shadow of its former size and opulent past under the Moors, but it must still have been a fascinating city. It is in Córdoba that Miguel de Cervantes went to an elementary school (he was seven years old when his family settled there) and acquired the rudiments of learning, perhaps at the school conducted by Father Alonso de Vieras. Later on, in 1555, he probably began the study of Latin at the Jesuit College of Santa Catalina. But 1557 was a bad year: the family was pressed by debts. There is no trace of Rodrigo and his family from that date until they reappear in Seville in 1564. Miguel was by then a handsome youth of seventeen. He must have enjoyed life in Seville, then on the verge of becoming a "boom town." He probably continued his studies at the Jesuit College. Much later, one of his characters, the wise dog Ciprón, would state: "I have heard it said [he describes the Jesuit teachers at Seville] of those saintly ones that in the matter of prudence there is not their like in the world, while as guides and leaders along the heavenly path few can come up to them. They are mirrors in which are to be viewed human decency, Catholic doctrine, and extraordinary wisdom, and, lastly, a profound humility that is the basis upon which the entire edifice of a holy life is reared."[1] Later, Cervantes would describe the agreeable character of student life: "In short, I led the life of a student, without hunger and without the itch—and I can give it no higher praise than that. For if it were not that the itch and hunger are the student's constant companions, there would be no life that is pleasanter or more enjoyable, since virtue and pleasure here go hand in hand, and the young find diversion even as they learn."[2] Miguel loved to read: he was a voracious reader, and we may assume that his long-lasting love affair with literature had already begun. The theatre fascinated him: it must have been a glorious day for him when Lope de Rueda, a famous actor who also wrote plays (among them his famous *pasos*, one-act plays or curtain raisers, that the modern reader finds still fresh and amusing) came to Seville and gave several performances there. This took place probably in 1564. In a prologue he later wrote to a collection of his own plays, he reminisces about that happy day. He is discussing the theatre in general, and his own childhood memories, with some of his friends: "I, as the oldest one there, said that I remembered having seen on the stage the great Lope de Rueda, a man distinguished in both acting and understanding. He was a native of Seville, and a goldsmith by trade, which means he was one of those that make gold leaf. He was admirable in pastoral poetry; and in this genre neither then nor since has anybody surpassed him."[3]

Bad luck once more besieged Cervantes' family. A certain Rodrigo de Chaves instituted a suit against Rodrigo, his father, and attached his goods. The family moved to Madrid in 1566. Miguel was now twenty. He probably continued his education there with private tutors and at the City School of Madrid under the learned López de Hoyos, who, as a follower of Erasmus, may have inculcated in his young pupil some of Erasmus' progressive and liberal ideas. Cervantes' culture was becoming broader and more solid. Nevertheless, as Richard L. Predmore states in his biography, "by the most generous estimate that the available facts will allow, young Cervantes cannot have enjoyed much more than six years of formal schooling. In most men this amount of study could not have created a sufficient base for the very considerable literary culture visible in Miguel's later writings, which reveal a good knowledge of the outstanding Latin authors, a smattering of Greek literature, a close familiarity with some of the great writers of the Italian Renaissance and the kind of acquaintance with his own literature that one might expect a boy with strong literary inclinations to possess. What he knew of the Latin language and literature was certainly grounded in his schooling; the rest must have been the product of his own reading. The five years he was soon to spend in Italy contributed decisively to his continued education and account for his extensive reading in Italian literature."[4]

At twenty Cervantes had a wandering spirit, which had been formed in his adolescence perhaps by his frequent travels through Spain. He also felt an intense yearning for both knowledge and freedom. All of this undoubtedly influenced his decision to go to Italy, which was then the mecca of all lovers of culture and of a free life. Nevertheless his trip to Italy may well have been the result of less lofty goals: it has been suggested that at this time Miguel first ran afoul of the law—since there exists in the General Record Office in Simancas a document dated September, 1569, which begins thus: "An Order of Arrest against Miguel de Cervantes. Without Right to Appeal. [signed by] Secretary Padreda. [Motive] A Crime." According to the document, he had stabbed a certain Antonio de Segura in Madrid during a challenge to a duel. No one knows for sure whether the Miguel de Cervantes alluded to in this document is *our* Miguel de Cervantes. The biographer Luis Astrana Marín, in his six learned volumes on the life of Cervantes, thinks this to be the case. In support of his charge, he cites in particular a verse of the *Voyage to Parnassus* in which the author confesses to a "youthful imprudence," from which many of his later misfortunes ensued. It is not wholly clear that we should pay much attention to this accusation, whether truly directed against our writer or not. If true, even if we conclude that Cervantes was guilty, it would only be a question of confirming one more trial, or rather one more accusation, of the many that the writer endured throughout his life. Finally, "it would not be defaming the author to admit that on occasion he was quick to reach for his sword. A gentlemen at that time never went forth without strapping on his sword, and its purpose was not simply for display alone."[5]

Towards 1569 we find Cervantes in Italy, where he had travelled as a member of the retinue of Cardinal Acquaviva. Shortly afterwards he enlisted in the Spanish army and was sent to sea. He fought heroically under the command of Don John of Austria in the sea battle of Lepanto in 1571 and was twice wounded: one wound paralyzed his left hand. He later took part in other campaigns, especially the raids against Tunis and the nearby fortress of La Goleta. In 1575 he embarked for Spain with his brother Rodrigo.[6] He carried with him warm letters of recommendation from his superiors. The galley in which he travelled was seized by Turkish pirates. Thus began five years of captivity, as a slave to his captor, the Greek renegade Dali Mamí. At the end of this period, and after several frustrated attempts to escape, he was ransomed by some Trinitarian monks and was able to return to Spain. Thus Cervantes had passed some twelve years outside Spain—and these were the decisive years in the life of any man, the years between twenty and thirty-three. He returned enriched by his experience; his thirst for adventure had been partially quenched; he longed for stability, a career, some kind of stable success. Success, however, was to prove out of reach.

When he returned to Spain in 1580, several unpleasant experiences still awaited him. He soon realized there was no hope of obtaining any reward for his services. A military career seemed hopeless since one of his arms was no longer useful. Thus began a ceaseless struggle against poverty and neglect. First he lived in Madrid, then he moved to Portugal for a short time. He found no place to root himself. He became a writer almost out of desperation: what else could he do? How could he earn a living? He began to write out of love for literature but also, probably, out of desperation, hoping to find in his literary career a source of income. He was thus from the very beginning a professional writer, although an unsuccessful one at first. The most popular genres were then the pastoral novel and the theater: he tried them both to little avail. A brief love affair made him a father: an illegitimate daughter, Isabel de Saavedra, was the consequence of his affair. In 1584 he married Catalina de Salazar, a woman somewhat younger than himself, and it seems that he found no happiness in his marriage. He lived for a time in Esquivias, a village of La Mancha where his wife had a farm. It was the heart of arid Spain, a poor land almost impossible to idealize: its inhabitants were ignorant and backward. From his memories of life in La Mancha, he would later create Don Quixote and his environment. Cervantes then turned to humble jobs, since literature had proved incapable of providing him with a living. He became quartermaster for the Invincible Armada: for ten years he was an itinerant buyer, living in Seville and other towns in Andalusia. He had separated from his wife, whom he never mentioned in his works. In 1597, because of the bankruptcy of a financier with whom he had deposited some state funds, he was jailed in Seville. In these years he became acquainted with people of the lower class: it seems obvious that he found them more outgoing and decent than the people of the middle and upper classes with whom he had dealings. He did not lack for occasion to study at firsthand the myriad forms of picaresque life, since Seville was the capital of the picaroons. The city was growing fast, having become the economic center of Spain and the main port of the overseas fleets. Gold and silver poured into Spain from Seville. Industry flourished. Rapid growth and change—plus a transient population—made for a minimum of social constraints. It is in Seville that Cervantes must have known the real-life counterpart of Monipodio, the good-tempered, humane Al Capone of the Golden Age.

There was another Spain, much less glamorous than the pageant of Seville, that also attracted his attention: life in the villages of Andalusia and along the winding, sun-drenched roads leading to these villages. Cervantes came to know it well: the poor inns, the wandering artisans and shepherds, the long convoys of mule trains, the humble yet proud peasants. It was another strand in the huge tapestry that unfolded before him. Cervantes was the perfect witness, observing every detail, noticing the delicate balance and the constant interaction between human beings, taking mental notes about their foibles and their moments of happiness.

Life was never boring. Yet Cervantes was always on the verge of bankruptcy: he was not a businessman, his records were not accurate, the financial rewards of his job were meager. It is not surprising, therefore, that in 1590 he petitioned to find a position in the Spanish colonies overseas. His hopes were dashed: an ungrateful administration rejected his petition. Perhaps his troubles with the law had convinced the bureaucrats that he was basically unreliable. Cervantes had pleaded: "Sire: Miguel de Cervantes Saavedra says that he has served Your Majesty for many years in the sea and land campaigns that have occurred over the last 22 years, particularly in the Naval Battle [Lepanto], where he received many wounds, among which was the loss of a hand from gunfire . . . and he has since continued to serve in Seville on business of the Armada, under the orders of Antonio de Guevara, as is on record in the testimonials in his possession. In all this time he has received no favors at all. He asks and begs as humbly as he can that Your Majesty be pleased to grant him the favor of a position in America, of the three or four currently vacant, namely, the accountant's office in the new Kingdom of Granada, or the governorship of the province of Soconusco in Guatemala, or the office of ship's accountant in Cartagena, or that of corregidor in the city of La Paz . . ."[7] As Richard Predmore observes, "influence and money won more jobs than merit, it seems. On 6 June 1590, an official of the Council of the Indies scribbled on the back of Cervantes' memorial: 'Let him look on this side of the water for some favor that may be granted him.' Perhaps the sympathetic reader will console himself with the proverb about the ill wind that blows no good. The action of the Council of the Indies unwittingly favored the birth of Don Quixote."[8]

There can be no doubt about Cervantes' honesty. Each new supervisor confirmed him in his job. There can be doubt neither about his bad luck. In 1602 he was again, for a short time, in jail at Seville. In 1604 he decided to move to Valladolid. The decisive moment was at hand: early in 1605 the first part of *Don Quixote* appeared. Yet Cervantes' joy at the instantaneous success of his novel was short-lived. Again he became involved with the police: a gentleman, Gaspar de Ezpeleta, was fatally wounded in a duel at the entrance of Cervantes' house. The investigation proved Cervantes and his family had nothing to do with this incident— yet it also revealed that Cervantes' sister and daughter led some-what irregular lives, were frequently visited by male friends and received gifts from them.

Cervantes' huge literary success did not bring him riches: his publisher and several pirate publishers kept most of the profits. But it did motivate him to go on writing.

In 1606 the Court settled again in Madrid: Cervantes and his family moved with it. Cervantes wanted to be in touch with other writers and was looking for new publishers; the women in his household, busy with fashion designing and sewing, were looking for customers. Miguel's last years in Madrid were relatively serene. He overcame through patience and wisdom all his adversities, the neglect of famous writers such as Lope de Vega—who seldom had a good word for his works—and the sadness of family crises: his daughter married but soon became the mistress of a wealthy middle-aged businessman; when Cervantes intervened in the in-terest of preventing scandal, she became estranged and never again visited him. Cervantes immersed himself in his work. It was harvest season for him: late in life, yet in full command of his talent, he produced in quick succession his *Exemplary Novels* (1613), the second part of *Don Quixote* (1615), and finally *Persiles and Sigis-munda*, a novel in which his imagination and his love for adventure found almost limitless scope. Cervantes knew his days were num-bered. He suffered from a disease which was diagnosed as dropsy—some modern biographers think it was diabetes—and had to stay in bed for long periods. He could not stop writing until the very end. Early in April, 1616, his doctor recommended a trip to Esquivias, in the hope that country air would reinvig-orate him. On April 19 he was back in Madrid: he busied himself with the final pages of his *Persiles* and the Prologue to the novel. In the Prologue he describes an encounter with a student on his way back from his recent visit to Esquivias. The student is very pleased to meet, as he says, "the famous one, the merry author, the jubilation of the Muses." They ride along for a while and the conversation turns to Cervantes' health. The student diagnoses Cervantes' disease as "dropsy" and advises him to curb his drinking. He replies, "Many have told me . . . but I find it as difficult not to drink my fill as though I had been born for that purpose alone. My life is coming to an end, and by the tempo of my pulse beats, I judge that their career and mine will be over on Sunday at the latest." He goes on to describe the parting of the new friends and closes with a general farewell: "Farewell to the Graces, farewell to wit, farewell to cheerful friends, for I am dying in the desire to see you soon contented in the other life."[9] He died in Madrid on April 23, 1616, at peace with himself and with the world, having received the last sacraments, and was buried in the convent of the Trinitarian nuns. He died without bitterness or regrets since he had been fully conscious of his merit, indeed of his genius, and was aware that his literary creations would endure: a writer cannot hope for a greater source of consolation.

Objectively, Cervantes' life was not a success story. He was seldom in full control: he was too poor; for many years he lacked public recognition. Yet, as Angel del Río points out, "there is no reason to lament Cervantes' misfortunes nor the mediocrity of his daily life. He could thus, through an experience which is seldom obtained when the writer is successful and wealthy, know, observe and feel the beat of Spanish life in its greatness and its poverty, in its heroic fantasy and in the sad reality of an imminent decadence. He was to leave in his books the most faithful image of this life, reflected in multiple perspectives with bittersweet irony and penetrating humor."[10]

If Cervantes' biography teaches us anything, it is that he was at the same time *inside* and *outside* the mainstream of Spanish life. As an insider he took part in the battle of Lepanto and wrote at least two successful books, *Don Quixote* and the *Exemplary Novels*. This is certainly much more than the level of achievement of most middle-class hidalgos of his time. As an outsider, he was always poor—almost to the point of being destitute—and not infrequently in jail; he lacked influential friends in a society where nothing could be done without them and without money; he was often unable to protect adequately the female members of his family; the influential critics and writers of his time did not recognize the quality of his work; his accomplishments as a soldier and as a loyal member of the Administration were ignored—while his every minor transgression was punished harshly. A complete outsider would have rebelled or subsided into depression and silence. A complete insider would have seen only the rosiest aspects of Spanish life. It was his fate, and our gain, that he saw both sides. Out of his twofold experience a complex picture of Spanish society was born. It was a picture that included irony and parody, idealism and criticism, realism and fantasy: it was so rich and complex that we can still see ourselves mirrored in it. This is what makes him a classic. He knew that criticism without love created a distorted image, love without criticism a bland, fuzzy image. Luckily for him—and for us—he was plentifully endowed with a critical eye and a compassionate heart.

A last footnote to his biography seems necessary, so much the more as most of his biographers (and this is the case even with his most recent ones, such as Richard Predmore) have chosen to ignore or neglect this point. It is a mere detail, almost meaningless to the modern reader, yet all-important to the inhabitant of Golden Age Spain: was Cervantes an "old Christian"? In other words, are we sure (and was he sure) that he did not belong to a "New Christian" family, a *converso* family, in other words, a family in which some ancestors were converted Jews? A critical, ironic bent, plus an affinity for the ideas of Erasmus seem to point in the direction of a *converso* ancestry. The documentary proofs are lacking. Yet some of the best modern Hispanists, Américo Castro and Stephen Gilman among them, lean towards the idea that Cervantes came from a *converso* family. As Gilman states, "Salvador de Madariaga was first to give printed expression to a suspicion that those readers who had perceived Cervantes' constant mockery of pretensions to lineage (not only in the *Retablo de las maravillas* [*The Marvelous Pageant*], but also in the *Persiles* and the *Quixote*) had fleetingly entertained.... Since then Castro in his *Cervantes y los casticismos* (*Cervantes and the Caste System*), Madrid, 1966, has brought additional information to the fore.... The presence of no less than five physicians in Cervantes' immediate family will seem highly significant to those familiar with the social history of the time."[11] We may never know for certain. If these suspicions were to be confirmed, they would help to explain Cervantes' official neglect, his failure to achieve social status, his ironic vision. Be it as it may, he was a "marginal man," according to the sociologists' cliché, and his work bears witness to this fact. Of course, a "marginal man" usually becomes a humorist—when at all possible, if bitterness or depression do not interfere. This was his case. His merry vision transcended each personal crisis, each disappointment. His robust laughter and his ironic smile can still help us to achieve the same goals.

Notes

1. *Three Exemplary Novels*, trans. Samuel Putnam (New York: Viking Press, 1950), 151.

2. Ibid., 152.

3. In *Obras completas* (Madrid: Aguilar, 1949), 179.

4. Richard L. Predmore, *Cervantes* (New York: Dodd, Mead, 1973), 49.

5. *Cervantes: His Life, His Times, His Works. Created by the Editors of Arnoldo Mondadori* (New York: American Heritage Press, 1970), 25.

6. The date traditionally given for Cervantes' departure from Naples is 20 September 1575. Professor Juan Bautista Avalle-Arce, however, has corrected this date and proved that Cervantes must have departed early in September. See "La Captura de Cervantes," *Boletín de la Real Academia Española* (1968): 237–80.

7. Quoted by Predmore, *op. cit.*, 138.

8. Ibid.

9. *Obras completas*, ed. *op. cit.*, 1529.

10. *Historia de la literatura española. Edición revisada* (New York: Holt, Rinehart and Winston, 1963), I. 288.

11. *The Spain of Fernando de Rojas. The Intellectual and Social Landscape of La Celestina* (Princeton: Princeton University Press, 1972), 20.

The Enchanted Dulcinea

ERICH AUERBACH

◆ ◆ ◆

—Yo no veo, Sancho, dijo Don Quijote, sino a tres labradoras sobre tres borricos.

—Ahora me libre Dios del diablo, respondió Sancho; ¿y es posible que tres hacaneas, o como se llaman, blancas como el ampo de la nieve, le parezcan a vuesa merced borricos? Vive el Señor, que me pele estas barbas si tal fuese verdad.

—Pues yo te digo, Sancho amigo, dijo Don Quijote, que es tan verdad que son borricos o borricas, como yo soy Don Quijote, y tú Sancho Panza: a lo menos a mí tales me parecen.

—Calle, señor, dijo Sancho, no diga la tal palabra, sino despabile esos ojos, y venga a hacer reverencia a la señora de sus pensamientos, que ya llega cerca: y diciendo esto se adelantó a recibir a las tres aldeanas, y apeándose del rucio tuvo del cabestro al jumento de una de las tres labradoras, y hincando ambas rodillas en el suelo, dijo:

—Reina y princesa y duquesa de la hermosura, vuestra altivez y grandeza sea servida de recebir en su gracia y buen talante al cautivo caballero vuestro, que allí está hecho piedra mármol, todo turbado y sin pulsos de verse ante vuesa magnífica presencia. Yo soy Sancho Panza su escudero, y él es el asendereado caballero Don Quijote de la Mancha, llamado por otro nombre el Caballero de la Triste Figura. A esta sazón ya se había puesto Don Quijote de hinojos junto a Sancho, y miraba con ojos desencajados y vista turbada a la que Sancho llamaba reina y señora; y como no descubría en ella sino una moza aldeana y no de muy buen rostro, porque era carirredonda y chata, estaba suspenso y admirado, sin osar desplegar los labios. Las labradoras estaban asimismo atónitas viendo a aquellos dos hombres tan diferentes hincados de rodillas, que no dejaban pasar adelante a su compañera; pero rompiendo el silencio la detenida, toda desgradiada y mohina, dijo:

—Apártense nora en tal del camino, y dejenmos pasar, que vamos de priesa.

A lo que respondió Sancho:

—Oh princesa y señora universal del Toboso, ¿cómo vuestro magnífico corazón no se enternece viendo arrodillado ante vuestra sublimada presencia a la coluna y sustento de la andante caballería?

Oyendo lo cual otra de las dos dijo:

—Mas yo que te estrego burra de mi suegro mirad con qué se vienen los señoritos ahora a hacer burla de las aldeanas, como si aquí no supiésemos echar pullos como ellos: vayan su camino, y déjenmos hacer el nueso, y serles ha sano.

—Levántate, Sancho, dijo a este punto Don Quijote, que ya veo que la fortuna, de mi mal no harta, tiene tomados los caminos todos por donde pueda venir algún contento a esta ánima mezquina que tengo en las carnes. Y tú, oh extremo valor que puede desearse, término de la humana gentileza, único remedio de este afligido corazón que te adora, ya que el maligno encantador me persigue, y ha puesto nubes y cataratas en mis ojos, y para sólo ellos y no para otros ha mudado y transformado tu sin igual hermosura y rostro en el de una labradora pobre, si ya también el mío no le ha cambiado en el de algún vestiglo para hacerle aborrecible a tus ojos, no dejes de mirarme blanda y amorosamente, echando de ver en esta sumisión y arrodillamiento

que a tu contrahecha hermosura hago, la humildad con que mi
alma te adora.

—Toma que me agüelo, respondió la aldeana, imiguita soy yo
de oír resquebrajos. Apártense y déjenmos ir, y agradecérselo he-
mos.

Apartóse Sancho y déjola ir, contentísimo de haber salido bien
de su enredo. Apenas se vió libre la aldeana que había hecho la
figura de Dulcinea cuando picando a su hacanea con un aguijón
que en un palo traía, dió a correr por el prado adelante; y como
la borrica sentía la punta del aguijón, que le fatigaba más de lo
ordinario, comenzó a dar corcovos, de manera que dió con la
señora Dulcinea en tierra: lo cual visto por Don Quijote, acudió
a levantarla, y Sancho a componer y cinchar el albarda, que también vino a la barriga de la pollina. Acomodada pues el albarda,
y queriendo Don Quijote levantar a su encantada señora en los
brazos sobre la jumenta, la señora levantándose del suelo le quitó
de aquel trabajo, porque haciéndose algún tanto atrás tomó una
corridica, y puestas ambas manos sobre las ancas de la pollina dió
con su cuerpo más ligero que un halcón sobre la albarda, y quedó
a horcajadas como si fuera hombre, y entonces dijo Sancho:

—¡Vive Roque, que es la señora nuestra ama más ligera que
un alcotán, y que puede enseñar a subir de la jineta al más diestro
cordobés o mejicano; el arzón trasero de la silla pasó de un salto,
y sin espuelas hace correr la hacanea como una cebra, y no le
van en zaga sus doncellas, que todas corren como el viento!

Y así era la verdad, porque en viéndose a caballo Dulcinea todas
picaron tras ella y dispararon a correr, sin volver la cabeza atrás
por espacio de más de media legua. Siguiólas Don Quijote con
las vista, y cuando vió que no parecían, volviéndos a Sancho le
dijo:

—Sancho, ¿qué te parece, cuán mal quisto soy de encanta-
dores?...

("I see nothing," declared Don Quixote, "except three farm
girls on three jackasses."

"Then God deliver me from the devil!" exclaimed Sancho. "Is
it possible that those three hackneys, or whatever you call them,

white as the driven snow, look like jackasses to your Grace? By the living God, I would tear out this beard of mine if that were true!"

"But I tell you, friend Sancho, it is as true that those are jackasses, or she-asses, as it is that I am Don Quixote and you Sancho Panza. At least, that is the way they look to me."

"Be quiet, sir," Sancho admonished him, "you must not say such a thing as that. Open those eyes of yours and come do reverence to the lady of your affections, for she draws near."

Saying this, he rode on to meet the village maids and, slipping down off his donkey, seized one of their beasts by the halter and fell on his knees in front of its rider.

"O queen and princess and duchess of beauty," he said, "may your Highness and Majesty be pleased to receive and show favor to your captive knight, who stands there as if turned to marble, overwhelmed and breathless at finding himself in your magnificent presence. I am Sancho Panza, his squire, and he is the world-weary knight Don Quixote, otherwise known as the Knight of the Mournful Countenance."

By this time Don Quixote was down on his knees beside Sancho. His eyes were fairly starting from their sockets and there was a deeply troubled look in them as he stared up at the one whom Sancho had called queen and lady; all that he could see in her was a village wench, and not a very pretty one at that, for she was round-faced and snub-nosed. He was astounded and perplexed and did not dare open his mouth. The girls were also very much astonished to behold these two men, so different in appearance, kneeling in front of one of them so that she could not pass. It was this one who most ungraciously broke the silence.

"Get out of my way," she said peevishly, "and let me pass. And bad luck go with you. For we are in a hurry."

"O Princess and universal lady of El Toboso!" cried Sancho. "How can your magnanimous heart fail to melt as you behold kneeling before your sublimated presence the one who is the very pillar and support of knight-errantry?"

Hearing this, one of the others spoke up. "Whoa, there, she-ass of my father!" she said. "Wait until I curry you down. Just look at the small-fry gentry, will you, who've come to make sport of us country girls! Just as if we couldn't give them tit for tat. Be on your way and get out of ours, if you know what's good for you."

"Arise, Sancho," said Don Quixote, "for I perceive that fortune has not had her fill of evil done to me but has taken possession of all the roads by which some happiness may come to what little soul is left within me. And thou, who art all that could be desired, the sum of human gentleness and sole remedy for this afflicted heart that doth adore thee! The malign enchanter who doth persecute me hath placed clouds and cataracts upon my eyes, and for them and them alone hath transformed thy peerless beauty into the face of a lowly peasant maid; and I can only hope that he has not likewise changed my face into that of some monster by way of rendering it abhorrent in thy sight. But for all of that, hesitate not to gaze upon me tenderly and lovingly, beholding in this act of submission as I kneel before thee a tribute to thy metamorphosed beauty from this humbly worshiping heart of mine."

"Just listen to him run on, will you? My grandmother!" cried the lass. "Enough of such gibberish. We'll thank you to let us go our way."

Sancho fell back and let her pass, being very thankful to get out of it so easily.

No sooner did she find herself free than the girl who was supposed to have Dulcinea's face began spurring her "cackney" with a spike on the end of a long stick that she carried with her, whereupon the beast set off at top speed across the meadow. Feeling the prick, which appeared to annoy it more than was ordinarily the case, the ass started cutting such capers that the lady Dulcinea was thrown to the ground. When he saw this, Don Quixote hastened to lift her up while Sancho busied himself with tightening the girths and adjusting the packsaddle, which had slipped down under the animal's belly. This having been accomplished, Don Quixote was about to take his enchanted lady in his arms to place her upon the she-ass when the girl saved him the trouble by jumping up from the ground, stepping back a few paces, and taking a run for it. Placing both hands upon the crupper of the ass, she landed more lightly than a falcon upon the packsaddle and remained sitting there astride it like a man.

"In the name of Roque!" exclaimed Sancho, "our lady is like a lanner, only lighter, and can teach the cleverest Cordovan or Mexican how to mount. She cleared the back of the saddle in one jump, and without any spurs she makes her hackney run like a zebra, and her damsels are not far behind, for they all of them go like the wind."

This was the truth. Seeing Dulcinea in the saddle, the other two prodded their beasts and followed her on the run, without so much as turning their heads to look back for a distance of half a league. Don Quixote stood gazing after them, and when they were no longer visible he turned to Sancho and spoke.

"Sancho," he said, "you can see now, can you not, how the enchanters hate me?")[1]

THIS IS A PASSAGE from chapter 10 of part II of Cervantes' *Don Quijote*. The knight has sent Sancho Panza to the hamlet of El Toboso to call on Dulcinea and announce his intention of paying her a visit. Sancho, entangled in his earlier lies, and not knowing how to find the imaginary lady, decides to deceive his master. He waits outside the hamlet for a time, long enough to make Don Quijote believe that he has done his errand. Then, seeing three peasant women on donkeys riding toward him, he hurries back and tells his master that Dulcinea and two of her ladies are coming to greet him. The knight is overwhelmed with surprise and joy, and Sancho leads him toward the peasant women, describing their beauty and splendid gear in glowing colors. But for once Don Quijote sees nothing except the actual reality, that is, three peasant women on donkeys—and this leads to the scene we have quoted.

Among the many episodes which represent a clash between Don Quijote's illusion and an ordinary reality which contradicts it, this one holds a special place. First because it is concerned with Dulcinea herself, the ideal and incomparable mistress of his heart.

This is the climax of his illusion and disillusionment: and although this time too he manages to find a solution, a way to save his illusion, the solution (Dulcinea is under an enchantment) is so intolerable that henceforth all his thoughts are concentrated upon one goal: to save her and break the enchantment. In the last chapters of the book, his recognition or foreboding that he will never achieve this is the direct preparation for his illness, his deliverance from his illusion, and his death. In the second place the scene is distinguished by the fact that here for the first time the roles appear exchanged. Until now it had been Don Quijote who, encountering everyday phenomena, spontaneously saw and transformed them in terms of the romances of chivalry, while Sancho was generally in doubt and often tried to contradict and prevent his master's absurdities. Now it is the other way round. Sancho improvises a scene after the fashion of the romances of chivalry, while Don Quijote's ability to transform events to harmonize with his illusion breaks down before the crude vulgarity of the sight of the peasant women. All this seems most significant. As we have here (intentionally) presented it, it sounds sad, bitter, and almost tragic.

But if we merely read Cervantes' text, we have a farce, and a farce which is overwhelmingly comic. Many illustrators have rendered the scene: Don Quijote on his knees beside Sancho, staring in wide-eyed bewilderment at the repellent spectacle before him. But only the stylistic contrast in the speeches, and the grotesque movement at the end (Dulcinea's fall and remounting), afford the fullest enjoyment of what is going on. The stylistic contrast in the speeches develops only slowly, because at first the peasant women are much too astonished. Dulcinea's first utterance (her request to be allowed to pass) is still moderate. It is only in their later speeches that the peasant women display the pearls of their eloquence. The first representative of the chivalric style is Sancho, and it is amusing and surprising to see how well he plays his part. He jumps off his donkey, throws himself at the women's feet, and speaks as though he had never heard anything in all his life but the jargon of romances of chivalry. Forms of address, syntax, metaphors, epithets, the description of his master's posture, and his supplication to be heard—it all comes out most successfully, although Sancho cannot read and owes his education wholly to the example set him by Don Quijote. His performance is successful, at least insofar as he gets his master to follow suit: Don Quijote kneels down beside him.

It might be supposed that all this would bring on a terrible crisis. Dulcinea is really *la señora de sus pensamientos*, the paragon of beauty, the goal and meaning of his life. Arousing his expectations in this way, and then disappointing them so greatly, is no harmless experiment. It could produce a shock which in turn could bring on much deeper insanity. But there is also the possibility that the shock might bring about a cure, instantaneous liberation from his idée fixe. Neither of these things happens. Don Quijote surmounts the shock. In his idée fixe itself he finds a solution which prevents him both from falling into despair and from recovering his sanity: Dulcinea is enchanted. This solution appears each time the exterior situation establishes itself as in insuperable contrast to the illusion. It makes it possible for Don Quijote to persist in the attitude of the noble and invincible hero persecuted by a powerful magician who envies his glory. In this particular case—the case of Dulcinea—the idea of so repellent and base an enchantment is certainly hard to endure. Still, it is possible to meet the situation by means available within the realm of the illusion itself, that is, by means of the knightly virtues of unalterable loyalty, devoted self-sacrifice, and unhesitating courage. And then there is the established fact that virtue will win in the end. The happy ending is a foregone conclusion. Thus both tragedy and cure are circumvented. And so, after a brief pause of disconcerted silence, Don Quijote begins to speak. He turns to Sancho first. His words show that he has recovered his bearings, that he has interpreted the situation in terms of his illusion. This interpretation has become so firmly crystallized in him that even the earthy colloquialisms in the directly preceding speech of one of the peasant women—however sharply they may contrast with the elevated style of knightly refinement—can no longer make him doubtful of his attitude. Sancho's stratagem has succeeded. Don Quijote's second sentence is addressed to Dulcinea.

It is a very beautiful sentence. A moment ago we pointed out how cleverly and amusingly Sancho handles the style of the romances of chivalry which he has picked up from his master. Now we see what sort of a master he had. The sentence begins, like a prayer, with an imploring apostrophe (*invocatio*). This has three gradations (*extremo del valor . . .* , *término . . .* , *único remedio . . .*), and they are very carefully considered and arranged, for it first emphasizes an absolute perfection, then a perfection in human terms, and finally the special personal devotion of the speaker. The threefold structure is held together by the initial words *y tú*, and ends, in its third, sweepingly constructed division, with the rhythmically conventional but magnificently integrated *corazón que te adora*. Here, in content, choice of words, and rhythm, the theme which appears at the end is already alluded to. Thus a transition is established from the *invocatio* to its obligatory complement, the *supplicatio*, for which the optative principal clause is reserved (*no dejes de mirarme . . .*), although it is still some time before we are allowed to reach it. First we have the multiple gradation—dramatically contrasting with both *invocatio* and *supplicatio*—of the concessive complex, *ya que . . .* , *y . . . y . . .* , *si ya también. . . .* Its sense is "and even though," and its rhythmic climax is reached in the middle of the first (*ya que*) part, in the strongly emphasized words *y para sólo ellos*. Only after this entire wonderful and dramatic melody of the concessive clause has run its course, is the long-restrained principal clause of the *supplicatio* allowed to appear, but it too holds back and piles up paraphrases and pleonasms until finally the main motif, which constitutes the goal and purpose of the entire period, is sounded: the words which are to symbolize Don Quijote's present attitude and his entire life, *la humildad con que mi alma te adora*. This is the style so greatly admired by Sancho in part I, chapter 25, where Don Quijote reads his letter to Dulcinea aloud to him: *¡y como que le dice vuestra merced ahí todo cuanto quiere, y qué bien que encaja en la firma El Caballero de la Triste Figura!* But the present speech is incomparably more beautiful; with all its art it shows less pedantic preciosity than the letter. Cervantes is very fond of such rhythmically and pictorially rich, such beautifully articulated and musical bravura pieces of chivalric rhetoric (which are nevertheless rooted in the tradition of antiquity). And he is a master in the field. Here again he is not merely a destructive critic but a continuer and consummator of the great epico-rhetorical tradition for which prose too is an art. As soon as great emotions and passions or sublime events are involved, this elevated style with all its devices appears. To be sure, its being so long a convention has shifted it slightly from the sphere of high tragedy toward that of the smoothly pleasant, which is capable of at least a trace of self-irony. Yet it is still dominant in the serious sphere. One has only to read Dorotea's speech to her unfaithful lover (part I, chapter 36), with its numerous figures, similes, and rhythmic clauses, in order to sense that this style is still alive even in the serious and the tragic.

Here, however, in Dulcinea's presence, it simply serves the effect of contrast. The peasant girl's crude, contemptuous reply gives it its real significance; we are in the realm of the low style, and Don Quijote's elevated rhetoric only serves to make the comedy of the stylistic anticlimax fully effective. But even this is not enough to satisfy Cervantes. To the stylistic anticlimax he adds an extreme anticlimax in the action by having Dulcinea fall off her donkey and jump on again with grotesque dexterity, while Don Quijote still tries to maintain the chivalric style. His being so firmly fixed in his illusion that neither Dulcinea's reply nor the scene with the donkey can shake him is the acme of farce. Even Sancho's exuberant gaiety (*Vive Roque*), which after all is nothing short of impertinent, cannot make him lose his bearings. He looks after the peasant women as they ride away, and when they have disappeared he turns to Sancho with words expressive much less of sadness or despair than of a sort of triumphant satisfaction over the fact that he has become the target of the evil magician's darkest arts. This makes it possible for him to feel that he is elect, unique, and in a way which tallies perfectly with the conventions of the knight-errant: *yo nací para ejemplo de desdichados, y para ser blanco y terrero donde tomen la mira y asesten las flechas de la mala fortuna.* And the observation he now makes, to the effect that the evil enchantment affects even Dulcinea's aura—for her breath had not been pleasant—can disturb his illusion as little as

Sancho's grotesque description of details of her beauty. Encouraged by the complete success of his trick, Sancho has now really warmed up and begins to play with his master's madness purely for his own amusement.

In our study we are looking for representations of everyday life in which that life is treated seriously, in terms of its human and social problems or even of its tragic complications. The scene from Don Quijote with which we are dealing is certainly realistic. All the participants are presented in their true reality, their living everyday existence. Not only the peasant women but Sancho too, not only Sancho but also Don Quijote, appear as persons representative of contemporary Spanish life. For the fact that Sancho is playing a rogue's game and that Don Quijote is enmeshed in his illusion does not raise either of them out of his everyday existence. Sancho is a peasant from La Mancha, and Don Quijote is no Amadis or Roland, but a little country squire who has lost his mind. At best we might say that the hidalgo's madness translates him into another, imaginary sphere of life; but even so the everyday character of our scene and others similar to it remains unharmed, because the persons and events of everyday life are constantly colliding with his madness and come out in stronger relief through the contrast.

It is much more difficult to determine the position of the scene, and of the novel as a whole, on the scale of levels between tragic and comic. As presented, the story of the encounter with the three peasant women is nothing if not comic. The idea of having Don Quijote encounter a concrete Dulcinea must certainly have come to Cervantes even when he was writing the first part of the novel. The idea of building up such a scene on the basis of a deceitful trick played by Sancho, so that the roles appear interchanged, is a stroke of genius, and it is so magnificently carried out that the farce presents itself to the reader as something perfectly natural and even bound to take place, despite the complex absurdity of all its presuppositions and relations. But it remains pure farce. We have tried to show above that, in the case of the only one of the participants with whom the possibility of a shift into the tragic and problematic exists, that is, in the case of Don Quijote, such a shift is definitely avoided. The fact that he almost instantaneously and as it were automatically takes refuge in the interpretation that Dulcinea is under an enchantment excludes everything tragic. He is taken in, and this time even by Sancho; he kneels down and orates in a lofty emotional style before a group of ugly peasant women; and then he takes pride in his sublime misfortune.

But Don Quijote's feelings are genuine and profound. Dulcinea is really the mistress of his thoughts; he is truly filled with the spirit of a mission which he regards as man's highest duty. He is really true, brave, and ready to sacrifice everything. So unconditional a feeling and so unconditional a determination impose admiration even though they are based on a foolish illusion, and this admiration has been accorded to Don Quijote by almost all readers. There are probably few lovers of literature who do not associate the concept of ideal greatness with Don Quijote. It may be absurd, fantastic, grotesque; but it is still ideal, unconditional, heroic. It is especially since the Romantic period that this conception has become almost universal, and it withstands all attempts on the part of philological criticism to show that Cervantes' intention was not to produce such an impression.

The difficulty lies in the fact that in Don Quijote's idée fixe we have a combination of the noble, immaculate, and redeeming with absolute nonsense. A tragic struggle for the ideal and desirable cannot at first blush be imagined in any way but as intervening meaningfully in the actual state of things, stirring it up, pressing it hard; with the result that the meaningful ideal encounters an equally meaningful resistance which proceeds either from inertia, petty malice, and envy, or possibly from a more conservative view. The will working for an ideal must accord with existing reality at least to such an extent that it meets it, so that the two interlock and a real conflict arises. Don Quijote's idealism is not of this kind. It is not based on an understanding of actual conditions in this world. Don Quijote does have such an understanding but it deserts him as soon as the idealism of his idée fixe takes hold of him. Everything he does in that state is completely senseless and so incompatible with the existing world that it produces only comic confusion there. It not only has no chance of success, it actually has no point of contact with reality; it expends itself in a vacuum.

The same idea can be developed in another way, so that further consequences become clear. The theme of the noble and brave fool who sets forth to realize his ideal and improve the world, might be treated in such a way that the problems and conflicts in the world are presented and worked out in the process. Indeed, the purity and ingenuousness of the fool could be such that, even in the absence of any concrete purpose to produce effects, wherever he appears he unwittingly goes to the heart of things, so that the conflicts which are pending and hidden are rendered acute. One might think here of Dostoevski's *Idiot*. Thus the fool could be involved in responsibility and guilt and assume the role of a tragic figure. Nothing of the sort takes place in Cervantes' novel.

Don Quijote's encounter with Dulcinea is not a good illustration of his relationship to concrete reality, inasmuch as here he does not, as elsewhere, impose his ideal will in conflict with that reality; here he beholds and worships the incarnation of his ideal. Yet this encounter too is symbolic of the mad knight's relationship to the phenomena of this world. The reader should recall what traditional concepts were contained in the Dulcinea motif and how they are echoed in Sancho's and Don Quijote's grotesquely sublime words. *La señora de sus pensamientos, extremo del valor que puede desearse, término de la humana gentileza,* and so forth—alive in all this are Plato's idea of beauty, courtly love, the *donna gentile* of the *dolce stil nuovo*, Beatrice, *la gloriosa donna della mia mente*. And all this ammunition is expended on three ugly and vulgar peasant women. It is poured into a void. Don Quijote can neither be graciously received nor graciously rejected. There is nothing but amusingly senseless confusion. To find anything serious, or a concealed deeper meaning in this scene, one must violently overinterpret it.

The three women are flabbergasted; they get away as fast as they can. This is an effect frequently produced by Don Quijote's appearance. Often disputes result and the participants come to blows. People are apt to lose their temper when Don Quijote interferes in their business with his nonsense. Very often too they humor him in his idée fixe in order to get some fun from it. The innkeeper and the whores at the time of his first departure react in this way. The same thing happens again later with the company at the second inn, with the priest and the barber, Dorotea and Don Fernando, and even with Maritornes. Some of these, it is true, mean to use their game as a way of getting the knight safely back home, but they carry it much further than their practical purpose would require. In part II the *bachiller* Sansón Carrasco bases his therapeutic plan on playing along with Don Quijote's idée fixe; later, at the duke's palace and in Barcelona, his madness is methodically exploited as a pastime, so that hardly any of his adventures are genuine; they are simply staged, that is, they have been especially prepared to suit the hidalgo's madness, for the amusement of those who get them up. Among all these reactions, both in part I and part II, one thing is completely lacking: tragic complications and serious consequences. Even the element of contemporary satire and criticism is very weak. If we leave out of consideration the purely literary criticism, there is almost none at all. It is limited to brief remarks or occasional caricatures of types (for example, the priest at the duke's court). It never goes to the roots of things and is moderate in attitude. Above all, Don Quijote's adventures never reveal any of the basic problems of the society of the time. His activity reveals nothing at all. It affords an opportunity to present Spanish life in its color and fullness. In the resulting clashes between Don Quijote and reality no situation ever results which puts in question that reality's right to be what it is. It is always right and he wrong; and after a bit of amusing confusion it flows calmly on, untouched. There is one scene where this might seem doubtful. It is the freeing of the galley slaves in part I, chapter 22. Here Don Quijote intervenes in the established legal order, and some critics will be found to uphold the opinion that he does so in the name of a higher morality. This view is natural, for what Don Quijote says: *allá se lo haya cada uno con su pecado; Dios hay en el cielo que no se descuida de castigar al malo ni de premiar al bueno, y no es bien que los hombres honrados sean verdugos do los otros hombres, no yéndoles nada en ello*—such a statement is certainly on a higher level than any positive law. But a "higher morality" of the kind here envisaged must be consistent and methodical if it is to be taken seriously. We know, however, that Don Quijote has no idea of making a basic attack on the established legal order. He is neither an anarchist nor a prophet of the Kingdom of God. On the contrary, it is apparent again and again that whenever his idée fixe happens not to be involved he is willing to conform, that it is only through his idée fixe that he claims a special position for the knight-errant. The beautiful words, *alla se lo haya*, etc., are deeply rooted, to be sure, in the kindly wisdom of his real nature (this is a point to which we shall return), but in their context they are still merely an improvisation. It is his idée fixe which determines him to free the prisoners. It alone forces him to conceive of everything he encounters as the subject of a knightly adventure. It supplies him with the motifs "help the distressed" or "free the victims of force," and he acts accordingly. I think it wholly erroneous to look for a matter of principle here, for anything like a conflict between natural Christian and positive law. For such a conflict, moreover, an opponent would have to appear, someone like the Grand Inquisitor in Dostoevski, who would be authorized and willing to represent the cause of positive law against Don Quijote. His Majesty's commissary who is in charge of the convoy of prisoners is neither suited for the role nor prepared to play it. Personally he may very well be ready to accept the argument, "judge not that ye be not judged." But he has passed no judgment; he is no representative of positive law. He has his instructions and is quite justified in appealing to them.

Everything comes out all right, and time and again the damage done or suffered by Don Quijote is treated with stoic humor as a matter of comic confusion. Even the *bachiller* Alonso Lopez, as he lies on the ground, badly mauled and with one leg pinned under his mule, consoles himself with mocking puns. This scene occurs in chapter 19 of book I. It also shows that Don Quijote's idée fixe saves him from feeling responsible for the harm he does, so that in his conscience too every form of tragic conflict and somber seriousness is obviated. He has acted in accordance with the rules of knight-errantry, and so he is justified. To be sure, he hastens to assist the *bachiller*, for he is a kind and helpful soul; but it does not occur to him to feel guilty. Nor does he feel any guiltier when at the beginning of chapter 30 the priest puts him to the test by telling him what evil effects his freeing of the prisoners had produced. He angrily exclaims that it is the duty of a knight-errant to help those in distress but not to judge whether their plight is deserved or not. And that settles the question as far as he is concerned. In part II, where the gaiety is even more relaxed and elegant, such complications no longer occur at all.

There is, then, very little of problem and tragedy in Cervantes' book—and yet it belongs among the literary masterpieces of an epoch during which the modern problematic and tragic conception of things arose in the European mind. Don Quijote's madness reveals nothing of the sort. The whole book is a comedy in which well-founded reality holds madness up to ridicule.

And yet Don Quijote is not only ridiculous. He is not like the bragging soldier or the comic old man or the pedantic and ignorant doctor. In our scene Don Quijote is taken in by Sancho. But does Sancho despise him and deceive him all the way through? Not at all. He deceives him only because he sees no other way out. He loves and reveres him, although he is half conscious (and sometimes fully conscious) of his madness. He learns from him and refuses to part with him. In Don Quijote's company he becomes cleverer and better than he was before. With all his madness, Don Quijote preserves a natural dignity and superiority which his many miserable failures cannot harm. He is not vulgar, as the above-mentioned comic types normally are. Actually he is not a "type" at all in this sense, for on the whole he is no automaton producing comic effects. He even develops, and grows kinder and wiser while his madness persists. But would it be true to say that his is a wise madness in the ironical sense of the romanticists? Does wisdom come to him through his madness? Does his madness give him an understanding he could not have attained in soundness of mind, and do we hear wisdom speak through madness in his case as we do with Shakespeare's fools or with Charlie Chaplin? No, that is not it either. As soon as his madness, that is, the idée fixe of knight-errantry, takes hold of him, he acts unwisely, he acts like an automaton in the manner of the comic types mentioned above. He is wise and kind independently of his madness. A madness like this, it is true, can arise only in a pure and noble soul, and it is also true that wisdom, kindness, and decency shine through his madness and make it appear lovable. Yet his wisdom and his madness are clearly separated—in direct contrast to what we find in Shakespeare, the fools of Romanticism, and Charlie Chaplin. The priest says it as early as chapter 30 of part I and later it comes out again and again: he is mad only when his idée fixe comes into play; otherwise he is a perfectly normal and very intelligent individual. His madness is not such that it represents his whole nature and is completely identical with it. At a specific moment an idée fixe laid hold on him; but even so it leaves parts of his being unaffected, so that in many instances he acts and speaks like a person of sound mind; and one day, shortly before his death, it leaves him again. He was some fifty years of age when, under the influence of his excessive reading of romances of chivalry, he conceived his absurd plan. This is strange. An overwrought state of mind resulting from solitary reading might rather be expected in a youthful person (Julien Sorel, Madame Bovary), and one is tempted to look for a specific psychological explanation. How is it possible that a man in his fifties who leads a normal life and whose intelligence is well developed in many ways and not at all unbalanced, should embark upon so absurd a venture? In the opening sentences of his novel Cervantes supplies some details of his hero's social position. From them we may at best infer that it was burdensome to him, for it offered no possibility of an active life commensurate with his abilities. He was as it were paralyzed by the limitations imposed upon him on the one hand by his class and on the other by his poverty. Thus one might suppose that his mad decision represents a flight from a situation which has become unbearable, a violent attempt to emancipate himself from it. This sociological and psychological interpretation has been advocated by various writers on the subject. I myself advanced it in an earlier passage of this book, and I leave it there because in the context of that passage it is justified. But as an interpretation of Cervantes' artistic purpose it is unsatisfactory, for it is not likely that he intended his brief observations on Don Quijote's social position and habits of life to imply anything like a psychological motivation of the knight's idée fixe. He would have had to state it more clearly and elaborate it in greater detail. A modern psychologist might find still other explanations of Don Quijote's strange madness. But this sort of approach to the problem has no place in Cervantes' thinking. Confronted with the question of the causes of Don Quijote's madness, he has only one answer: Don Quijote read too many romances of chivalry and they deranged his mind. That this should happen to a man in his fifties can be explained—from within the work—only in aesthetic terms, that is, through the comic vision which came to Cervantes when he conceived the novel: a tall, elderly man, dressed in old-fashioned and shabby armor, a picture which is beautifully expressive not only of madness but also of asceticism and the fanatic pursuit of an ideal. We simply have to accept the fact that this cultured and intelligent country gentleman goes suddenly mad—not, like Ajax or Hamlet, because of a terrible shock—but simply because he has read too many romances of chivalry. Here again there is nothing tragic. In the analysis of his madness we have to do without the concept of the tragic, just as we have to do without the specifically Shakespearean and romantic combination of wisdom and madness in which one cannot be conceived without the other.

Don Quijote's wisdom is not the wisdom of a fool. It is the intelligence, the nobility, the civility, and the dignity of a gifted and well-balanced man—a man neither demonic nor paradoxical, not beset by doubt and indecision nor by any feeling of not being at home in this world, but even-tempered, able to weigh and ponder, receptive, and lovable and modest even in his irony. Furthermore he is a conservative, or at least essentially in accord with the order of things as it is. This comes out wherever and whenever he deals with people—especially with Sancho Panza—

in the longer or shorter intervals during which his idée fixe is quiescent. From the very beginning—although more in part II than in part I—the kindly, intelligent, and amiable figure, Alonso Quijano el Bueno, whose most distinguishing characteristic is his naturally superior dignity, coexists with the mad adventurer. We need only read with what kindly and merry irony he treats Sancho in part II, chapter 7, when the latter, on the advice of his wife Teresa, begins to present his request for a fixed salary. His madness intervenes only when he justifies his refusal by referring to the customs of knights-errant. Passages of this kind abound. There is evidence everywhere that we have to do with an intelligent Don Quijote and a mad one, side by side, and that his intelligence is in no way dialectically inspired by his madness but is a normal and, as it were, average intelligence.

That in itself yields an unusual combination. There are levels of tone represented here which one is not accustomed to finding in purely comic contexts. A fool is a fool. We are used to seeing him represented on a single plane, that of the comic and foolish, with which, at least in earlier literature, baseness and stupidity, and at times underhanded malice, were connected as well. But what are we to say of a fool who is at the same time wise, with that wisdom which seems the least compatible with folly, that is, the wisdom of intelligent moderation? This very fact, this combination of intelligent moderation with absurd excesses results in a multiplicity which cannot be made to accord altogether with the purely comic. But that is by no means all. It is on the very wings of his madness that his wisdom soars upward, that it roams the world and becomes richer there. For if Don Quijote had not gone mad, he would not have left his house. And then Sancho too would have stayed home, and he could never have drawn from his innate being the things which—as we find in delighted amazement—were potentially contained in it. The multifarious play of action and reaction between the two and their joint play in the world would not have taken place.

This play, as we think we have been able to show, is never tragic; and never are human problems, whether personal or social, represented in such a way that we tremble and are moved to compassion. We always remain in the realm of gaiety. But the levels of gaiety are multiplied as never before. Let us return once more to the text from which we set out. Don Quijote speaks to the peasant women in a style which is genuinely the elevated style of courtly love and which in itself is by no means grotesque. His sentences are not at all ridiculous (though they may seem so to many readers in our day), they are in the tradition of the period and represent a masterpiece of elevated expression in the form in which it was then alive. If it was Cervantes' purpose to attack the romances of chivalry (and there can be no doubt that it was), he nevertheless did not attack the elevated style of chivalric expression. On the contrary, he reproaches the romances of chivalry with not mastering the style, with being stylistically wooden and dry. And so it comes about that in the middle of a parody against the knightly ideology of love we find one of the most beautiful prose passages which the late form of the tradition of courtly love produced. The peasant women answer with characteristic coarseness. Such a rustically boorish style had long been employed in comic literature (although possibly never with the same balance between moderation and verve), but what had certainly never happened before was that it should follow directly upon a speech like Don Quijote's—a speech which, taken by itself, could never make us suspect that it occurs in a grotesque context. The motif of a knight begging a peasant woman to hear his love—a motif which produces a comparable situation—is age old. It is the motif of the *pastourelle*; it was in favor with the early Provençal poets, and, as we shall see when we come to Voltaire, it was remarkably long-lived. However, in the *pastourelle* the two partners have adapted themselves to each other; they understand each other; and the result is a homogeneous level of style on the borderline between the idyllic and the everyday. In Cervantes' case, the two realms of life and style clash by reason of Don Quijote's madness. There is no possibility of a transition; each is closed in itself; and the only link that holds them together is the merry neutrality of the playful scheme of puppet-master Sancho—the awkward bumpkin, who but a short time before believed almost everything his master said, who will never get over believing some of it, and who always acts in accordance with the momentary situation. In our passage the dilemma of the moment has inspired him to deceive his master; and he adapts himself to the position of puppet-master with as much gusto and elasticity as he later will to the position of governor of an island. He starts the play in the elevated style, then switches to the low—not, however, in the manner of the peasant women. He maintains his superiority and remains master of the situation which he has himself created under the pressure of necessity but which he now enjoys to the full.

What Sancho does in this case—assuming a role, transforming himself, and playing with his master's madness—other characters in the book are perpetually doing. Don Quijote's madness gives rise to an inexhaustible series of disguises and histrionics: Dorotea in the role of Princess Micomicona, the barber as her page, Sansón Carrasco as knight-errant, Ginés de Pasamonte as puppet-master—these are but a few examples. Such metamorphoses make reality become a perpetual stage without ever ceasing to be reality. And when the characters do not submit to the metamorphosis of their own free will, Don Quijote's madness forces them into their roles—as happens time and again, beginning with the innkeeper and the whores in the first tavern. Reality willingly cooperates with a play which dresses it up differently every moment. It never spoils the gaiety of the play by bringing in the serious weight of its troubles, cares, and passions. All that is resolved in Don Quijote's madness; it transforms the real everyday world into a gay stage. Here one should recall the various adventures with women which occur in the course of the narrative in addition to the encounter with Dulcinea: Maritornes struggling in Don Quijote's arms, Dorotea as Princess Micomicona, the lovelorn Altisidora's serenade, the nocturnal encounter with Doña Rodriguez (a scene which Cide Hamete Benengeli says that he would have given his best coat to see)—each of these stories is in a different style; each contains a shift in stylistic level; all of them are resolved by Don Quijote's madness, and all of them remain within the realm of gaiety. And yet there are several which need not necessarily have been thus restricted. The description of Maritornes and her muleteer is coarsely realistic; Dorotea is unhappy; and Doña Rodriguez is in great distress of mind because her daughter has been seduced. Don Quijote's intervention changes nothing of this— neither Maritornes' loose life nor the sad plight of Doña Rodriguez' daughter. But what happens is that we are not concerned over these things, that we see the lot and the life of these women through the prism of gaiety, and that our consciences do not feel troubled over them. As God lets the sun shine and the rain fall on the just and the unjust alike, so Don Quijote's madness, in its bright equanimity, illumines everything that crosses his path and leaves it in a state of gay confusion.

The most varied suspense and wisest gaiety of the book are revealed in a relationship which Don Quijote maintains throughout: his relationship with Sancho Panza. It is not at all as easy to describe in unambiguous terms as the relationship between Rocinante and Sancho's donkey or that between the donkey and Sancho himself. They are not always united in unfailing loyalty and love. It frequently happens that Don Quijote becomes so angry with Sancho that he abuses and maltreats him; at times he is ashamed of him; and once—in part II, chapter 27—he actually deserts him in danger. Sancho, for his part, originally accompanies Don Quijote because he is stupid and for the selfishly materialistic reason that he expects fantastic advantages from the venture, and also because, despite all its hardships, he prefers a vagabond life to the regular working hours and monotony of life at home. Before long he begins to sense that something must be wrong with Don Quijote's mind, and then he sometimes deceives him, makes fun of him, and speaks of him disrespectfully. At times, even in part II, he is so disgusted and disillusioned that he is all but ready to leave Don Quijote. Again and again the reader is made to see how variable and composite our human relationships are, how capricious and dependent on the moment even the most intimate of them. In the passage which was our point of departure Sancho deceives his master and plays almost cruelly on his madness. But what painstaking humoring of Don Quijote's madness, what sympathetic penetration of his world, must have preceded Sancho's conceiving such a plan and his being able to act his role so well! Only a few months earlier he had not the slightest inkling of all this. Now he lives, after his own fashion, in the world of knightly adventure; he is fascinated by it. He has fallen in love with his master's madness and with his own role. His development is most amazing. Yet withal, he is and remains Sancho, of the Panza family, a Christian of the old stock, well known in his village. He remains all that even in the role of a wise governor and also—and indeed especially—when he insists on Sanchica's marrying nothing less than a count. He remains Sancho; and all that happens to him could happen only to Sancho. But the fact that these things do happen, that his body and his mind are put in such violent commotion and emerge from the ordeal in all their unshakable and idiosyncratic genuineness—this he owes to Don Quijote, *su amo y natural señor.* The experience of Don Quijote's personality is not received by anyone as completely as it is by Sancho; it is not assimilated pure and whole by anyone as it is by him. The others all wonder about him, are amused or angered by him, or try to cure him. Sancho lives himself into Don Quijote, whose madness and wisdom become productive in him. Although he has far too little critical reasoning power to form and express a synthetic judgment upon him, it still is he, in all his reactions, through whom we best understand Don Quijote. And this in turn binds Don Quijote to him. Sancho is his consolation and his direct opposite, his creature and yet an independent fellow being who holds out against him and prevents his madness from locking him up as though in solitary confinement. Two partners who appear together as contrasting comic or semi-comic figures represent a very old motif which has retained its effectiveness even today in farce, caricature, the circus, and the film: the tall thin man and the short fat one; the clever man and his stupid companion; master and servant; the refined aristocrat and the simple-minded peasants; and whatever other combinations and variants there may be in different countries and under different cultural conditions. What Cervantes made of it is magnificent and unique.

Perhaps it is not quite correct to speak of what Cervantes made of it. It may be more exact to say "what became of the motif in

his hands." For centuries—and especially since the romanticists—
many things have been read into him which he hardly foreboded,
let alone intended. Such transforming and transcendent interpretations are often fertile. A book like *Don Quijote* dissociates itself
from its author's intention and leads a life of its own. Don Quijote
shows a new face to every age which enjoys him. Yet the historian—whose task it is to define the place of a given work in a
historical continuity—must endeavor insofar as that is still possible, to attain a clear understanding of what the work meant to
its author and his contemporaries. I have tried to interpret as
little as possible. In particular, I have pointed out time and again
how little there is in the text which can be called tragic and
problematic. I take it as merry play on many levels, including in
particular the level of everyday realism. The latter differentiates
it from the equally unproblematic gaiety of let us say Ariosto;
but even so it remains play. This means that no matter how
painstakingly I have tried to do as little interpreting as possible,
I yet cannot help feeling that my thoughts about the book often
go far beyond Cervantes' aesthetic intention. Whatever that intention may have been (we shall not here take up the problems
presented by the aesthetics of his time), it most certainly did not
consciously and from the beginning propose to create a relationship like that between Don Quijote and Sancho Panza as we see
it after having read the novel. Rather, the two figures were first
a single vision, and what finally developed from them—singly
and together—arose gradually, as the result of hundreds of individual ideas, as the result of hundreds of situations in which
Cervantes puts them and to which they react on the spur of the
moment, as the result of the inexhaustible, ever-fresh power of
the poetic imagination. Now and again there are actual incongruities and contradictions, not only in matters of fact (which
has often been noted) but also in psychology: developments
which do not fit into the total picture of the two heroes—which
indicates how much Cervantes allowed himself to be guided by
the momentary situation, by the demands of the adventure in
hand. This is still the case—more frequently even—in part II.
Gradually and without any preconceived plan, the two person-

ages evolve, each in himself and also in their relation to each other. To be sure, this is the very thing which allows what is peculiarly Cervantean, the sum of Cervantes' experience of life and the wealth of his imagination, to enter the episodes and speeches all the more richly and spontaneously. The "peculiarly Cervantean" cannot be described in words. And yet I shall attempt to say something *about* it in order to clarify its power and its limits. First of all it is something spontaneously sensory: a vigorous capacity for the vivid visualization of very different people in very varied situations, for the vivid realization and expression of what thoughts enter their minds, what emotions fill their hearts, and what words come to their lips. This capacity he possesses so directly and strongly, and in a manner so independent of any sort of ulterior motive, that almost everything realistic written before him appears limited, conventional, or propagandistic in comparison. And just as sensory is his capacity to think up or hit upon ever new combinations of people and events. Here, to be sure, we have to consider the older tradition of the romance of adventure and its renewal through Boiardo and Ariosto, but no one before him had infused the element of genuine everyday reality into that brilliant and purposeless play of combinations. And finally he has a "something" which organizes the whole and makes it appear in a definite "Cervantean" light. Here things begin to be very difficult. One might avoid the difficulty and say that this "something" is merely contained in the subject matter, in the idea of the country gentleman who loses his mind and convinces himself that it is his duty to revive knight-errantry, that it is this theme which gives the book its unity and its attitude. But the theme (which Cervantes, by the way, took over from the minor and in itself totally uninteresting contemporary work, the *Entremés de los romances*) could have been treated quite differently too. The hero might have looked very different; it was not necessary that there should be a Dulcinea and particularly a Sancho. But above all, what was it that so attracted Cervantes in the idea? What attracted him was the possibilities it offered for multifariousness and effects of perspective, the mixture of fanciful and everyday elements in the subject, its malleability, elasticity, adaptability. It was ready to absorb all forms of style and art. It permitted the presentation of the most variegated picture of the world in a light congenial to his own nature. And here we have come back to the difficult question we asked before: what is the "something" which orders the whole and makes it appear in a definite, "Cervantean" light?

It is not a philosophy; it is no didactic purpose; it is not even a being stirred by the uncertainty of human existence or by the power of destiny, as in the case of Montaigne and Shakespeare. It is an attitude—an attitude toward the world, and hence also toward the subject matter of his art—in which bravery and equanimity play a major part. Together with the delight he takes in the multifariousness of his sensory play there is in him a certain Southern [European—ED.] reticence and pride. This prevents him from taking the play very seriously. He looks at it; he shapes it; he finds it diverting; it is also intended to afford the reader refined intellectual diversion.

But he does not take sides (except against badly written books); he remains neutral. It is not enough to say that he does not judge and in the author's style. For Cervantes, a good novel serves no other purpose than to afford refined recreation, *honesto entretenimiento*. No one has expressed this more convincingly in recent times than W. J. Entwistle in his book on Cervantes (1940) where he speaks of recreation and connects it very beautifully with re-creation. It would never have occurred to Cervantes that the style of a novel—be it the best of novels—could reveal the order of the universe. On the other hand, for him too the phenomena of reality had come to be difficult to survey and no longer possible to arrange in an unambiguous and traditional manner. Elsewhere in Europe men had long since begun to question and to doubt, and even to begin building anew with their own materials. But that was in keeping neither with the spirit of his country nor with his own temperament, nor finally with his conception of the office of a writer. He found the order of reality in play. It is no longer the play of Everyman, which provides fixed norms for the judgment of good and evil. That was still so in *La Celestina*. Now things are no longer so simple. Cervantes undertakes to pass judgment only in matters concerning his profession as a writer. So far as the secular world is concerned, we are all sinners; God will see to it that evil is punished and good rewarded. Here on earth the order of the unsurveyable is to be found in play. However arduous it may be to survey and judge phenomena, before the mad knight of La Mancha they turn into a dance of gay and diverting confusion.

This, it seems to me, is the function of Don Quijote's madness. When the theme—the mad hidalgo who sets forth to realize the ideal of the *caballero andante*—began to kindle Cervantes' imagination, he also perceived a vision of how, confronted with such madness, contemporary reality might be portrayed. And the vision pleased him, both by reason of its multifariousness and by reason of the neutral gaiety which the knight's madness spreads over everything which comes in contact with it. That it is a heroic and idealized form of madness, that it leaves room for wisdom and humanity, was no doubt equally pleasing to him. But to conceive of Don Quijote's madness in symbolic and tragic terms seems to me forced. That can be read into the text; it is not there of itself. So universal and multilayered, so noncritical and nonproblematic a gaiety in the portrayal of everyday reality has not been attempted again in European letters. I cannot imagine where and when it might have been attempted.

Note

From Erich Auerbach, *Mimesis: The Representation of Reality in Western Literature,* trans. W. Trask (Princeton: Princeton University Press, 1953).

1. Miguel de Cervantes Saavedra, *Don Quixote,* trans. Samuel Putnam (New York: Viking Press, 1949).

The Genesis of *Don Quixote*

RAMÓN MENÉNDEZ PIDAL

◆　◆　◆

From the twelfth century onward, France, relying primarily on Bretonian legends, had set the model for the versified romance of chivalry, the taste for which spread throughout Europe, thanks to the charm of works such as *Tristan, Lancelot, Perceval,* and, *Merlin,* by Chrétien de Troyes or Robert de Boron, and to that of a body of prose literature that made its appearance in the first half of the thirteenth century. Heroic verse, which reflected traditional, political, and martial ideas and was characterized by domestic austerity and the absence of love as a poetic theme, was now succeeded by a new kind of narrative poetry, which, like the lyric, assumed the essential character of love poetry, with its scenes unfolding in a courtly, elegant world far removed from the stern feudalism of the epic.

The several and new emotions that enriched these poems of adventure were embellished by very diverse means. Through the famous works of Béroul, Chrétien, and Thomas, France was especially smitten by the poetry of fatal and turbulent love, whose poisoned shafts struck the breast of Tristan. Germany, in the poem by Wolfram von Eschenbach, contemplated the battles of inner purification fought in Parsifal's soul, winning for him the kingdom of the mystical city of the Holy Grail. Spain refined the legends of Bretonian inspiration into the anonymous *Amadís*, inventing the innocent first love of the Doncel del Mar and Lady Oriana, which was destined to last from childhood until death "in such a manner that never for a single hour did they cease to love one another," despite the temptations and hardships that relentlessly conspired against them.

Amadís, whose stout heart beats comfortably only at the shock of danger and in the midst of battles against deadly attacks, nevertheless trembles and turns into a coward in the presence of his lady, at whom he hardly dares to gaze. He goes numb upon merely hearing Oriana's name, and he would actually fall off his horse were it not for his faithful squire Gandalín, who steadies and supports him. The romance of chivalry inherits this trait from the love poems. But because the latter originate immediately after the epic, it is not surprising that they, like the later romances of chivalry, have certain points of contact with the ancient heroic poems. Like heroic poetry, the romances of chivalry conceive their heroes within very similar ideals of chivalric perfection, placing them in a world made up of only two bands, one of the noble personages, the other of the wicked, who are locked in eternal antagonism with one another. Moreover, the struggle between them is settled in battles that use formulas and narrative techniques found both in the romances of chivalry and epic poetry.

Apart from the inspiration of love, other very profound differences in the conception of poetic life nevertheless separate the new literary productions from the old. In the romances of chivalry the struggle between the two forces previously mentioned is not carried out in an organized fashion, as in the epic—where the contest is generally played out before the king and his court—nor does it extend to entire nations. It is instead a purely personal struggle. The life of the ancient vassals, set in the midst of a powerful family group, faithful to or rebellious against their lord, abandons its national and political dimensions to assume a human and merely individual quality with the advent of the new knights-errant, who wander about alone in search of adventures, stimulated by whim and chance. The horrible revenges based on inherited enmities that characterized the epic are now replaced by what the *Amadís* calls "glorious vengeances," which the knight executes in the name of justice as if following a professional protocol without himself being personally involved in the wrong he seeks to redress. The knight-errant fights as if to the death for any reason, whether it be to prevent the harmful enchantments of Archelaus or merely to compel a strange knight to declare his secret name. Heroic action is replaced in the romances of chivalry by actions that are arbitrary and more than human, both in the brutal acts of violence of the evil knight and in the lance thrusts of the good ones, which always cut through perversity's strongest coats of mail. The epics' heroic deeds unfold slowly in the middle of the life of societies of great historical density; meanwhile, the adventures of the romance of chivalry take place brusquely and swiftly against a lonely landscape, typically in a vast forest where the laments of the aggrieved go unheeded until the avenging knight hears them. If there arises on the edge of the forest a well-turreted castle inhabited by some powerful lord, or by a giant or an enchanter, be he evil or kindly, it is only for the purpose of initiating further complicated adventures which the good knight untangles and resolves with the blows of his invincible arm. If farther on a king's court is occasionally found, it is only because the valiant knight-errant, who all by himself is more powerful than the entire kingdom, is awaited. How far removed is all this from the *Poem of Mío Cid!* The Corpes Woods, where the Cid's daughters are ravaged, is not the center of the heroic life. The greatest of affronts committed against the hero in the oak woods is not immediately avenged on the spot, as a romance of chivalry would demand, but rather at the court of Toledo and under its authority. However, the romance of chivalry is actually not very far removed from the later epic—the new decadent epic of the Cid—in which the vassal repudiates his king and the entire nation and goes on to fight alone.

In Spain, this medieval romance had a very late revival. Around 1492 Garci Ordóñez de Montalbo adapted and expanded the old *Amadís* with such timeliness and good fortune—typical at the time of all Spanish endeavors—that the work, which for two centuries had been confined to the Peninsula, now sallied forth brilliantly and impetuously into the realm of universal literature, being translated and meriting repeated editions in a great many foreign languages. The romance of chivalry, which during the Middle Ages had scarcely produced any original works in Spain and which in France was completely forgotten, enjoyed in the plenitude of the Renaissance a profuse flowering which spread from the Peninsula throughout Europe. There came forth an entire series of sequels to the *Amadís* which recounted the lives of the sons and grandsons—Esplandianes, Lisuartes, Floriseles—of the fortunate Doncel del Mar. Additional series of Palmerines, Primaleones, and a hundred other knights, who came from the strangest and most archaic realms of fiction, entertained the spirits of those generations that deserved the more refined art of Bembo, Garcilaso, Ronsard, and Sidney. The last highly successful romance of chivalry, the one that survived the longest, was Diego Ortúñez de Calahorra's *El Caballero del Febo* (1562), whose adventures furnished plots to the courtly theater of Queen Elizabeth of England and inspired Henry Pettowe and perhaps even Shakespeare himself.

With some basis in fact, but also considerable exaggeration—justified by the exuberance of popular opinion on the matter—it has been claimed that chivalric and adventurous ideals were at odds with the Spanish character and spirit. For some, an unfathomable abyss existed between the Spanish epics (like the *Poem of Mío Cid*) and the romances of chivalry which, some had asserted, never enjoyed real popularity among us. It is true that the romance of chivalry is not derived from the ancient Spanish epic, but it is nevertheless linked to it, even if only by a tenuous thread. It is also true that it is primarily a reflection of foreign models, but this fact neither cancels out its popularity nor stands in the way of the intimate Spanishness of the *Amadís*, which was a happy adaptation to the Spanish spirit of a French trend. And if chivalric literature captivated the Spanish public from the remote times of King Don Pedro to those of Philip III, filling bulky tomes for the more cultured classes; if it descended the social scale in the form of cheaply produced broadsides for the humble classes and invaded even the beautiful ballads of the *Romancero*; if it inspired the national Hispano-Portuguese theater; if it found its way into seigneurial events and public fiestas; if its lengthy tales provided absorbing reading, capable of filling with bitter remorse the conscience of the old Chancellor Ayala, Juan de Valdés, or Santa Teresa, and of worrying the solicitors in the Cortes of the kingdom as well as the moralists Luis Vives and Fray Luis de Granada, then we must concede that this literary genre was not only popular but exceedingly so. The romances of chivalry did not triumph, as some believe, because they were the only narrative works of fiction available in the sixteenth century, but rather because they practically had no competition, as their adventures had long beforehand captured the Spanish imagination. These works spawned continuations and sequels because readers' imaginations wanted to prolong the pleasure of living vicariously the life of exciting adventure with its victorious, avenging great deeds.

This literature was not dying of old age even as late as 1602, when Don Juan de Silva, Lord of Cañadahermosa, published his *Crónica de don Policisne de Boecia*. Then came the well-known moment when Cervantes decided to better the reading habits and morals of his homeland by discrediting the romances of chivalry.

Don Quixote is thus born with a special literary purpose, stated repeatedly by the author, according to which it may be believed that the novel bears only a negative relationship to such books and to the chivalric spirit that informs them. Lord Byron (in his *Don Juan*) thinks that Cervantes destroyed the Spanish feeling for chivalry and that he was thus responsible for his country's ruin. Likewise, León Gautier (upon dedicating his monumental volume on the chivalric life to Cervantes himself), bitterly lamented the fact that ancient chivalry—his love of loves—was ridiculed and put to death by the great novelist. To forgive Cervantes for the imperishable yet demolishing pages of *Don Quixote*, Gautier was forced to evoke the heroic soldier of Lepanto, preferring the man over the book. Menéndez y Pelayo, at the opposite pole, maintained that Cervantes did not write a work antithetical to chivalry nor one of dry and prosaic negation but, rather, a work of purification and perfection: He came not to kill an ideal but to transfigure and exalt it. All the poetic, noble and human elements of chivalry were incorporated into the new work with the loftiest of meanings. In this way, *Don Quixote* was considered to be the last of the romances of chivalry, the definitive and most perfect one.

Between this latter point of view, which in itself seems paradoxical, and the other, more generally accepted one, we shall endeavor to develop our own judgment concerning the fundamental meaning of *Don Quixote* by taking a genetic approach.

Regarding the introduction of a comic dimension into a heroic domain, *Don Quixote* appears as the last exemplar of a series. This intertwining of the comic and the heroic had existed in literature for many centuries, since the very time of the epic's splendor. It is sufficient to recall, as the most notable instance, the epic poem *Pèlerinage de Charle Magne*. The Renaissance stressed this way of understanding heroic poetry, because in that period, which contemplated serene classical beauty with great seriousness, the characters of the *chansons de geste* must have been seen as extremely simple poetic fictions, as monotonous in their turns of thought as in the wild blows of their swords. Spirits nourished by the ideas of Roman antiquity understood much less the empire of Charlemagne than that of Augustus, and they were unable to truly appreciate the simple grandeur of the medieval epic. Thus the Italian Renaissance, from the end of the fifteenth century, finding itself with Pulci and Boiardo confronting Carolingian and Bretonian poetic material that the northern Italian tradition transmitted to it, could not take that tradition seriously. By making Roland fall in love, Boiardo amused himself by presenting the unconquerable paladin as an awkward and timid lover, a stupid fellow, a *babbione* ever deceived by Angelica. Later, Ariosto (1516–32) continued this ridicule of the hero, making him a spurned lover, and exaggerating the furious madness of his jealousy to tragicomic proportions. With regard to these culminating scenes, the poet, whimsically and with a barely veiled smile, intertwines the knights of Charlemagne with those of Marsilio in a tangle of adventures—adventures replete with love affairs, battles, and enchantments, each one being interrupted and overtaken by the following one, like the calm waves of the sea, always continuous, always monotonous, foaming forever with playful novelty.

Almost a century after Ariosto, Cervantes took up chivalric adventures from a comic point of view. The Spanish author knew and admired Boiardo as well as Ariosto. He frequently imitated the *Orlando Furioso,* and Don Quijote even prided himself in being able to sing some stanzas of the poem. Still, face to face with his much admired predecessors, Cervantes achieved a strange kind of originality. While Pulci, Boiardo, and Ariosto carried forward the narration of the old poems with mocking humorism, Cervantes, on aiming to satirize the tales of chivalry in prose, did not set out to write a poem but rather a novel which took him into an artistic realm very different from that of the Italians. That is, Cervantes did not seek the initial source of his inspiration in their works, lofty as they were with artifices and the exquisiteness of monumental endeavors; instead, following the instincts of his Spanish nation, he sought inspiration in a simpler, more popular kind of literature.

Along with the comic scenes of the old French epic and the unbelievable narration of chivalric fiction created by Boiardo and Ariosto, there had long existed, in works of a lesser literary magnitude, another more openly hostile way of looking at chivalry: that of embodying its ideals in a poor madman whose fantasies are dashed to pieces against hard reality. For example, in the second half of the fourteenth century, I find in the work of the Italian novelist Franco Sacchetti a figure of the most exact quixotic appearance. In Agnolo di Ser Gherardo, Sacchetti created an extravagant personality, afflicted with a chivalric monomania in spite of his seventy years of age, who, mounted on a tall, lean horse that was the very image of hunger itself, goes from Florence to a nearby town to attend jousting matches. As his assistants help him put on his helmet and give him his lance, mischievous wags place a thistle under the tail of his nag, which begins to run, leaping and bucking, and does not stop until galloping all the way to Florence. There, amid general laughter, a woman takes in the battered equestrian, puts him into bed to cure him of the blows caused by his helmet and armor, and upbraids him for his foolish chivalric madness. Not only the comic structure but also the narrative details are similar to those in *Don Quixote*. Who can forget the old Manchegan hidalgo atop his lean Rocinante on the beach at Barcelona, where he, too, has gone to participate in certain jousts, and by his strange bearing arouses wonder in the merrymakers who surround him? Who does not remember the boys who place a bundle of gorse beneath his horse's tail, producing the beast's bucking that sends Don Quijote crashing to the ground?

Cervantes must have known Sacchetti's story or a similar one, either in manuscript or in its oral telling, although he must have come to it late, only upon writing part II of the novel, where he exploits it. He also must have been familiar with some of the various stories then in circulation about comic delusions suffered by readers of books of chivalry, like the one about the student at the University of Salamanca who, because of these books, abandoned his studies and one day interrupted the solitude of his reading with loud shouts and sword thrusts in the air in defense of one of the characters in the novel he was reading; to such a point it had saturated his brain.

While Cervantes must have known stories of this sort, perhaps not knowing or remembering them until after beginning *Don Quixote*, it is certain that he conceived the first episodes of the novel as a response to the stimulus of a work of another type, a contemptible "Entremés de los Romances" ("Interlude of the Ballads") whose importance, in my opinion, has not yet been understood by the critics.[1] Adolfo de Castro happened to exhume this sorry theatrical composition, stating that Cervantes himself was its author and thereby attracting to himself the most justifiable and widespread disgrace among critics. Nevertheless, his foolish affirmation ought not to prevent us from examining the question without prejudice.

The "Entremés" must have been written about 1591 or shortly afterward. Its intention was to make fun of the extraordinary vogue of the *Romanceros*, the volumes of which had been published without pause for half a century, especially the *Flor de Romances*, which was reprinted and augmented from 1591 to 1597.

This "Entremés" introduces us to a poor peasant, Bartolo, who from "reading the ballads so much" goes crazy, as Don Quijote did from reading the books of chivalry. Bartolo insists on ridiculously imitating the knights in the ballads. His ravings bear the most striking resemblance to those of Don Quijote during his first adventure, that of the Toledan merchants. Having become a soldier in his madness, Bartolo believes himself to be the Almoradí or the Tarfe of the Morisco ballads, and he attempts to defend a shepherdess who is being harassed by her shepherd boyfriend. But the latter takes Bartolo's lance and mauls him with it, leaving him flattened on the ground. In like manner, Don Quijote is beaten with his own lance by one of the merchant's muleteers. Unable to get up, Bartolo consoles himself by thinking that not he but rather his horse was to blame for his misfortune. Don Quijote says the same thing, without being able to raise himself from the ground: "It is not through my fault that I lie here, but through that of my horse." Resemblances increase when Bartolo, recalling the well-known "Ballad of the Marqués de Mantua," now believes himself to be the enamored Valdovinos, who lies wounded in the deserted woods and exclaims: "Where art thou, my lovely lady/Feel'st thou not my cruel pain?" Don Quijote likewise believes himself to be Valdovinos, and he bursts forth reciting these same verses. Meanwhile, members of Bartolo's family arrive, and he now thinks that it is the Marqués himself arriving; thus he greets them with more verses from the ballad: "O noble Marquis of Mantua/My uncle and carnal lord!" These are verses that Don Quijote also repeats when a peasant from his own town approaches him.

The "Entremés" goes on stringing together parts of the ballad, first in the mouth of Bartolo, then in those of the other characters who, humoring the madman, give themselves over to a foolish parody concerning the very famous history of the Marqués de Mantua. As would have been expected, Cervantes rejected such a grotesque parody, and he reduced it to a short narrative in which he says that Don Quijote only replied to all of his neighbor's questions with verses from this ballad, recounting Valdovinos's misfortunes as his own. In this short sequence, early in his novel, Cervantes allows himself to be swayed by the parodic system of the "Entremés." He recalls that the Marqués, on approaching the wounded knight,

> From his head and face his helmet
> And his beaver first he drew;
> Then with gore beheld him cover'd,
> All of one ensanguin'd hue.
> With his handkerchief he wipes him;
> When his face from blood was clean,
> Then, alas! too true the story,
> Then too plain the truth was seen.

Cervantes tells us that, upon approaching Don Quijote, the peasant, "taking off the visor of his helmet . . . wiped off the dust that covered his face, and presently recognized the gentleman and said to him . . ." Created by Cervantes without any burlesque intent, this parody is a significant vestige of his unconscious imitation of the ballads, as suggested by the "Entremés."

Bartolo and Don Quijote are carried away in the same fashion to their respective villages, and while on the road the madness of both takes a violent leap from the ballad of the Marqués de Mantua to those on Morisco themes. Bartolo now imagines that he is the mayor of Baza, who laments with his friend Abencerraje the unfaithfulness of his beloved Zaida, and Don Quijote fancies that he is Abencerraje's captive, who tells the mayor of Antequera about his loves. Both madmen finally reach their homes, and once in bed, they fall asleep. But in a short time both are back to alarming their concerned relatives, disturbing them with new follies: Bartolo ranting about the burning of Troy and Don Quijote about the tournaments of the twelve peers.

"May the devil take the ballads which have put you in such a plight!" says Bartolo's neighbor. "May a hearty curse . . . light upon those books of chivalry that have put you in this pickle," says Don Quijote's housekeeper when he reaches home. The "Entremés" aims to make sport of imprudent readers of the ballads and treads its ground firmly when it makes Bartolo believe that he is a character drawn from them. Cervantes wants to censure the reading of chivalric romances, and he is very much out of his element when he repeatedly makes Don Quijote rave about the same ballad characters as Bartolo. It can be readily seen that the first idea of the madman who dreams that he is Valdovinos belongs to the "Entremés," and that only thanks to its general, undue influence is it found in Cervantes' novel. If we should claim for an instant that the "Entremés" was written after the novel and created in imitation of *Don Quixote*, we would be forced to confront the fact that it reaches into the very foundation of both works.

We should still add yet another substantial consideration on behalf of the precedence of the "Entremés." A madman in whose head his own personality dissolves in order to be substituted by that of a famous personage is the crass and sole type of lunacy that governs the "Entremés," which is mindful only of provoking the spectators' laughter. But in *Don Quixote* this kind of madness only appears in the first adventure, in the fifth and seventh chapters about which we have been speaking. It is, moreover, a madness that is at odds with the one that always afflicts Don Quijote, whose personality remains on every other occasion steadfast and firm in the presence of those heroes who are the cause of his insanity. One must consider, then, in examining the foundations of that which is quixotically comic in the adventure of the Toledan merchants, that Cervantes did not conceive the episode by freely mixing the resources of his own fantasy, but that his imagination was constrained and limited by the indelible recollection of the "Entremés de los Romances," which had left a strong comic impression in his mind. This tenacious, immoderate impression not only imposed on Cervantes an unconscious and incomprehensible substitution by the ballads of the *Romancero* tradition of the books of chivalry as the cause of Don Quijote's madness, but rather, and in addition, implied a form of madness and a parodic procedure that were quite foreign to the untrammeled imagination of the novelist.

This is the fundamental element in the genesis of *Don Quixote*. Cervantes discovered a productive kind of humor in the "Entremés," which poked fun at the mental derangement caused by the injudicious reading of the *Romancero*. This literary satire seemed to him an excellent theme. But he shifted it away from the ballads— an admirable poetic form—in order to transfer it to a literary genre despised by many, that of the romances of chivalry, which at the same time were as popular as the *Romancero*. There were authors, too, who, like Lorenzo de Sepúlveda, wished to apply a corrective to the influence of the old ballads, so "full of many lies and very little merit," but Cervantes was not to proceed either in the manner of Sepúlveda or of that of the writer of the "Entremés."

As soon as Don Quijote arrives home and goes to sleep, resting from the madness of having been the Valdovinos of the ballad, the priest and the barber proceed to the scrutiny of the deranged hidalgo's library. In it, besides the great profusion of romances of chivalry, there are the *Dianas*, the *Galatea*, and other pastoral romances. There are heroic poems in the Italian style and the *Tesoro de varias poesías*, but we notice with surprise that there are none of the many *Cancioneros*, *Silvas*, *Flores de Romances*, or other *Romanceros* that had been published over the previous half century.[2] To Cervantes, the brief poems contained in these collections were, so to speak, the poetic output of the entire Spanish people. They could not be the cause of the madness of the very noble knight of La Mancha, nor should they be subjected to the judgment of the priest and the barber. What really drove Don Quijote insane were those bulky old books of chivalry which were condemned to the fire, like the unwieldy *Don Florisel de Niquea* and that fat barrel of a tome, *Don Olivante de Laura*. Still, the first instance of Don Quijote's immortal madness was not provoked by any of these but rather by a thin, cheaply produced broadside containing the "Romance del Marqués de Mantua," which does not figure in any way in the witty and grand scrutiny because it entered not into Cervantes' plans but rather into those of the mediocre author of the "Entremés."

Solely through the immediate influence of the "Entremés" are we able to discover that the ballads, not the romances of chivalry, lie at the heart of *Don Quixote*. And this is not only the case in the adventure of the Toledan merchants but also in other events of chapter 2. At dusk on that hot July day which saw Don Quijote's first longed-for sally through the Montiel plain, when he arrives at the inn where he is to be dubbed a knight, is he contented with the poor lodging that the innkeeper offers him, recalling the words of the mysterious ballad *La Constaneira*: "My only gear is arms,/My only rest, the fray"? And when the inn's female attendants help him remove his armor, he goes on with his insanity by garbling lines from the ballad of Lancelot:

> Oh, never, surely, was there a knight
> So served by hand of dame,
> As served was he, Don Quijote hight,
> When from his town he came.

But all this changes completely as soon as Cervantes puts the "Entremés" behind him.

When a superior work of literature is in question, the study of the literary sources of an author, which is always an excellent way of understanding the sum of human culture of which the poet forms a part, should not be undertaken for the purpose of determining what that work takes from them in order to subtract from its originality. (That could only be done by those who do not understand what truly constitutes artistic invention.) On the contrary, the study of sources should serve to show how a poet's conception rises above those sources, how it frees itself, and evaluates and transcends them.

Paradoxically, Cervantes is more original than ever precisely when he follows the "Entremés" most closely. Of that fresh, keen, and profound comic delicacy which makes the episode of the Toledan merchants one of the best in the novel, not a single element is derived from the "Entremés," which imposed on Cervantes' imagination only sporadically the most peripheral details of the adventure. The grotesque and clownish Bartolo resembles Don Quijote from the outset only in the crass materiality of some of his actions. To make use of the "Entremés" in the first chapters of *Don Quixote*, a gigantic creative effort was needed; this fact is forgotten by many eminent critics who are reluctant to believe that Cervantes' (or Dante's) inventive genius could have had more sources of inspiration than those commonly attributed to them. After providing Cervantes with a point of departure, the "Entremés" did not help but rather became a hindrance because it obligated him to carry out a corrective procedure that we are able to observe only partially and that to some degree was carried out not at the time of the work's gestation but in the course of its execution.

Several inconsistencies in the sequence of the episodes and their relationship to one another can easily be observed in *Don Quixote*. This phenomenon has stimulated some critics to speak of Cervantes' creative haste in writing his work, while others believe such a view to be merely a common misconception because it is known that Cervantes corrected and produced more than one draft of his writings. It should be clear that there are traces of every possible cause in the lapses that have been noted in the novel; there are cases of evident carelessness, half-made corrections, and bold displays of willful incongruities and absurdities. Forever changing direction because of the hero's deranged imagination, the overall plan of the plot of *Don Quixote* received less attention than that which the author devoted to the *Exemplary Novels*. Cervantes wanted to allow the action to be fraught with all the trifling inconsistencies of improvisation, very much in the Spanish style. But that improvisation in no way presupposes indifference but rather gives a keen, lively, and profound impression that refuses to be bogged down by useless detail. Cervantes' art is not a careless one because he happens to draw liberally from popular fiction; he knows how to carve out of that raw material facets of extraordinary poetic brilliance. It is not a careless art made simply to satisfy the shallow joviality of those who say: "Let us have more quixotic stunts, let Don Quijote attack and let Sancho comment, come what may, and with this we will be quite content!" Cervantes was perfectly aware that he was infusing his work with lasting human value. He writes, in the prologue to part II, that he believes "that there is not going to be . . . a language into which it will not be translated." Yet in contrast to the carelessness we observe in some details, how much meditation is evident in the distillation of the quixotic type! What an intimate and prolonged cohabitation between the artist and his creation!

Our point of departure is that Cervantes' fantasy did not conceive the type spontaneously but rather that it was in a certain fashion held in check by the outline of the "Entremés." He did not create his protagonist according to a plan well defined at the outset; he worked instead from a somewhat imprecise and synthetic vision. Only during the development of the work did he, at times groping tentatively, draw forth and call to life all the complicated grandeur that was latent in his brilliant initial conception. One can easily understand how felicitously the gradual development of an idea may be in a long novel of adventures. Far from being a wearying repetition of the original type of the hero, Don Quijote's adventures are a never-ending series of revelations, even for the artist himself, and they are therefore ever more gratifying to the reader. The character of the protagonist is not perfectly and completely revealed until the very end of the novel.

Don Quijote's particular madness on his first sally, imagining himself at one time to be Valdovinos laying wounded on the ground, believing himself immediately thereafter to be Abindarráez the prisoner, and next Reinaldos, indignant with Don Roldán, was, as we have already indicated, very damaging to the personality of the ingenious hidalgo. Cervantes abandoned this course completely after he had exhausted the "Entremés," his first source of inspiration. From then on Don Quijote would always and only be Don Quijote.

His character immediately receives firm support. In that same seventh chapter in which his delusions about his identity come to an end, Sancho enters the scene. He, too, comes from popular literature. An old proverb goes: "There goes Sancho with his donkey." And here comes Sancho, inexhaustible reciter of proverbs, like an archaic type of squire who had first appeared in the fourteenth century in the oldest known romance of chivalry, *El*

Caballero Cifar. In the very first conversations that Don Quijote holds with his squire there is already an anticipation of the hidalgo's axiomatic mental habits that later will give weight to his madness and soon afterward, in the eleventh chapter, blossom forth in the eloquent speech on the Golden Age. Master and squire will continue to gradually complement (and complete) one another in such a way "that the madness of the master without the servant's gaffes would not be worth a penny." Rubió rightly adds that when Don Quijote is left alone in the Sierra Morena and at the home of the Duke and Duchess, which are the only two occasions on which the genial pair is separated, we feel for Sancho the same yearnings that the knight experiences in his own golden heart.

As soon as he put an end to the adventure suggested by the "Entremés de los romances," Cervantes clearly understood that the kind of humor produced by the collision of a half-witted fantasy with cruel reality, which was consequent with the popular art of Sacchetti or the author of the "Entremés," could not reach humoristic perfection by being based on the heroic and national ideals of the ballads. It is true that the *Romancero* and the romances of chivalry were half brothers as offspring of the medieval epic, but the *Romancero*, as a legitimate child, remained within the patrimonial legacy of the heroic world, while the bastard child (the romances of chivalry) went in search of adventures and lost its wits by pursuing them. Cervantes venerated the world of the epic, and as soon as he saw himself free from the influence of the "Entremés" he withdrew Don Quijote's madness from the verses of the *Romancero* and made it take refuge, as if in its own castle, in the fantastic chivalric deeds of the prose romances. These, then, in the mind of Don Quijote, are elevated to the level of heroic fictions. The hidalgo claims to know that in the armory of the kings of Spain, next to the saddle of the Cid's horse Babieca, stands the enormous peg, big as a wagon tongue, with which the valiant Pierres guided his wooden horse through the air. And he even places the world of the romances of chivalry above that of the epic, holding the Knight of the Blazing Sword in higher esteem than the Cid himself. Scandalized by this nonsense, the

canon, on the contrary, discriminates between the epic heroes
and the phantoms of chivalry, and he connects the former in a
general way with historical personages. He had never seen in the
Armory in Madrid the peg belonging to Pierres, but he believes
in the authenticity of Babieca's saddle (which archaeological
scholarship has now banished from the royal collection), and he
counsels Don Quijote to stop reading about the fanciful deeds of
Felixmarte de Hircania and the Emperors of Trebizond and to pay
heed to the (real) ones of Viriatus, Caesar, Alexander, Fernán
González, and the Cid.

Without uncertainty we may say that Cervantes definitely understood that his Don Quijote could not continue reliving the
episodes of the *Romancero*, of which the Spanish imagination was
so notably fond, and that he knew that the comic force of his
book would have to rely solely on the clash between the knight-
errant's asocial perfection and the life of society tightly organized
and structured by the powerful institutions of the state. Don
Quijote not only stops believing himself to be a character drawn
from balladry; he also ceases to apply to himself the ballads'
verses. He only appropriates later a certain famous vow from the
Marqués de Mantua ballad ("My arms are my only gear; my only
rest, the fray!") as indelible memories of the first manifestation
of his madness as influenced by the "Entremés." Apart from this,
it seems as if Cervantes instinctively wished to remove himself as
far as possible from the wrong road along which he had initially
embarked, and in all the rest of the part I of *Don Quixote* he makes
but few allusions to the ballads in spite of the fact that they were
then in fashion and even used in ordinary conversation. Don
Quijote cites only the ballad about Lancelot and the one about
the Cid being excommunicated by the Pope, treating them as
historical matters. By contrast, in part II of the novel, written
when Cervantes was already free from the objectionable "Entremés," the resonance of the *Romancero* tradition occurs twice as
often as it appears in the first part and, as we shall see, it is much
more fully developed there than in part I.

Even when Cervantes expressly avoided making reference to
the *Romancero* in part I, he had it very much in mind and made

use of it for his own personal inspiration. When he wanted to enliven part I of *Don Quixote*, crafting the plot with care and making the greatest effort that a novelist could make according to the art then in fashion, he created the series of episodes in the Sierra Morena. There came to his mind a ballad worthy of imitation, although its thrust was quite different from that which held sway in the parodic "Entremés." It is the figure of Cardenio, taken bodily from a ballad by Juan del Encina that circulated along with the traditional ones in *Cancioneros* and broadsides. Rejected by his beloved, this Cardenio, leaving his dead mule behind, penetrates into the most rugged and remote part of the Sierra, and leaps from hedge to hedge amid brambles and thickets. Then, surrounded and pitied by the shepherds he encounters, he weeps, gives signs of madness, becomes speechless, and fixes his eyes on the ground:

> A sorrowing knight presses
> into the forges of a dark mountain
> His steed, dead, he forsakes,
> and scales the cliffs alone.
> Deeper and deeper,
> from bush to bush,
> into the thickest of the forest
> he penetrates.
> With eyes downcast,
> he does not stop lamenting.
> His beloved has scorned him,
> and never before has he felt such pain.
> "Who hath brought thee here, Sir Knight,
> into this dark forest?"
> "Alas, shepherd, only my misfortune!"

Cervantes' learned critics have failed to see the correspondence between this ballad and Cardenio's actions, but it is clear to us, and it reveals how in the mind of Cervantes his inspiration in romance has shifted its focus.

Once Cervantes modified the relationship between the hidalgo's madness and the *Romancero*, he was easily able to lead the protagonist to his perfection. Ever since his first sally, Don Quijote had proposed to right wrongs and punish the proud, but in this respect he does not yet differ greatly from the grotesque Bartolo, who confronted the shepherd pursuing the shepherdess. Only in the seventh chapter, cited earlier, in which the influence of the "Entremés" comes to its end, does the hidalgo elevate his madness to a comprehensive reflection, expressing the need for knight-errantry to be, through him, revived in the world. He is thus invested with a mission and this fleeting phrase signals the moment of genius of Cervantes' conceptualization. For it is then that the author begins to look upon the madman's fantasies as an ideal deserving of respect; it is then that he decides to depict him as grand in his purposes but inadequate in their execution. Perhaps the initial, flawed introduction of the *Romancero* into the novel helped Cervantes to rescue the heroic element still present in the romances of chivalry. These elements coincided with the epic, as we have noted, in the ideal of chivalric perfection. Don Quijote gradually fulfills in himself both the ideals of the epic and those of the romances of chivalry. He is steadfast in his love of glory and tenacious in his struggles in the face of danger; he displays a loyalty to which all ingratitude is foreign, and he will not tell a lie, even though he be shot for it. He interprets and applies the law correctly, aids all those in need, defends those not present, is liberal and generous, eloquent, and even listens to omens, daring to challenge those which are adverse to him, as did the ancient Spanish heroes. The romances of chivalry had added a further perfection to the epic ideal: that of being in love. Dulcinea rises up before Don Quijote because the "knight-errant without a beloved was a tree without either fruit or leaves, a body without a soul." Thus, from the intricate adventures of the romances of chivalry, Don Quijote's confused mind derived a pure heroic ideal that came down from the same stock as that of the ancient epic.

"Poor Don Quijote!" exclaims Paulin Paris, considering the superior beauty of the French poems of chivalry from which the romances of chivalry took their inspiration. "Poor Don Quijote!

The romances responsible for your madness were nothing more than long colorless paraphrases. What would have become of you if you had read the French originals?" But no, if Don Quijote had read only *Tristan* and *Lancelot* with "that recounting, so sweet and smooth, of his brave and amorous deeds," he would have been an ordinary madman, fortunate only in tragic loves. The parody would have come to an end and exhausted itself after a few scenes verging on buffoonery in which the knight of la Mancha would win Dulcinea, the "Tobosan dove," by the might of his arm, realizing an accomplishment that Cervantes often had in mind and that he had announced in the introductory verses of Urganda's prophecy. The French poems might well have maddened Don Quijote more, but only the happy Spanish adaptation of the *Amadís* could lend a superior nobility to his madness. After much racking of his brains in long meditations, Don Quijote decides to imitate not the madness of Orlando Furioso but rather the penitence of the knight from Gaul on the Peña Pobre. "And now," he exclaims, "oh famous deeds of the great Amadís, come to my remembrance, and instruct me in the means by which I may begin to imitate you!" This is the moment in which his madness offers a glimpse of all the moral grandeur of which he is capable.

From that time onward, the gradual refinement of the quixotic type is assured. If before that moment the fidelity and veneration that Don Quijote feels for Dulcinea reveal some vacillation and serious lapses of reverence (part I, chapters 21, 25, 26), from now on the figure of the faithful lover is definitively established, especially in chapter 30 in which the knight-errant slights the Princess Micomicona. Recall the subsequent chapter in which Sancho, telling of his mission to El Toboso and its message, describes Dulcinea as a mannish country wench winnowing reddish wheat; the more the squire seeks to undo all the illusions of Don Quijote, the more successfully the knight-errant reconstructs them with delicate and untiring care.

This stubborn restoration of the ideal of the beloved is likewise treated a little earlier, in chapter 25. Yet how much more infelicitously, because of the vacillation and irreverence already mentioned! And still the progression continues. The peasant girl Aldonza, who had a better hand for salting pork than any other woman in all of La Mancha, with whom Sancho is acquainted, and whom Don Quijote has looked upon occasionally in respectful silence, disappears in part II of the novel and is converted into an ideal lady whom her knight has never seen, being in love with her solely on the basis of hearsay.

In like manner, the novel's comic disposition, which at first manifested itself in confused fashion, gradually reaches its highest inner perfection. At the end of part I Don Quijote can say: "ever since becoming a knight-errant, I am brave, courteous, bountiful, well-bred, generous, civil, bold, affable, patient, and a sufferer of hardships, imprisonments and enchantments." He has distanced himself from the allures of love and violence that the anarchical and fantastic world of chivalry offered in order to accept only harsh sacrifices, always placing before his imagination "the goodness of Amadís, the flower and mirror of knights-errant." Firm in the idea that chivalry is a religion, he ennobles all his ridiculous life with profound mystical sentiment. He ascends to the purest sources of the heroic and, with the corporeal indifference of a martyr, he endures the greatest pains "as if he were not a man of flesh, but a statue of stone." He is sustained by the most steadfast faith: "Get upon thy ass, good Sancho, and follow me once more; for God, who provides for every creature, will not fail us, especially since we have set about a work so much to His service; thou seest that He even provides for the little flying insects of the air, the wormlings in the earth, and the spawnings in the water. In His infinite mercy, He makes His sun shine on the righteous and on the unjust, and the rains fall upon the good and the malevolent." Don Quijote always places his hopes in God, even though he always finds his expectations frustrated. He wishes to "improve this depraved age of ours" and to restore to it the purity of chivalry though the whole world be ungrateful to him for it. He seeks all about himself to entrust his downtrodden honor to those who show him the most sympathy: "I have redressed grievances, and righted the injured, chastised the insolent, vanquished giants, and trod elves and hobgoblins under my feet! ... My intentions are all directed toward virtuous ends and to do no man wrong, but good to the entire world. And now let your Graces judge, most excellent Duke and Duchess, whether a person who makes it his only endeavor to practice all this, deserves to be upbraided as a fool!" It is all in vain. The Duke and Duchess, to whom he appeals in his sadness, are at that very moment playing a vicious trick on him in order to ridicule his misguided ideals. The most holy hopes of heaven and earth are frustrated. Is it because they are impossible? It does not matter. The hero's noble madness assumes a bitter, tragicomic meaning. It is a madness sustained by an ideal which, although never realized, is deserving of humankind's warmest sympathy.

At times we let ourselves be overwhelmed with the hidalgo's comic aspect and think like his niece: "You should know so much, sir uncle, as to be able, if there were occasion, to get up into a pulpit and go to preach in the streets, and yet be so strangely mistaken, so grossly blind of understanding, as to fancy that a man of your years and infirmity can be strong and valiant; that you can set everything right, and force stubborn malice to bend, when you yourself stoop beneath the burden of age; and, what is yet more odd, that you carry yourself like a knight, when it is well known that you are none! For, though some gentlemen may be knights, a poor gentleman can hardly be so." Nevertheless, when all is said and done, we believe that the ideal force of Don Quijote overcomes his abandonment of reason as well as all the other limitations imposed by reality. Being poor, he amazes us with his generosity; being weak and sickly, he is a hero possessed of unyielding courage in the face of misfortune; being old, he yet moves us with his absurd, mad first love; being crazy, his words and actions always stir vital chords in the enthusiastic heart.

Nine years after the publication of part I of *Don Quixote* there appeared an imitation which is of keen interest to us. Avellaneda seems to have written another *Don Quixote* solely to give us a tangible measure of Cervantes' own value. The outstanding characteristics and qualities of the comic type are in Avellaneda, but they miss the mark of genius. This judgment can never be sufficiently emphasized if we are to avoid inadequate assessments of the novel. Every appreciation of *Don Quixote* which can be likewise applied to Avellaneda contains nothing unique to Cervantes. Avellaneda's *Don Quixote* can be used as another touchstone for measurement.

From the point of view of the issues under consideration here, Avellaneda dwelt on both the hero's delusions in which he assumed other identities as well as his ravings over the ballads; far from understanding how much harm they did to his hero, Avellaneda thus tediously insisted on the vulgar madness of the "Entremés" and *Don Quixote*'s early chapters. Avellaneda's Don Quijote, wounded and defeated by a melon dealer, begins to recite the ballad of King Don Sancho, believing himself wounded by Vellido Dolfos, and he orders Sancho Panza to call himself Diego Ordóñez and to go challenge the people of Zamora and the venerable old Arias Gonzalo. Again, Avellaneda "strings together a thousand beginnings of old ballads without rhyme or reason," just like the Bartolo of the "Entremés." Mounting his horse, he recites the beginning of the ballad "Ya cabalga Calaínos." Upon entering Zaragoza he speaks as if he were Achilles; he later takes himself to be Bernardo del Carpio; in Siguenza he believes himself to be Ferdinand the Catholic; in the Prado of Madrid he imagines himself to be the Cid Rui Díaz; still later he says that he is Fernán González and stuffs his speeches with irrelevant ballad verses. This fool who, puffed up with vanity and boasting, appropriates the identities of heroes and kings, makes us appreciate all the more the vigorous personality of Cervantes' Don Quijote, from whose mouth discretion and madness flow in gentle alternation. It is instructive to observe how, in the hands of Avellaneda, the same popular theme of the madman enamored of chivalry is punished by reality and ends in failure. Meanwhile, Cervantes, using that very same idea, tapped a powerful source of inspiration. Avellaneda's gifts as a narrator are not accompanied by a profound poetic genius, and so his Don Quijote does not resemble the real one at all. In the false *Don Quixote* the worst kind of literary coarseness is shockingly combined with a pleasing form, at times in a solemn and labored way, just as immorality can coexist with superficial devotion to the rosary, self-flagellation, and hair shirts—

all so far removed from the mystical religiosity of the real *Don Quixote*. The structure that Cervantes erects upon a popular idea is so much his own that, even after it has been assembled, it cannot be copied by the likes of an Avellaneda.

But a fact that cannot be denied is that Avellaneda's work served as one of Cervantes' sources of inspiration when he wrote part II of his novel. I believe that Cervantes had some fairly definite information about his competitor's work before writing chapter 59, in which he refers expressly to it, and which marks the moment when it appeared in print. What is certain is that he wanted to derive the most reasonable profit from Avellaneda's envy, that is, to have his work resemble in no way his resentful rival. It would appear as if in Avellaneda he saw clearer than ever the dangers of triteness and coarseness that the story contained, and that he struggled all the harder to eliminate them upon writing part II of *Don Quixote*. He no longer thought of drawing those two or three crude pictures elaborated in part I, even though they were far removed from the coarseness of his imitator. The superiority of part II of *Don Quixote*, unquestionable for me as for most people, may be attributed in great measure to Avellaneda. There are sources of literary inspiration that operate by rejection, and they may be as important as, or more so than, those that are mobilized by attraction.

The blundering way in which Avellaneda takes hold of the ballads contrasts strongly with the new use which Cervantes makes of them in part II. Having now forgotten his aversion to the "Entremés," he again begins to use the ballads in profusion, but now, of course, never to impair the personality of the hero in the form of impertinent nonsense, as did the author of the "Entremés" and Avellaneda. The ballads reappear in order to render Cervantes' prose agreeable with poetic reminiscences that at that time were remembered by all, and which everybody used in polite conversation: The novelty now is that this poetic resonance appears not only in the mouth of Don Quijote and in those of the more educated characters but, rather, principally, in the mouth of Sancho. The Sancho of the proverbs is now, at times, the Sancho of the ballads.

This evolution can be observed from the very beginning of part II of *Don Quixote* when, in chapter 5, Sancho refers to a ballad for the first time. It is the one concerning the Infanta doña Urraca's self-assuredness. It is true that this chapter is jokingly labeled apocryphal by Cide Hamete's translator on account of containing "judgments that exceed Sancho's capacity." But its intimate authenticity is guaranteed by the dialogue that Don Quijote later has with his squire: " 'Truly, Sancho, every day thy simplicity lessens, and thy sense improves!' 'And there is good reason why!' quoth Sancho, 'Some of your worship's wit must needs stick to me.' " Without doubt, Sancho is improving and being refined, too, at the same time that Don Quijote and Dulcinea are undergoing their own evolution. Avellanedas's Sancho, gluttonous, brutal, and clownish to the point of not even understanding the proverbs that he chaotically heaps up pell-mell, rises up between the primitive Sancho of part I and the new Sancho of Cervantes' part II. He makes us appreciate in all his perfection the Sancho of poor and kind heart, a faithful spirit who is skeptical of everything and believes in everything, and in whom prudence in abundance shows through his coarse shell of craftiness, achieving the keenest kind of folk wisdom as governor in decisions comparable to those of Solomon and Peter the Cruel.

The Sancho of part II of *Don Quixote* recalls verses from the *Romancero* several times in his conversation: "Aquí morirás, traidor, enemigo de doña Sancha," "Mensajero, sois amigo," "no diga la tal palabra," or he alludes to the ballad of the Conde Dirlos, to that of Calaínos, to that of the *Penitencia del rey Rodrigo*, or to that of Lanzarote about which, as he declares, he learned by hearing them from his master.

Moreover, Cervantes used the *Romancero* not only for its phraseology but also for the very invention of the novel, although in a very different way than he had used it in the adventure of the Toledan merchants. In this as in everything else, one sees the superiority of part II of *Don Quixote* over part I. Savi López, an adherent to the opposite opinion, affirms that part I is predominantly comical, while in part II the grotesque dominates. But I believe in fact that quite the opposite is true. Limiting ourselves to the special point that we are considering, the grotesque elements that appear in the adventure of the ballad of the Marqués de Mantua are completely absent from the episode that has its inspiration in the Montesinos ballads and succeeds because of its delicate comic sentiment.

While in part I of the novel, only a single adventure contains a resonance of the *Romancero*, in part II several adventures do so.

When Don Quijote enters El Toboso on that mournful night, looking in the darkness for the ideal palace of his Dulcinea, he hears a farmhand approaching, who, on his way to work before dawn, sings this ballad: "Ill you far'd at Roncesvalles,/Frenchmen . . ." His song, like an evil omen, startles and disturbs the mind of the knight-errant.

Later, the ballad of the undauntable Don Manuel de León, who enters a lion's den for the purpose of retrieving a lady's glove, is invoked for the great adventure of the lions. There the so frequently audacious madness of Don Quijote borders on extremes that approximate more the epic than the comic mode. The victory won before the lion which turns his hindside to the knight is ridiculous, but the valor of the Manchegan hero, comparable to that of Don Manuel de León, is realized not solely in his imagination as on other occasions; it is, instead, actually materialized in the midst of the fear of all those who witness his boldness in the presence of the savage beast, free to attack. He rightly feels himself strong: "No, these magicians may well rob me of success, but they can never take from me my strength and courage of mind!" He is so beside himself that he sends Sancho to remunerate the lion keeper with two crowns of gold; it is the first time that history records that Don Quijote has given a gratuity! Generosity, an essentially chivalric virtue, stands out only in part II of the novel. Is it not evident that here the hidalgo's comic success far surpasses the repeated beatings by which the adventures of the first part are resolved?

Nor is there in part I as rich a development of the frequent quixotic delusions as appear in part II, in the adventure, for example, of Maese Pedro's puppet show, so wisely and admirably commented upon by José Ortega y Gasset. Here we are interested in remarking only on one thing: Delusion in the presence of a theatrical spectacle was a common theme of popular anecdotes old and new, and it had already been incorporated in the quixotic fable by Avellaneda, when his Don Quijote, taking for reality the performance of Lope de Vega's play, *El testimonio vengado*, leaps into the actors' midst to defend the unprotected queen of Navarre. As if he had seen here an excellent theme poorly developed and now wished to use it, Cervantes even gave his competitor the advantage of being first! Hence he described the madman's exaltation not before a performance of actors but of puppets, and the topic was not an original and cleverly dramatized action but a well-known ballad adventure familiar to young and old. The ballad recounts how the forgetful Don Gaiferos recovered his wife Melisendra from captivity. Cervantes' success here is one of stylistic and psychological refinement. The picturesque narration by the boy who explains the action of the figures onstage is animated with such descriptive force that he brings to life that poor world of balladry and puppetry. Nevertheless, Don Quijote listens and watches everything with cool sanity, even commenting upon the archaeological accuracy of the representation. But when the boy's words project real emotion and anguish over the danger in which the fleeing lovers find themselves, the flash of chivalric obsession suddenly flares in Don Quijote's mind and he hurls himself into the midst of the adventure to destroy with his sword the stage upon which the Moors of Sansueña ride at full speed in pursuit of the lovers. Reality soon again takes possession of the deluded knight and imprisons him in its powerful bonds; Don Quijote now agrees to the undeceived appraisal and payment for the broken clay figures. But in the presence of the most fleeting recollection of the dangerous adventure, his fragile and inconsistent imagination again goes wild and he once again escapes to live, as if it were reality, in the world of the ideal that is his and from which he sorrowfully feels banished.

The perfection so often attained in the real adventures was nevertheless not enough for the novel. Cervantes sought a type of adventure that could rise above the realm of the ordinary, "of the possible and verisimilar," in which other adventures, crafted according to the aesthetic doctrines that he followed, could develop. He wanted a fantastic adventure that could serve as a sort of nucleus for part II, and he created it in the Cave of Montesinos, the visit to which he announces with solemn anticipation, relating it to subsequent adventures right up to the very end of the novel. Just as in the profoundly humorous episode of the galley slaves, where he had coupled his chivalrous hidalgo with the heroes of the picaresque novel, he wished now to associate him with the true and venerated heroes of medieval fiction. He did not seek them out in any book of chivalry. Once more, his mind turned to the ballads, although not, as we might suppose, to those of Spanish themes, but rather to the Carolingian.

Through an extravagant allusion, Don Quijote appears among Charlemagne's knights for a second time in an adventure derived from the ballads. But this time he appears more nobly and rationally, so to speak, than in the adventure of the Toledan merchants. The ballads had given those first chapters the appearance of a caricatural parody. Now in part II they provide the best moment of the burlesque ideal, in which it seems as if Cervantes were making amends for having earlier allowed himself to be too greatly influenced by the "Entremés."

If in Italy and Spain the Carolingian heroes had second homelands, conquered for them by Charlemagne's campaigns in both countries, they had multiplied in our own with new characters such as Durandarte and Montesinos. La Mancha, at the time a frontier between Christendom and Muslims and a bulwark that the three powerful military orders defended, had made itself worthy of being inhabited by poetic figures prouder and more gallant than, though not as universally admired as, that of their belated compatriot, Don Quijote. A certain castle in ruins, with its fountain which stood on a rocky outcrop in the middle of one of the lagoons of Ruidera where the river Guadiana has its source, was singled out by Manchegan tradition as the wonderful castle of which the ballad sang: "The castle called Roca/And the fountain called Frida." Silver battlements had been erected there on a foundation of gold, as the ballad states, studded with sapphires that shone in the dark of night like suns. In that castle had lived the maid Rosaflorida, disdainful of all suitors until she burned with love for the French Montesinos and, bringing him there, strew his path with pearls and precious stones. About the nearby cave, named for the same Montesinos, they told such marvelous things through all that realm that Don Quijote's curiosity was aroused. This was a great good fortune for the Guadiana, a hapless river in which the poets of the Golden Age, who lavished their efforts on the Duero, the Tagus, and the Henares, could find not a single nymph, except perchance one who had been turned into a frog in its muddy pools! Don Quijote found in the medieval Rosaflorida the nymph who would endow those marshlands with poetry, converting them into the enchanted fortress of the chivalry of long ago. The lagoon and cave, along with the dusty roads, the burning hot oak groves, and all the monotony of the vast, disconsolate horizon of La Mancha, were exalted to the dignity of a landscape that was poetical, familiar, and pleasing to humankind—no less so than the sacred olive groves of Attica and the luxuriant groves of the Cephisus, which were never penetrated by the summer sun or the winds of winter but indeed were frequented by the choruses of muses and bacchantes and by Aphrodite, driver of the golden chariot.

The exceptional quality in this adventure of Montesinos's cave, so insistently called to the attention of his readers by Cervantes, is that, for me, Don Quijote's heroic ideal does not manifest itself, as usual, in conflict with reality but, rather, finds itself emancipated, free from annoying and painful contact with it. Don Quijote descends to the bottom of the cave and, slackening the rope held by Sancho and the guide—the only link that connects him to the outer world—finds himself removed from it, alone in the midst of the cold, cavernous darkness. The cave is then illuminated by the light of the Manchegan hidalgo's imagination, as noble as it is unbalanced, and he finally finds himself among the heroes of the old ballads. He discourses amid the gloomy shades of Durandarte and Balerma, comic–heroic figures shrouded in a warped ideal. He appeases his mind with the placid and pitiful appearance of the enchanted Dulcinea, and in that mansion of ancient chivalry, where the lugubrious and the comic are powerfully blended in a fantastic picture of incomparable beauty and humorism, the eager spirit of the hidalgo realizes its supreme aspiration, the crowning of his effort through the mouths of the admired masters. Montesinos himself extols the restorer of knight-errantry and entrusts to him the important mission of revealing to the world the mysteries of the ancient heroic life and that of disenchanting the ancient paladins and the new Dulcinea. The novel's entire machinery, built on the opposition between fantasy and reality, is suspended on this sole occasion.

Upon reaching the summit of his exaltation, the hero nevertheless also reaches the edge of the abyss. When Don Quijote, hanging onto the rope, returns to the land of mortals and relates the supreme success that he has achieved, he encounters more than ever in his faithful Sancho a bold, impudent skepticism, and finally he, too, falls into doubt. That firm soul, who always restored his idealism so energetically whenever it was crushed by the vicious blows of reality, does not know how to defend himself against doubt in this glorious adventure devoid of torments. In vain he tries to put his uncertainty at rest by questioning the soothsayers as to whether his experiences with the ballad heroes in the enchanted cave had been a dream or the truth. The ambiguous clichés of the replies obtained from such oracles gradually filter into his heart, and dejection holds sway over him. The hour of being reduced to ordinary thinking has arrived. The hero is convinced that he will not attain the promise of Montesinos, that he will not see Dulcinea in all the days of his life, and he dies of sorrow . . . and of sanity. He has recovered his reason but lost the ideal by which he lived and breathed, so nothing is left for him but to die.

In Sophocles' tragedy, the offended Minerva sets in motion in Ajax's mind the whirlwind of a chimera, and the maddened hero attacks a flock of sheep, believing that he is beheading the Atrides who have wronged him. On recovering from his delirium and seeing himself surrounded by dead animals, he realizes that spilled blood is a dishonor to his invincible courage and to all his achievements, and he runs himself through with his own sword. His madness is divine because it is a punishment of the gods, while that of Don Quijote is a divine creation of his ailing soul.

The hero of Salamis takes his own life upon feeling himself ludicrous in the face of the reality that he contemplates. He kills himself out of shame. The Manchegan hero dies of the sadness of life upon discovering that reality is inferior to him and upon seeing that the Dulcinea to whom he gave his being is fading away forever into the world of impossible enchantment.

Is this novel of a madman one more book of chivalry, the last, the definitive and perfect one, as some say? Or, is it the ruination of chivalry and heroism, as others contend? It was not when writing *Don Quixote* that Cervantes attempted to produce a modern romance of chivalry, but afterward, when he composed his last, and for him, his most valuable work, *The Trials of Persiles and Segismunda*. This the good canon seems to announce in chapter 47 of part I when, cursing the books that have caused the Manchegan hidalgo's madness, he nevertheless finds in them something good, and this is "the subject that they furnished to a man of understanding with which to exercise his parts, because they allowed a large scope for the pen to expand upon without restriction, describing shipwrecks, storms, skirmishes and battles." All this is found in *Persiles*, the real novel of adventures, not only because of the influence of the Byzantine novel but also because of the romances of chivalry. The latter are influential even through their conventional episodes, as when Periandro, at the head of the company of fishermen, goes out to sea righting wrongs—a seafaring *Amadís*, created by the author of *Don Quixote*.

As for *Don Quixote*, we cannot help considering it simply and plainly as antagonistic to the romances of chivalry, which it tries to condemn to oblivion by satirizing not only their unpolished and careless composition but also their subject matter, a blend of childish fantasy, unbelievable deeds, and elemental passions.

Yet on the other hand, because these books, far from being essentially exotic to the Spanish people, are deeply saturated with that part of their spirit that consists of the exaltation of the universal feelings of selfless generosity and of honor, Cervantes' satire does not seek to damage the reputation of the eternal ideal of chivalric nobility. When he observes the ideal come to naught by its collision with daily life, he does not blame the ideal as much as he does reality itself for not turning out to be exactly as the heroic spirit would want it. Far from wishing to destroy that world adorned by the purest moral feelings, Cervantes holds it up for our respect and sympathy, showing us its ruins, bathed in a light of supreme hope, as a lofty refuge for the soul. Dulcinea del Toboso will always be the most beautiful woman in the world, as her unfortunate knight proclaims, even when he falls vanquished to the ground and begs his opponent to slay him.

In short, far from combating the spirit and fictions of heroic poetry, Cervantes received from the *Romancero* the first impulse to portray Don Quijote's ideal madness, and he sought in the *Romancero* a great portion of the work's inspiration and embellishments. Thus, popular heroic poetry was present at the creation that destroyed the molds in which the romances of chivalry were cast, removing its fictions from the world of chimeras to bring them to contend with the world of mundane reality. Thus Cervantes forged the first and inimitable prototype to which every modern novel, in close concert or somewhat distantly, is ultimately subordinated.

Notes

1. An *entremés*, literally a dish served between main courses of a meal, was a brief, one-act skit, a comic interlude performed in the interval between the acts of a play. *Romance* is the Spanish for ballad, a narrative poem in popular meter and rhyme. The first *romances* were derived from the epic poems, such as the *Poem of Mío Cid*, but as time went on they acquired a variety of themes, including the wars against the Moors and topics derived from the romances of chivalry. *Romancero* is the sum of all the romances and also a compendium or anthology of them. These popular, anonymous ballads enjoyed a great revival in the sixteenth century among cultivated poets, and they became a standard form in Spanish poetry that has endured up to the present. Menéndez Pidal was the foremost expert on the *romances*, which he placed at the core of Spanish literary history. [For further details, see Introduction.—ED.]

2. *Cancioneros* were anthologies of poetry in the courtly love tradition with much circulation in the fifteenth and sixteenth centuries. [Editor's note]

Canons Afire

Libraries, Books, and Bodies in Don Quixote's *Spain*

GEORGINA DOPICO BLACK

❖   ❖   ❖

T HIS ESSAY OPENS in the smoke of a fire, "in a village in
La Mancha," in the early years of the seventeenth century.
The scene is a familiar one: a "public trial" presided over by a
priest, a barber, a housekeeper, and a girl in her teens, this last,
the niece of Alonso Quijano, who dubs her uncle's books "heretics" and opens his library to the "amusing and exhaustive scrutiny" that will be its undoing. On that very day, as Don Quijote's
books are consumed by flames, another fire is burning, in another
village in La Mancha, or perhaps Toledo, Cuenca, or Seville. The
smoke that fills the air of this second fire does not carry the
distinctive smell of burning books, however, of words and
thoughts ablaze, but the equally distinctive smell of burning flesh.
I conjure these two images—the burning of a library and the
burning of heretics at any one of the inquisitorial *autos-da-fé* that
were celebrated in any number of Spanish towns throughout the
sixteenth and seventeenth centuries—not only because of the
haunting symmetry of these two scenes but because they speak
eloquently, if disquietingly, to the topic of this essay: the relation

between books and bodies, between canons and cannons, between libraries and power.

The idea or dream of the library is intimately linked in the early modern period—perhaps in every period—with the consolidation of empire, with national definition, and with the acts of incorporation and exclusion that canon formation—whether literary or national—inevitably mobilizes, foregrounding the ways in which questions of nationalism, variously and broadly defined (cannons), are brought to bear on the creation of cultural or literary histories (canons). As such, the library provides us with a privileged point of entry to the cultural politics of early modern Spain and, moreover, to the relation between cultural politics and political culture. By library I understand not only the physical space that houses manuscripts, books and other printed matter but, more important, the tensions that animate that space as well as the historic, epistemological, and even readerly conditions of its possibility. In this sense, the library is perhaps best understood as a "heterotopic space," a place in which, according to Foucault, "all the other real sites that can be found within the culture are represented, contested and inverted."[1]

In this essay I follow—and also critique—Foucault, but I do so by way of Borges, Roger Chartier, Walter Benjamin, Tony Bennett, Fernando Bouza Alvarez, Américo Castro, Lucien Febvre, Anthony Grafton, Roberto González Echevarría, and Irving Leonard, to name but a few. Chartier's work in particular opens up a brilliant space of inquiry in the library, one situated between order and transgression.[2] Order is reflected on one hand in the arrangement of books according to branches of knowledge, branches that are themselves ordered into a coherent system, and on the other in the regulation of the library—the circulation of books, the rules of access, its very etiquette. Transgression is the province of the readers who violate those two senses of order: finding connections between disparate texts, rearranging the order of books, writing in the margins, speaking aloud. I am interested here in these tensions as well, but I am more interested in seeing how that heterotopic space between order and transgression is haunted or informed by questions of origins, of genealogies, by the his-

tories that bring together bodies and books and those that bodies
and books bring together.

In the case of early modern Spain, we might question the
extent to which the library—the project of the library—at once
colludes with and resists the ongoing political project of defining
a national canon and, by extension, the inclusions and exclusions
of books—and of bodies—that such definition putatively required. The library serves, then, not only as a space to think the
canon but the nation or the empire as well. Bringing these questions to bear upon the library (and in particular upon foundations
and destructions of libraries) is useful in thinking about how we
construct the canon, how we imagine the nation, indeed, how
we remember the past. Libraries, I argue, have both histories and
genealogies. It is along these two axes—the historical and the
genealogical—that this essay is organized: the first part, a brief,
schematic history of the library in Spain through the seventeenth
century; the second, a close reading of genealogies in *Don Quixote*,
a text that is at the very center of the Golden Age library and
that has a library at its very center.

While my focus here is on the libraries of sixteenth- and
seventeenth-century Spain (a period that witnessed the establish-
ment both in Spain and in the American colonies of the library
as a politicocultural institution much as we know it today), the
story of course is much older. We might begin that story in Cordoba, about 1,000 years ago, before Spain was Spain or much less,
Spanish. By the mid-tenth century, some 200 odd years after a
tribe of Berber Muslims first crossed the strait of Gibraltar and
decided to stay, the city of Cordoba, capital of the Umayyad dynasty, was second in size only to Constantinople. In cultural
splendor, it was second to none. Al-Andalus boasted more than
seventy libraries in this other *Siglo de Oro* which, together with
Cordoba's famed book bazaar, attracted scholars—Islamic, Christian, and Jewish—from all corners of the world. The University
of Cordoba became an important center not only for the study
of Islam but for astronomy, mathematics, philosophy, and medicine. The royal library of Cordoba, founded by Abderrhaman III
in the ninth century and lovingly nurtured by his heirs was the

uncontested jewel in the crown. Under caliph al-Hakim (961–76), a consummate book collector and a scholar in his own right, the library grew to house over 400,000 volumes and to employ as many as 500 copyists, illuminators, bookbinders, and librarians on its regular staff. The royal library would suffer numerous vicissitudes over the course of the next half century (the regent-vizir who ruled for al-Hakim's son, for example, burned many of the library's scientific and philosophical holdings to appease religious conservatives) until its collection was dispersed in 1031, with the collapse of the Umayyad dynasty.[3]

We next travel north several hundred miles and forward several hundred years to mid-thirteenth-century Toledo, home to the brilliant and heterodox school of translators that plays a deciding role in the cultural production of Alfonso el Sabio. Like the Baghdad school on which it was modeled, the Toledo school of translators—and the libraries that it fed and fed off of—were largely responsible for the transmission of many of the foundational texts of the "Western" canon to the "West." The vast Alphonsine project of translation and cultural incorporation is perhaps best understood as the foundation of a symbolic library, a library of translations, and, moreover, a "national" library containing the earliest texts in a vernacular language produced anywhere in Europe: astronomical and scientific works, legal treatises, chronicles, books of games, mathematical charts, and universal histories, among many others. The foundation of this library is inseparable from Alfonso's aspirations to the imperial crown (in 1257 Alfonso was in fact elected Holy Roman emperor, although he never obtained papal recognition, his claims contested by a rival candidate) and, within his Spanish realms, from the political goal of centralization and unification. The cultural project, then, at once underwrites and is underwritten by the political one. Alfonso's revolutionary turn to Castilian Spanish as a language of legal, scientific, and cultural prestige is not so much a sign of Castilian linguistic or even political hegemony in the thirteenth century (Castile was in many ways the poor cousin of Alfonso's Andalusian kingdoms) as it is of the wise king's recognition that *romance* was the language most accessible to the majority of his subjects and hence a particularly apt language with which to rule them.

The central place of this Toledo library is no doubt occupied by Alfonso's monumental history, the *Estoria de Espanna*, dubbed *Primera Crónica General* by Ramón Menéndez Pidal, a history that sets out to trace a legitimizing genealogy for Spain, to stretch the national past to a Visigothic, and further still, a Genesic origin. In the prologue to that text (a prologue that translates and recycles an earlier prologue by archbishop of Toledo Rodrigo Jiménez de Rada, himself an important bibliophile), Alfonso relates the loss of memory, of history, and of identity represented by the loss of the written record, by the burning of libraries during the wars of Reconquest. "And thus" he writes, "all the deeds [*los fechos*] of Spain were lost with the books that were lost and destroyed as power changed hands, so that the origins of those who peopled her can hardly [*apenas*] be known."[4] The adverb *apenas* [hardly] is doubly weighted in the passage. On one hand it confirms the historiographic void that justifies the writing of a *new* history: to fill the silence of the libraries lost to political unrest as power changed hands. On the other the *apenas* [hardly] points to the *auctoritas* (the textual authorities that have not been lost, the books that have survived the pillaging of libraries) that will authorize Alfonso's history by inserting it within a legitimate textual genealogy. Alfonso clears the ground on which a new library can be erected even as he recovers the traces that will gird its foundation. It is not surprising that what immediately follows this act is the monarchical authorization, one that is sustained on *both* geopolitical and genealogical grounds and that ends with the ordering of the new history: "And thereby, we, don Alfonso, by the grace of God king of Castile, of Toledo, of Leon, of Galicia, of Seville, of Cordoba, of Murcia, of Jaen and the Algarbe, son of the very noble king don Fernando and of the queen doña Beatriz, ordered a collection of as many books as could be had of histories that in some way recounted the deeds of Spain."[5]

Alfonso's intense labor of cultural incorporation is carried out somewhat unevenly by his heirs over the next two hundred odd years; not until the end of the fifteenth century does it find a worthy scion in the queen who plays a crucial role in a defining moment of modern Spanish history, a queen who inherits the crown obliquely (on the rumor of her half brother's impotence), but wears it with aplomb: Isabel la Católica. My interest is not only in reading Isabel's library—or, rather, libraries—she founds important libraries in Toledo, at the Segovia Alcázar and in the Capilla Real de Granada or the particular (or even permissible) articulations of power and gender that a *queen's* library represents, but in the politics and the histories that infiltrate that library.

There is a notable difference between the Isabelline libraries and any that had come before them; in the years around 1450, a goldsmith from Mainz, Johann Gensfleisch, better known as Gutenberg, had radically redefined the contours of the library, forever transforming the shape of reading and writing and, with it, the alliance of knowledge and power. The movable-type printing press is imported to Spain within a decade of its invention (the oldest extant book printed in Spain dates from 1472) and very rapidly expands under the auspices of the Catholic Monarchs: By 1480, there are printers in Seville, Salamanca, Valencia, Tortosa, Barcelona, Lérida, and Saragossa; by 1492, the press has reached Toledo, Coria, Guadalajara, Huete, Murcia, Gerona, Burgos, Pamplona, Valladolid, Zamora, Santiago, and San Cucufate. It is in the context of that banner year that we can best understand the relation between three figures who play prominent roles in Isabel's Spain and in Isabel's library. The convergence of three landmark events—the fall of Muslim Granada, the expulsion of the Jews, and Columbus's voyage to the Americas—makes 1492 a determining date not only for Spain and for what would become the New World but for the cultural and geopolitical configuration of the globe.[6]

While neither as tragic nor as momentous as the other events that marked that year, the 1492 publication of Antonio de Nebrija's *Gramática de la lengua castellana*, the first grammar of Spanish or of any other vernacular language, rightly belongs beside the other three. Not only is it equally critical for Spain and for the definition of a Spanish canon (of what may properly be called "Spanish" and in this case, notably, "Castilian"), but it suggests the extent to which "textual" events and the more properly "historical" ones are bound up with one another. "Language was always the companion of empire,"[7] Nebrija writes in the dedication of his grammar to Isabel, spelling out in no uncertain terms what the savvy Queen knew all along: that the project of imperial consolidation was as much a matter of linguistic and cultural acts as it was of military and political ones. Invoking the memory of Alfonso el Sabio, Nebrija cites the usefulness of his *Gramática*: first, as an instrument at the service of an imperial historiography, a work essential not so much for the creation as for the preservation of a national memory, and second, as an indispensable tool in the work of conquest and conversion, a kind of linguistic catechism to help the *vencedor* [conqueror] impose his laws on the *vencido* [defeated]. It is not by chance that the *Gramática* is imported to the New World more than any other book in the period.[8]

The second figure in this 1492 library is only three years old when Columbus stumbles upon the Bahamas. At that tender age, he is already implicated in its genealogy: Fernando Colón, illegitimate Spanish son of Isabel's "Admiral of the Ocean Sea," humanist, historiographer, translator, and editor is also, and above all, a librarian. By the time of his death in 1539, Fernando Colón's library in Seville contained more than 16,000 volumes.[9] It was the ambition of the younger Colón (a goal that in the early years of the fifteenth century was not inconceivable) to assemble a universal library, a complete *corpus*: to own a copy of *every* book ever published both inside and *outside* Christendom.[10] He enlists (and in 1536 obtains) the financial assistance of the emperor himself, Isabel and Fernando's grandson Charles V, who had reaped the benefits of the older Colón's navigations. Fernando Colón mortgages his father's contested legacy in exchange for imperial support of his universal library, a library intended to support the universal empire. If Colón's work as collector and editor of texts (his father's among others) is an indispensable chapter in the history of early modern Spanish libraries, no less so is his work as bibliographer, as compiler of what are quite likely the first modern subject and author catalogs in Spain. It is through this bibliographic work and the virtual library of knowledge it assembles that we can perhaps best see the hidden fissures between the expansion of the empire and the expansion of the library or, to put it differently, between the older Colón's reading of maps and the younger Colón's maps of reading.

The third figure in the Queen's library is her confessor, her courtier and one of her closest confidantes: Cardinal Francisco Jiménez de Cisneros, Archbishop of Toledo, Inquisitor General in 1507, and regent of Castile upon Isabel's death. Intense contradictions (or what appear to us today as contradictions) surround Cisneros: the same brilliant humanist thinker who founds the University of Alcalá and its rich library, who reforms the Franciscan order, who brings German printers to Spain, who commissions the Polyglot Bible, and who finances the translation of medieval treatises on mysticism (texts that Teresa de Avila would read) burns more than 80,000 volumes—many of them expatriates from the Cordoba collection—at a purge by fire in the plaza de Vivarrambla in Granada. He spares only scientific and medical works in order to incorporate them to his Alcalá library.[11]

The same year that the good cardinal was burning books in Granada, at the height of the reign of the Catholic Kings, a printer in Burgos—Fadrique de Basilea—very possibly one of the same printers Cisneros invited to Spain, publishes a little book written by a first-generation *converso* on semester break from the University of Salamanca, where it is likely he took courses with Nebrija. It is a dark, intensely secular, and, to some, immoral work about sex, corruption, violence, greed, and ultimately death that would scandalously become a runaway bestseller. There are no libraries per se in Fernando de Rojas's *La Celestina*; its scenes of reading involve bodies rather than books. But the *tragicomedia* occupies a foundational—if uncomfortable—place in the Golden Age library, a book that has been more censured and more circulated than almost any other. *La Celestina* would not be officially expurgated until the early seventeenth century, but she is immediately banned from the libraries of women, children, and Native Americans, for fear of what she might teach them in hushed tones. It is these whispers in the library, the ministering and movements of Celestina's mouth and, in particular, her tongue ("the most harmful part") that at once threaten and confirm her place in the canon.[12] A tongue that is agent of transgressions and token of empowerment, ("What does my life depend upon?" Calisto implores. "My tongue," she responds[13]): a tongue that is a striking *compañera* to Nebrija's *lengua compañera del imperio* [language/tongue, companion of empire], a tongue that irreverently speaks what Cisneros had tried to silence with tongues of fire.

From the Spain of Fernando de Rojas, we turn to the Spain of Philip II (and of Cervantes), specifically to the site the prudent king planned as the intellectual and political center of that Spain: the Real Biblioteca del Escorial, sometime during the second half of the sixteenth century. There is an event that is determining for that library and all others in early modern Spain. In 1558, the very year that Charles V dies at Yuste and Philip II begins planning the construction of the Escorial as a fitting mausoleum for his emperor father, a *Pragmática* is passed at the Cortes de Valladolid ordering, under penalty of death, that all books printed in or imported to Spain be licensed by the Consejo de Castilla. As a parallel measure, the *Pragmática* calls for the inspection of all libraries and bookstores. It relinquishes this task to the Inquisition, which enforces it with swift and "unprecedented severity,"[14] in the words of J. H. Elliott. The next year, under Inquisitor General Fernando Valdés, the first native Spanish Index of Prohibited Books appears, followed by updated and expanded indices in 1570–71 and 1583–84. These would be followed by five additional indices in the course of the seventeenth century. Under the new laws, the process of obtaining license to publish was arduous: If a manuscript was approved for publication, every page had to be stamped and counted by an official of the Consejo. Publication could proceed only from this signed and sealed original. Once published, the manuscript and several copies of the printed book were resubmitted to the censor, to ensure that no liberties had been taken. If there were even minor discrepancies between them, a *Fe de Erratas* had to accompany the edition. Inquisitorial censorship came into play once a manuscript was already licensed; after that point, however, it could occur at literally any stage of the process: in the printing press, at the bookshop, on shipboard, or even within the walls of the library. Book censorship could take either of two forms: outright burning (if an entire book or the entire corpus of an author was prohibited) or *expurgación* (if only certain passages were deemed problematic).

The anonymous *Lazarillo de Tormes* of 1554 appears already on the Valdés Index of 1559, which not only prohibits the book but prohibits authorial anonymity: to obtain approval for publication, works must bear their authors' names. This disciplinary imposition of the author's name has important consequences for our conception of early modern authorship. It revises Foucault in two ways. First, it suggests—with Chartier—a much earlier date for the emergence of a modern author function (casting doubts on the theory of Spain's belated modernity). Second, it suggests that if that emergence is partly the result of new conceptions of intellectual property (the rise of copyright and booksellers' privileges), it is much more profoundly related to penal responsibility. To the extent that the *Lazarillo*'s anonymity may have been what prompted the more general prohibition of anonymity (the requirement of the name)—a prohibition directly tied to the emergence of an author function—the picaresque work becomes indispensable to any subsequent discussion of early modern authorship. With the *Lazarillo*, we can almost pinpoint the moment when the *name* of the author is made to arise as subject of both state and inquisitorial discipline. There is an important corollary to all of this: the 1559 Index that bans authorial anonymity prohibits editorial anonymity as well, suggesting the emergence of a "printer-function" alongside the "author-function." The Holy Office recognized early on the terrific power and the terrific threat posed by mechanical reproduction.[15] In their capacity for disseminating heresy, printers were viewed as potentially far more dangerous than authors.

One outcome of the simultaneous rise of inquisitorial and civil censorship was the devising of means to circumvent them. Resistance took many forms: forged licenses, apocryphal names, misattributed authorships, manuscript circulation, secret readings. It is worth noting here that these strategies could be deployed for other reasons as well: literary rivalries (Avellaneda's covert attack on Cervantes, for example) or financial profit (the numerous plays falsely attributed to Lope, seeking to capitalize on his popularity). A favorite strategy of printers was to publish prohibited books with false covers, so that what on the surface appeared to be a prayer manual might actually have contained a text by one of the Valdés brothers whose entire *corpus* was placed on the 1559 index. This stratagem was particularly useful for books destined for the New World which not only had to pass through an additional layer of scrutiny (inspection at Seville) before they could board ship but which were subject to other controls. A *Real Cédula* of 1531, for example, prohibits the shipment to America of "books of romance, vain and profane histories, and books of chivalry" all deemed too dangerous for native readers.[16] This textual *passing*— of books pretending to be what they were not in order to avoid the flames—has striking resonances in a society in which passing was an everyday affair. The impact of the indices on libraries cannot be overstated: Its effects were both material and formal, not only ordering what books and what authors would be allowed entry within its walls but effectively *re* ordering the library's shelves. The publication of a new index inevitably meant a new cycle of "scrutiny of libraries" both public and private, and, in their wake, a new cycle of arrests. Reading had high stakes.

Censorship of books is pretty well institutionalized by the time the first stone of the Escorial's foundation is ceremoniously laid in 1563. Philip II, perhaps the consummate Renaissance collector,[17] begins building the Escorial's collection almost immediately, with the same untiring energy and micromanagement style by which he rules. His initial donation to the library (in 1565) includes more than 4,000 of his own books and manuscripts. The collection would nearly triple in size during the course of the next decade. The sources of this growth—which continued throughout the seventeenth century—were various. The collection expanded first through the incorporation of other libraries (two notable examples are those of Diego Hurtado de Mendoza in the sixteenth century and of the Count Duke of Olivares in the seventeenth), second, through the intense acquisition process that Philip II set in motion (a process largely advanced by Benito Arias Montano whom Philip summons to the Escorial to order its books and serve as official librarian; this is the same Arias Montano who authors the 1570–71 index), and third, through acts we might term "cultural pirating." In 1614, for example, as the last of the *moriscos* are expelled from Spain, 4,000 Arabic manuscripts are incorporated to the Escorial. These manuscripts, destined for the library of the Sultan of Morocco, were seized by Pedro de Lara, captain of the Spanish galleys in the Mediterranean, from two of the Sultan's ships traveling along the Barbary Coast. The apparent paradox (*morisco* bodies out of Spain, Arab manuscripts in) is resolved if we imagine the Escorial library as a machine of incorporation that swallows whole the cultural output of a group expelled as waste from the national body.

This same appetite accounts for the presence on its shelves of works and authors that appear on Inquisitorial indices: the first inventory of the Escorial's holdings lists 139 prohibited books, books that the Inquisition had seized but *not* burned, turning them over, instead, to the king's librarian. In his master plan for the Escorial library ("Traza de la librería de San Lorenzo"), Juan Bautista Cardona had recommended to Philip II not only that he reserve a separate room to house prohibited books (keeping them isolated from the rest), but, moreover, that he obtain special papal dispensation in the form of a bull authorizing him to collect banned books with a free conscience. In the end, the prohibited books would not be quarantined to a room of their own, as Cardona had counseled, but would instead be placed on the top shelves of the main library.

A persistent criticism of the Escorial was, precisely, that it ingested books, swallowing texts whole, burying them in a paradoxically remote center: "magnificent sepulcher [*magno sepulcro*] of books where the cadavers of manuscript codices are conserved and rotted."[18] But the Escorial was, primarily, a *magno sepulcro* where royal cadavers were conserved and rotted. The basilica (complete with its *pudrideros* [rotting rooms]) was San Lorenzo's *raison d'être*, one inseparable, in many ways, from Philip II's immense relic "library" (a library that would include nearly 8,000 pieces by the time of Philip's death in 1598).[19] The central relic in the Escorial was (and still is) the body of the Emperor Charles V, the last Spanish king to wear the imperial crown. There is an important legitimizing relation between the Emperor's dead body and the *corpus* of the national library, a relation reflected in the very placement of the library, and one, moreover, with an illustrious history that was not unknown to Philip: the founding presence of the body of Alexander the Great in the "Museum," the Great Library of Alexandria, and, prior still, the body of Rameses II near the *bibliotheke* in the "Mausoleum."[20]

LET US LEAVE suspended the mythic genealogy of the Escorial and return to Alonso Quijano's library to explore a question that has been haunting us all along but that becomes unavoidable the moment we open that particular library's door. The "donoso y grande escrutinio" that, as we have seen, has all the makings and all the markings of an inquisitorial *auto-da-fé*, is largely predicated on genealogies. The priest and the barber who preside over the trial of the books repeatedly appeal to a genealogical argument that entangles heresy with heredity: *Amadís* is first condemned as the dogmatizing father of a heretical sect ("all the others have their origin and beginning in it") and then, improbably, pardoned for his seminal role.[21] *Las sergas de Esplandián*, "Amadis of Gaul's legitimate son," is sentenced to the fire, in part because he *is* his father's son: "the excellence of the father isn't going to be of any avail to the son" (I, 6). The rest of the progeny are likewise condemned because they are "members of that same family [lineage]" (I, 6). The priest goes so far as to say he would burn the father who begat him "if I catch him going about as a knight errant" (I, 6). The genealogical model of guilt similarly applies to the other books that complete the hidalgo's library and, quite explicitly to translations, sentenced to the flames on account of their secondariness: "they can never recreate it in the full perfection of its original birth" (I, 6).

The question of genealogy is not an idle one in 1605 Spain; the early seventeenth century saw increasingly heated debates over *limpieza de sangre* [purity of blood] statutes. A war of paper is fought between proponents of a softening or *relajamiento* [relaxation] of those statutes (including Pope Nicholas V who forcefully opposes them as unchristian; this position would eventually become linked to Olivarista politics and to the Crown's economic interests) and those who not only favored stricter application of existing purity of blood statutes but who called for the total expulsion of the *moriscos* and, in its wake, a second, more rigorous Jewish expulsion (Quevedo, a case in point; his *Execración contra los judíos*, a text discovered in very recent years in the library of the Catedral de Santiago, makes just this argument).

But the possibility of reading a relation between genealogies of books and genealogies of bodies is rooted in a more fundamental relation between body and book. It is a relation *Don Quixote* repeatedly confronts us with, both inside and outside the library's walls. The *escrutinio* chapter in fact opens with an explicit reference to *cuerpos de libros* [bodies of books]. The practice of referring to books as bodies was common enough in early modern Spain: *cuerpo* [body] where books were concerned referred in the first place to the materiality of the book—a materiality that was given the contours of a body—with face [*carátula*], spine [*lomo*], and even fingers [*índices*]. We need look no further than the *Preliminares* of any number of early modern texts to find, in the royal censor's *aprobación y licencia* [approbation and license], permission for printing and selling a specified quantity of *cuerpos de libros*.[22] *Cuerpo* referred also to the composition of the text as a kind of body, based on Aristotelian norms of proportion. Early modern rhetorical and philological texts—Luis de León's and el Pinciano's, for example—invoked just such a language, tending even, to spiritualize it.[23] It is precisely this Aristotelian model that informs the canon's censure of books of chivalry at the end of Book I: "I've never seen a book of chivalry that could be regarded as a whole body complete with all its members [. . .], on the contrary, their authors give them so many members that their intention seems more to produce a chimera or a monster than a well-proportioned figure" (I, 47). Their physiological disproportion and their spiritual inadequacies are so acute, he argues, that they "deserve to be thrown out [expelled] of a Christian society" (I, 47).

The attribution of bodies to books makes them, as the canon

is quick to recognize, immediately subject to all the accidents that can befall a body: They can be banished ("*desterrados*" [I, 47]) or burned ("*a la hoguera*" [I, 6]), or even turned over to civil authorities for execution ("*entregados al brazo seglar*" [I, 6]). It is no coincidence that these accidents all involve the participation of the body of the state or of the Holy Office as agents of discipline, further consolidating the relationship between the emergence of authorship and institutional controls. We might ask if books are assigned (symbolic) bodies because bodies are somehow more pliable—more readily disciplined—than words.

Bodies can also be both subjects and objects of contagion. It is precisely in relation to disease that the anatomical body, the textual body, and the national body are most stubbornly entwined in early modern Spain. Books are banned or burned so they will not infect their readers. Live bodies are quarantined, dead ones burned in the devastating plague that assails Castile at the turn of the seventeenth century. The body of the nation is symbolically figured as diseased and in need of remedies in the *arbitrista* literature that explodes in these years. It is these various ailments that make bodies subject to the ministering of both physical and spiritual healers: to wit, priests and barbers (barbers effectively functioned in the early modern period as local surgeons, cutting bodies open and sewing them together).

Don Quixote as book first assigns itself a body in the Prologue to part I; it is there that an argument concerning natural and textual generation first surfaces. The 1604/1605 Prologue stages perhaps the most famous case in literature of writer's block: a defining moment of impotence.[24] That impotence is cast in a language of natural and unnatural generation, legitimate and illegitimate fatherings, fruitful inseminations and incontinent disseminations. *Don Quixote* is not only engendered from sterility and infirmity ("to what can my barren and ill-cultivated mind give birth?" [I, Prologue]), but the engendering takes place at the very site where the body of the state imposes its discipline upon the body of the subject ("born, after all, in prison" [I, Prologue]). This debilitated, but natural, line of generation ("son of my brain" [I, Prologue]) is immediately fractured by a competing line ("but though I seem like Don Quijote's father, I am his stepfather" [I, Prologue]). This second, artificial line inscribes either the father's death (there is no divorce in counter-Reformation Spain) or his being made a cuckold. If we believe Sebastián de Covarrubias, it also inscribes an imminent threat to the stepchild: "his stepfather will harm him, if he can."[25]

These two models of generation bring to a head the problem of similitude in the text, on which hangs the status of representation itself. On the surface, the natural model—"like give births to like" (I, Prologue)—appears to be linked with genetic similitude, with faithful mimesis, with correspondence between the original and the copy (or alternately, the translation), between things and the words that name them. The *padrastro–padrino* [stepfather–godfather] model is, by contrast, the province of difference, of monstrous mimesis, where *imitatio* is under siege and signs run rampant. Remember here the painter of Úbeda who must label his paintings to make the figures in them recognizable. But the models chiasmically cross one another where we least expect it: The father's resemblance to his "ugly, charmless son" blinds him to his son's faults which he takes for "gifts and graces" (I, Prologue). The stepfather, on the other hand, not only sees clearly but exempts the disoccupied reader from repeating the father's blindness. The terms of that exemption are suggestive, extending the nonfamilial line to the impassive reader: "you are neither his relative nor his friend" (I, Prologue). But the lines become impossibly entangled with the entrance of the author's anonymous *amigo*, who interrupts [*a deshora*] the interruption of writing (the block) that the prologue represents. The way to authorize the textual body of *Don Quixote*, the friend advises, is by violating Aristotelian proportion, grafting onto it pieces of other bodies, claiming unnatural paternities, or forging *ahijamientos* [baptisms]. Ironically, these falsifications (reminiscent of some of the ways in which real authors countered censorship) depend on perfect Aristotelian *imitatio*.

Strange paternities and questionable genealogies crop up repeatedly in the chapters leading up to the "Inquisition of the Library." During his dinner at the first castle-inn, for example,

Don Quijote expounds on the equivalence between many *truchuelas* and one *trucha*. The substitutability he argues for, however (and casts in monetary terms), is based on a monstrous conception of synecdoche that confuses nominal with genetic similitude: Neither are *truchuelas* parts of a whole *trucha*, nor will they ever grow up to become one; the analogy (*truchuela* to *trucha* as *ternera* to *vaca* or *cabrito* to *cabrón*) is both logically and rhetorically flawed. But it is in the eighth and ninth chapters where paternities fully explode in *Don Quixote*. Or, rather, in the space between the two, a space in which we literally run out of text, where we are left hanging ("colgados," "suspensos") like the books of Don Quijote's library—Cervantes' own *La Galatea* among them—that are sequestered in the barber's house, their sentences suspended until the publications (births) of their sequels (children). Here, the threat of bodily division is visited upon the body of the book.[26]

> In the first part of this history we left the valiant Basque and the famous Don Quijote with naked swords aloft, about to deliver two such devastating downstrokes that if their aim was true they would at the very least split each other from top to bottom and cut each other open like pomegranates; and at this critical point the delightful history stopped short and was left truncated. (I, 9)

Let us see how and on what terms that cleaved body is reassembled and how that reassembly mobilizes the various contested paternities of both book and body. It should not surprise us that the scene of discovery should take place in the Alcaná de Toledo. Toledo, as we have seen, has a rich history of Hebrew and Arabic translation, sustained by a long history of Jewish and Muslim presence. It is a history the narrator is well aware of: "and so I looked around to see if there was some Spanish-speaking Moor ... and it wasn't very hard to find one, because even if I'd been looking for a translator from another better and older language, I should have found him, too" (I, 9). After the burning and walling of Alonso Quijano's library, the Alcaná in fact serves as a kind of open-air library, a space where fragmented and devalued texts circulate. But Toledo has a different history, too: It is there, in 1547, the same year that Cervantes was born, that Spain's first purity of blood statute is made law, and it is there, in that very Alcaná, that more than 1,000 Jews had been massacred centuries earlier.

The brilliant irony of chapter 9 is the attribution—in 1605—of authorial paternity to an *historiador arábigo* [Arab historian/storyteller], who would have no place in a seventeenth-century library (the Escorial notwithstanding). The attribution is, moreover, immediately displaced onto a second-generation *morisco aljamiado* who promises to "make a good and faithful translation" of the Arabic manuscript (I, 9). (We already know the infernal fate reserved for translations in the burning library.) But the version we are reading is not just a translation but includes the translator as character, suggesting at least *one* other hand, one more *padrastro manco* [maimed stepfather]—the presumably Christian narrator of chapter 9, who may or may not be the narrator of chapters 1 through 8, or of the prologue, but who *is*, he confesses, an obsessive and undiscriminating reader, a reader of broken parts, of fatherless street-texts: "since I'll read anything, even scraps of paper lying in the gutter . . ." (I, 9). We are at a moment that disoccupies all past and future authorial and genealogical positions. Cide Hamete's *hijo-libro* [child-book] undergoes a conversion in language, *apadrinado* [godfathered] by a *morisco,* and then adopted by a Christian stepfather of dubious lineage.[27]

There is more here. The name of the father, Cide Hamete Benengeli (*Berenjena* [eggplant] in Sancho's lexicon), has been thought to be an Arabized perversion of Cervantes' own (and Cervantes' name appears in the library chapter, as a second-class author). But in 1605 and in the forty years leading up to 1605 (and the narrator tells us this is a *historia moderna* [modern story], a fact he ascertains from the publication dates of the books on Don Quijote's shelves), no one in Spain could, by law, bear the name Benengeli or, for that matter, own an Arabic book authored by a Benengeli. In 1567, Philip II had passed a series of ordinances of cultural repression, implemented first in Granada (and it is these measures that prompt the second revolt of the Alpujarras in 1568), later in the rest of Spain. Under penalty of death, the ordinances prohibited written and spoken Arabic, moorish dress, the veiling of women, moorish baths, moorish celebrations (including musical instruments, song, and dance), and the use of Arabic names. The matter of naming is central to *Don Quixote*, and, at least since Spitzer, to its readings. Names are also central to the ordering and disordering of libraries, to its occupation by zealous priests and barbers armed with indices and its disoccupation according to genealogies. The constant confusion of lineages (Quijada, Quesada, Quejana) and willful forgetting of names in the novel ("the name of which I [do not want to] recall" [I, 1]) take on special poignancy when considered alongside the forced christenings and false genealogies of early modern Spain: attempts by power, attempts against power to forget the name of the father *and* of the mother.

One effect of the constant confusion and circulation of names is to cast doubt on the "truth of the history" ["*verdad de la historia*"]. There is a remarkable—and remarkably cited—passage in chapter 9 that reflects on the status of truth and the matter of history. It is the passage that Borges gives us in both Pierre Menard's and Cervantes' versions:

> If there is any objection to be made about the truthfulness of this history, it can only be that its author was an Arab, and it's a well-known feature of Arabs that they're all liars; but since they're such enemies of ours, it's to be supposed that he fell short of the truth rather than exaggerating it. And this is, indeed what I suspect he did, because where he could and should have launched into the praises of such an excellent knight, he seems to have been careful to pass them over in silence, which is something he shouldn't have done or even thought of doing, because historians should and must be precise, truthful and unprejudiced, without allowing self-interest or fear, hostility or affection, to turn them away from the path of truth, whose mother is history: the imitator of time, the storehouse of actions and the witness to the past, an example and a lesson to the present and a warning to the future. (I, 9)

There is much that merits comment here from the accusation of liar [*mentiroso*] hurled against the Arabic author on the grounds of national origins to the lie that exists only as its own absence: in the silence of what remains unspoken or unwritten. What is striking for our troubled paternities, however, is the status of the mother here or, rather, the status of history, as *mother* of truth. It is a genealogy that turns (*tuerce el camino*) from the expected one: a history (daughter) legitimately born of—and thus authorized by—truth. But "*madre*" [mother] Covarrubias reminds us is not only "*mater.* Correlative of child" but "among printers [it means] the matrices [*hembras*] with which letters are emptied."[28] The maternal line, then, is also connected with the material reproduction (*mater, materia*) that generates the story that will in turn manufacture truth. This mechanical *madre,* repeatedly filled and emptied (occupied and disoccupied) with ink and letters, is vital to the very existence of the library, the library that will house the stories and histories that mother (or doctor) the truth about the nation—its proclaimed or its silenced genealogies.

There are other mothers in *Don Quixote,* but one in particular reappears several times, aligned with purity—both sexual and racial. One of the most stunning instances where this mother is made flesh occurs just before the penance in the Sierra Morena: "I would venture to swear that my Dulcinea del Toboso has never seen a real Moor in real Moorish clothes in all her life, and that she is today as intact as the mother who bore her" (I, 25). There is good reason, for Dulcinea's never having seen "a real Moor in real Moorish clothes" after the 1567 ordinances. That not seeing, however, is immediately attached to her corporeal integrity: By virtue of her sightlessness, Dulcinea is as pure and whole as her mother bore her (and the expression is used a number times to guarantee virginity). But that's not what the passage says at all: "se está hoy como la madre *que* la parió": by means of the *que* [who], the daughter is identified with the body of the mother, a mother that in the very act that produces the daughter, loses not only her own intactness but, alarmingly, her daughter's as well. Dulcinea's purity—where *moros* are concerned—is radically undermined, then, by the force of the innocuous *que* on which the wordplay turns (a typical Cervantine wordplay in which a tremendous semantic change is effected by a minimal syntactic one): a *que* that points back to the mother's *im*purity: a "mancha" that the daughter is not allowed to forget. The maternal line, in the end, is no less tainted than the paternal.

A BOOK ABOUT BOOKS, about the dangers and seductions of the printed page, about a man maddened by reading, who confuses the fictions of his books with the fictions of reality, *Don Quixote* has aptly been dubbed the most bookish of books. But that bookishness has persistently led, from the Romantics on, to readings that stress the novel's disconnection or disengagement from its own historical circumstance, a disengagement often expressed in terms of quixotic idealism or in corroboration of a transcendent universality. While this view has by no means stood unchallenged—on the contrary, it has elicited vigorous responses, Américo Castro's the most comprehensive—it remains stubbornly entwined to the privileged place *Don Quixote* is afforded in the Spanish and, more broadly, the Western canon, as if the centrality of books—indeed of the written word—in the novel at once canonized and condemned *Don Quixote* to the library, one imagined as shelter (and sheltered) from the world.

Libraries, however—and particularly national or imperial libraries—are fully *in* the world. Their foundations, their constitutions, their very destructions are inseparable from the ebbs and flows of power and resistance. It would be possible to write not just a cultural or literary history of a people, or a language, or an empire through the story of its libraries (who and what is permitted access, who or what is expelled), but a national and political history as well. If the library is a space that archives history, it also instances it, is everywhere riddled with it. Alonso Quijano's library is no exception. Even, perhaps especially, at those moments when *Don Quixote* is at its most bookish—in its authorial games, its forays in the library, its metatextual mirrorings (or mirages), it never escapes its historical grounding. It is not just that *Don Quixote* is enmeshed in its time and place—the same is true of all books, of all stories, from the most archetypal to the most locally colored—it is that that enmeshing is perhaps most poignantly inscribed in those same bookish games and forays that are consistently invoked as evidence of its detachment. The constant confusion between book and body in *Don Quixote* points not only to the irreducible materiality of the two, a materiality that challenges idealist readings, imbuing both book and body with gravity, weighing them with history, but the book–body relation in the novel points also to the body of the nation behind them, a body that calls them into being as subjects or objects, even as it disciplines them. *Don Quixote* playfully and starkly reminds us that behind every book is a body, and with it, a madness, real or imagined, a genealogy, authentic or forged, a history, remembered or forgotten.

DON QUIXOTE OPENS with a willful act of forgetting and closes with "Don Quixote's weary mouldering bones at rest in his tomb" (II, 74), safe from the misrememberings of the "false writer from Tordesillas." I would like to close by turning to a different scene of forgetting, very near the book's end, as innocent, on the surface, as the excessive *que* that transforms Dulcinea's putative mother from virgin to not; it takes place in part II, when Don Quixote and Sancho are approaching Barcelona: ". . . riding off the road, night overtook [them] in a dense copse of evergreen oaks or cork-oaks—on this point Cide Hamete isn't as meticulous as usual" (II, 60). Several times in the novel, particularly in the last dozen chapters of the second part, we are told that Cide Hamete is careless in his arboreal description. We have it again some eight chapters later during the *aventura cerdosa* (when he is run over by pigs): "Don Quijote, leaning against the trunk of a beech or a cork-oak (Cide Hamete Benengeli doesn't specify which it was), sang as follows, to the accompaniment of his own sighs . . ." (II, 68).

It seems a gratuitous detail on either the translator or the narrator's part, one meant, perhaps, to cast further shadow on the *verdad* [truth] of this *historia* [history/story]. But I suspect there is more to the story. We might read Cide Hamete's lack of precision following (or anticipating) Borges who reads the *absence* of camels in the Koran as proof of its Arabness. "Muhammad, as an Arab, was secure; he knew he could be Arab without camels."[29] Perhaps what is at stake in the *Quixote*'s *alcornoques* is, precisely, the Spanishness of its *autor arábigo y manchego*.

But it is neither camels nor, more locally, bulls that Cide Hamete represses, it is trees. In sixteenth- and seventeenth-century Spain, as now, the tree was the central metaphor for genealogy: *linajes* [lineages], and consequently *limpieza de sangre* [purity of blood], were traced through trees.[30] We are faced, then, with a silence that may not be so innocent after all (and recall that it is Cide Hamete's silences that expose him as liar, or to put it another way, as author of fictions). The close etymological connection between *estirpe*[31] [genealogy] and *estirpar*[32] [uproot] should not surprise us; neither perhaps should the predominant use of *estirpar* in early modern Spain: "To uproot heresies," according to Covarrubias, "is to yank from the roots everything that can cause or foster them, punishing heretics, banning suspicious books, etc., as is done by the ministers of the Holy Inquisition."[33] At a moment when trees—their roots, their trunks, their branches, but mostly their names—are of central concern, Cide Hamete "isn't as meticulous as usual," confusing *encinas* [evergreen oaks] and *hayas* [beech trees] with *alcornoques* [cork-oaks]. I will not rehearse here a reading of Avellaneda's name in this line, although we can see where it might lead us, particularly when we recall that the stepfather of the prologue describes his malformed son as *"seco y avellanado"* [dry and shriveled/hazel-nut] (I, Prologue).

We seem to have traveled a long way from the library to arrive at the shade of this improbable oak, but really we have not left it at all. Trees, after all, are both materially and etymologically linked to *libros* [books] and *librerías* [libraries]. Covarrubias writes: "Book [libro] comes from the Latin word *liber,* which means the covering of the tree." The Arabic genealogy of *alcornoque* remits precisely to its covering: The word means nakedness, on account of that covering—bark—the tree is repeatedly made to give up. It is with respect to the generosity of trees—*alcornoques* and *enci-*

nas—that *Don Quixote* defines a lost Golden Age, *siglos dorados* [golden centuries] when *encinas* [evergreen oaks] freely gave their *bellotas* [acorns] and *alcornoques* [cork-oaks] their *cortezas* [bark].[34]

Like Cide Hamete, I may be mixing my trees here, *pidiéndole peras al olmo, bellotas al alcornoque*, but I want to connect this golden moment with another moment in *Don Quixote* that bears upon fruit: upon the flowering of an unexpected fruit. It is yet another act of monstrous generation inscribed in the first prologue: the improbable moment at which "even the most barren muses [. . .] become fertile and bring forth a progeny to fill the world with wonder and delight" (I, Prologue). These *muses* who inseminate texts make their homes—and in fact name—the *Museum*, a "museum" that in Golden Age Spain at least was remembered as the most magnificent library imaginable: the Great Library of Alexandria. But let us not forget our genealogies: The muses who haunt the library are daughters, after all, of Zeus and Mnemosyne, of power and memory. It is this uncertain territory between power and memory that the library claims as its own: a ground for deliberate acts of forgetting and powerful acts of remembering, a space for the books and the bodies that survived the fires and the cinders of those that did not. The scrutiny of the library chapter of *Don Quixote* brilliantly opens the door to this haunted, enchanted space, a place in which reading is both refuge and risk, in which the traces of power and memory are grafted on skin or on paper, in which bodies and books are fraught with history and desire: madness to surrender, madness not to.

Notes

1. Michel Foucault, "Of Other Spaces." *Diacritics* 16, no. 1 (Spring 1986): 22–27.

2. See Chartier's brilliant study of readers, writers, and libraries from the fourteenth to the eighteenth century. Roger Chartier, *The Order of Books* (Stanford, Calif.: Stanford University Press, 1994). See also Fernando Bouza Álvarez's suggestive *Del escribano a la biblioteca* (Madrid: Editorial

Síntesis, 1997) and François Géal's *Figures de la bibliothèque dans l'imaginaire espagnol du Siècle d'Or* (Paris: Champion, 1999).

3. It is worth noting that there were a number of important monastic libraries at this time in Spain, but even the most richly endowed of these—the library of the Monastery of Ripoll, for example, a library whose dates correspond almost perfectly with the Abderrhaman's royal library (it is founded by Wilfredo el Velloso in the ninth century and reaches its peak under the abad Oliba in the eleventh) could not compete with the majesty of Cordoba.

4. Alfonso X, el Sabio, *Primera crónica general de España*. Ramón Menéndez Pidal, ed. (Madrid: Gredos, 1977): "Prólogo." Translation mine. The original reads: "E desta guisa fueron perdudos los fechos d'|Espanna| por los libros que se perdieron e fueron destroydos en el mudamiento de los sennorios, asi que apenas puede seer sabudo el comienço de los que la poblaron."

5. Ibid., translation mine. "E por end, nos don Alfonso, por la gracia de Dios rey de Castilla, de Toledo, de León, de Gallizia, de Sevilla, de Cordoba, de Murçia, de Jaén e del Algarve, fijo del muy noble rey don Fernando e de la reyna doña Beatriz, mandamos ayuntar cuantos libros pudimos aver de istorias en que algun|a| cosa contasse de los fechos d'Espanna."

6. For a more detailed account of the coincidences ciphered in this date (and the events leading up to them), see "The Horse Latitudes," in María Rosa Menocal, *Shards of Love* (Durham, N.C.: Duke University Press, 1994).

7. "Siempre la lengua fue compañera del imperio." Antonio Nebrija, *Gramática de la lengua castellana*. Antonio Quilis, ed. (Madrid: Centro de Estudios Ramón Areces, 1989). Translation mine.

8. See Irving A. Leonard, *Books of the Brave*, with Rolena Adorno's important Prologue (Berkeley: University of California Press, 1992).

9. This figure includes books, pamphlets, as well as any other sort of bound, printed matter.

10. On Fernando Colón's library, see Tomás Marín Martínez, José Manuel Ruiz Asencio and Klaus Wagner, eds., *Catálogo concordado de la biblioteca de Hernando Colón* (Madrid: Fundación Mapfré-América, 1993). See also Agustín Millares Carlos, *Introducción a la historia del libro y de las bibliotecas* (México: Fondo de Cultura Económica, 1993), 262; Hipólito Escolar, *Historia de las bibliotecas* (Madrid: Fundación Germán Sánchez, 1990), 281–86; and Francisco Rico, "El nuevo mundo de Nebrija y Colón. Notas sobre

la geografía humanística en España y el contexto intelectual del descubrimiento de América," in *Nebrija y la introducción del renacimiento en España*, Victor García de la Concha, ed. (Salamanca: Ediciones Universidad de Salamanca, 1996), 157–85.

11. An anonymous *qasida* of 1501—a letter-poem sent to the Ottoman Sultan Bayazid II, requesting his intervention in Spain—gives an idea of the sense of loss this represented.

41. transgredió [el rey Fernando de Aragón] las Capitulaciones con que nos había engañado y nos convertimos al cristianismo por la fuerza, con dureza y severidad,

42. quemando los libros que teníamos y mezclándolos con excrementos e inmudicias.

43. Todos los libros que trataban de asuntos de nuestra religión fueron presa del fuego entre la mofa y la irrisión.

44. No dejaron ni un solo libro que perteneciera a un musulman, ni un solo tomo con quien uno pudiera refugiarse en soledad y leer.

45. Aquel que ayunaba o rezaba y esto llegaba a saberse, iba a parar a las llamas. . . .

"Casida morisca enviada al sultán otomano en petición de ayuda," in Mercedes García Arenal, *Los moriscos* (Granada: Universidad de Granada, 1996), 36–37.

In his 1882 *Historia de los heterodoxos españoles*, Marcelino Menéndez Pelayo gives an account of the Vivarrambla book burning: "[Cisneros] entregó a las llamas en la plaza de Vivarrambla gran número de libros árabes de religión y supersticiones, adornados muchos dellos con suntuosas iluminaciones y labores de aljófar, plata y oro, reservando los de medicina y otras materias científicas para su biblioteca de Alcalá." Marcelino Menéndez Pelayo, *Historia de los heterodoxos españoles. Erasmistas y protestantes. Sectas místicas. Judaízantes y moriscos. Artes mágicas* (Mexico: Porrúa, 1995), 373.

12. Fernando de Rojas, *The Celestina. A Novel in Dialogue*, trans. Lesley Bird Simpson (Berkeley: University of California Press), 53. The original reads: "el más empecible miembro." Fernando de Rojas, *La Celestina*, Dorothy Severin, ed. (Madrid: Cátedra), 270.

13. *The Celestina. A Novel in Dialogue*, 122–23. Calisto: "No sé en qué está mi vida." Celestina: "En mi lengua." *La Celestina*, 270.

14. John Elliott, *Imperial Spain. 1469–1716* (New York: Mentor Books, 1966), 223.

15. The historical argument linking the spread of Protestantism to the rise of the printing press could be understood as a corollary to this.

16. "libros de romances, historias vanas y profanas, y libros de caballería"

17. For a provocative account of the connection between the Renaissance and the accumulation of material goods, see Lisa Jardine, *Worldly Goods* (New York: Doubleday, 1996).

18. "Magno sepulcro de los libros donde se conservan y se pudren los cadáveres de los códices manuscritos." Cited in Manuel Sánchez Mariana, *Bibliófilos españoles* (Madrid: Biblioteca Nacional–Ministerio de Cultura, 1993), 42, translation mine.

19. The classic reference on Philip II's immense relic library is J. M. del Estal, "Felipe II y su archivo hagiográfico de El Escorial," *Hispania Sacra* 23 (1970): 193–335.

20. See Luciano Canfora's stunning history of the Library of Alexandria. Luciano Canfora, *The Vanished Library* (Berkeley: University of California Press, 1989).

21. English translation: Miguel de Cervantes, *Don Quixote*, trans. John Rutherford (New York: Penguin, 2001), I, 6. Further references to this edition will be parenthetically cited within the text by book and chapter. For the Spanish text of the *Quixote*, I have used Francisco Rico's meticulous edition: Miguel de Cervantes, *Don Quijote de la Mancha*, Francisco Rico, ed. (Barcelona: Crítica, 1999).

22. The "aprovaciones" that preface Quevedo's *Buscón*, for example, state: "se ha hallado que no tiene cosa contra nuestra santa Fe Catholica. . . . Por tanto por tenor de los presentes, de nuestra cierta sciencia, y por la Real Autoridad que vsamos en esta parte, damos licencia y facultad al dicho Roberto Duport . . . pueda imprimir y vender, y hazer imprimir y vender el susodicho libro, y todos los *cuerpos* que del quisiere" Francisco de Quevedo, *Vida del Buscón llamado Don Pablos*, Fernando Lázaro Carreter, ed. (Barcelona: Editorial Juventud, 1968), 33–34.

23. In a striking passage of Luis de León's *De los nombres de Cristo*, one character praises another's exegetical skills, drawing on a text–body analogy: "soys el primero de los que he visto y oydo yo que, juntando cada una cosa con su igual cuya es, y como pareándolas entre sí y poniéndolas en sus lugares, travándolas todas y dándoles orden, avéys hecho *como un cuerpo* y como un texido de todas ellas." Fray Luis de León, *De los nombres de Cristo*, Federico de Onís, ed. (Madrid: Espasa Calpe, 1949), 101.

24. On the impotence of the Prologue's writer, see Hugo Rodríguez

Vecchini's remarkable "La imitación perfecta y la imitación depravada," in *En un lugar de la Mancha. Ensayos cervantinos en honor de Manuel Durán*, Georgina Dopico Black and Roberto González Echevarría, eds. (Salamanca: Almar, 1999).

25. "|S|u padrastro, si puede, le hará daño." Sebastián de Covarrubias, *Tesoro de la lengua castellana o española*, Martín de Riquer, ed. (Barcelona: S.A. Horta, 1943), 844. English translation mine.

26. For a different take on this, see Jacques Lezra's extraordinary reading of the *Quijote* in his *Unspeakable Subjects. The Genealogy of the Event in Early Modern Europe* (Palo Alto, Calif.: Stanford University Press, 1997).

27. The custody arrangement is oddly reminiscent of that proposed in the early years of the seventeenth century for *morisco* children. The idea—which was put into practice at different moments both before and during the expulsion—was to separate them from their own parents who might infect them of heresy, not via blood but by mere contact. (Note the different model of racial and cultural pollution proposed here: one that paradoxically gives the lie to a *limpieza de sangre* ideology.)

28. Covarrubias, *Tesoro*, *op. cit.*, 778.

29. "Mahoma, como árabe, estaba tranquilo: sabía que podía ser árabe sin camellos." Jorge Luis Borges, "El escritor argentino y la tradición," in *Obras completas* (Barcelona: Emecé, 1989), I, 270. English translation mine.

30. Covarrubias writes: "Árbol... en las genealogías, la descripción figurada a modo de árbol, poniendo en el *tronco* el que es *principio y origen* de aquel linage." Covarrubias, *Tesoro*, *op. cit.*, 122. We might remember, in this context, our *cuento "destroncado,"* or the priest's comment in the library about the *Amadís*: "todos los demás han tomado *principio y origen* déste" (I, 6).

31. "Estirpe: comunmente llamamos la decendencia de cada uno y su origen discurriendo hasta el tronco y rayzes del linaje, aludiendo al tronco del árbol. En esta sinificación es el nombre *stirps*, |...| vale *originem, progeniem, sobolem.*" Covarrubias, *Tesoro*, *op. cit.*, 566.

32. "Estirpar. Arrancar de rayz y de quajo las malas plantas y yervas. ..." Ibid., 566.

33. "Estirpar heregías es arrancar de rayz todo lo que las puede causar o fomentar, castigando los hereges, vedando los libros sospechosos, etc. como lo hacen los ministros de la Santa Inquisición. ..." Ibid., 566, translation mine.

34. "Díxose libro de la palabra latín *liber*, que vale *corteza* de árbol." "Eran en aquella santa edad todas las cosas comunes, a nadie le era

necesario, para alcanzar su ordinario sustento tomar otro trabajo que alzar la mano y alcanzarle de las robustas encinas, que liberalmente les estaban convidando con su dulce y sazonado fruto. [...] Los valientes alcornoques despedían de sí, sin otro artificio que el de su cortesía, sus anchas y livianas cortezas con que se comenzaron a cubrir las casas" (I, 11).

FIGURE 1. Paris, 1869. Gustave Doré. Don Quijote reading chivalric romances.

FIGURE 2. London, 1858. The scrutiny of Don Quijote's library.

FIGURE 3. Paris, 1862. Albert Chereau. Don Quijote and the galley
slaves.

FIGURE 4. London, 1818. Don Quijote lowered into Montesinos's Cave.

FIGURE 5. London, 1755. F. Hyman. Don Quijote attacks Maese
Pedro's puppet show.

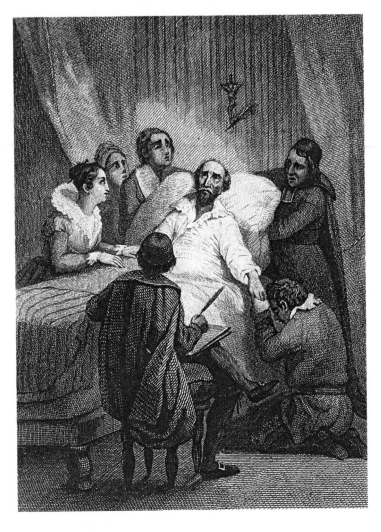

FIGURE 6. Paris, 1858. Horace Vernet, Ch. Paquin. Don Quijote on his deathbed.

Literature and Life in *Don Quixote*

E. C. RILEY

◆ ◆ ◆

The true hero is a poet, whether he knows it or
not; for what is heroism if not poetry?

Unamuno

THE INTERACTION OF LITERATURE and life is a fundamental theme of *Don Quixote*.[1] The subject is not literary
theory itself (no one would be so foolish as to suggest that *Don
Quixote* was a sort of dramatized treatise), but it is useful to approach it from the standpoint of Cervantes' novelistic theory,
with which it is firmly connected. This may throw more light
not only on the theory but on the motivation and methods of
the author in what looks at times like a waggish, bewildering,
and complicated game or a protracted private joke. We must
confine ourselves to the literary and artistic aspects of matters
susceptible of unlimited philosophical extension. The epistemological questions which the *Quixote* poses are also literary problems
of professional interest to Cervantes as a novelist.

There is a basic preoccupation with literary fiction in the expressed purpose of the book and in the most elemental conception of the hero. However far the author transcended his purpose,
his declared aim was to debunk the novels of chivalry. Whatever
else the hero may be, he is, quite simply, a man who cannot
distinguish between life and literary fiction: 'everything that our
adventurer thought, saw or imagined seemed to him to be done
and to happen in the manner of the things he had read' (I, 2).

The discussion of history (matters of fact) and poetry (fiction) in II. 3, as Toffanin first showed, springs therefore, like other such passages, from the very heart of the novel.[2]

The critique of the novels of chivalry is made in two ways: by more or less direct judgements within the fiction and also *as* the fiction. Criticism in fictional form is conventionally parody, and to some extent the *Quixote* is parody, but it is unusual in containing the object of the parody within itself, as a vital ingredient. The novels of chivalry exist in the book in just the same way as Rocinante or the barber's basin. They are so palpably present that some of them can be burnt. Cervantes' originality lies not in parodying them himself (or only incidentally), but in making the mad Knight parody them involuntarily in his efforts to bring them, by means of imitation, literally to life.

A more essential characteristic of Don Quixote's delusions than the fact that they have to do with chivalry is their bookish, fabulous nature. The golden age of chivalry that he wanted to resurrect had little to do with the real Middle Ages; it was an age that never was, the imaginary storybook age of 'Once upon a time'. History only inspired him when it merged distantly with fiction as legend. Byron's foolish remark that Cervantes 'smiled Spain's chivalry away' is a confusion of history and literature not far removed from that of the mad Knight himself. Quixote's Utopian and messianic ideals may have proved more important in the end, but it was fabulous romance, Cervantes tells us in the first chapter, that originally captivated his fancy: "His imagination became filled with everything he had read in his books, with enchantments, affrays, battles, challenges, wounds, gallantries, amours, torments and impossible extravagances" [*disparates imposibles*] (I, 1).

In 1752 Mrs. Lennox published her *Female Quixote* about a lady whose head had been turned by heroic romances, and a modern Cervantes could as easily create a twentieth-century Quixote obsessed, say, with science fiction. Don Quixote the reader of popular romances is the grandfather of Emma Bovary and Joyce's Gertie McDowell. What distinguishes him from them is an obsession with the most impossibly fabulous form of fiction that could be imagined.

His imitation of the heroes of chivalresque novels aims at such completeness that it becomes an attempt to live literature. He is not inspired to a vague sort of emulation, nor does he merely ape the habits, manners, and dress of knights errant; he does not simply adapt chivalresque ideals to some other cause, like St. Ignatius of Loyola; he is not even acting a part, in the usual sense. He is content with nothing less than that the whole of the fabulous world—knights, princesses, magicians, giants and all— should be part of his experience. Once he believes he really is a knight errant, and believes in his world of fiction, he steps off the pinnacle of inspired idealistic emulation into madness. He cannot play his part as he would like except in this fabulous world. In this sense he is trying to live literature.

His choice of literature is a debased and supremely fictitious form of epic; he its idealized and superhuman hero. He has epic aspirations to honour and glory through hardship and danger, the chivalric ideal of service and the hero's urge to shape the world to his pattern. He goes farther than that: in effect he is trying to cast off his earthly, historical existence and live in the rarefied region of poetry. (Since Cervantes' story of this endeavour is itself a poetic fiction—since what is 'life' in the story is a literary creation by Cervantes—we begin to see some of the complications of the novel.) Don Quixote is trying to turn life into art while it is yet being lived, which cannot be done because art, and idealistic art more than any, means selection, and it is impossible to select every scrap of one's experience. Life is one thing and art is another, but just what the difference is was the problem that baffled and fascinated Cervantes. If the Knight is like the wise man of Epicurus who would rather 'live poems' than write them, his efforts to do this literally are madness. Unamuno identified poetry and heroism in a wide sense, but they cannot be literally identical, if words mean anything at all.

Now the obvious and practicable way for Don Quixote to imitate the books of chivalry would have been through a recognized artistic medium—to have written romances himself, for instance. In fact, he was initially tempted to do so. He many times felt the urge to complete the unfinished novel *Don Belianís de Grecia* and would undoubtedly have done so, and very well too, 'if other and continual thoughts of greater moment had not prevented him' (I, 1). The books had too strong a hold on him. He was impelled to take up not the pen but the sword.

Don Quixote is, among a great many other things, an artist in his own peculiar way. His medium is action and, secondarily, words. Consciously living a book and acting for a sage enchanter to record, he is in a sense the author of his own biography. Even when he has abandoned the idea of conventional literary expression he retains many of the writer's characteristics. He composes verse on occasion. He imitates the archaic language of the novels of chivalry. At the start of his venture he anticipates his chronicler by putting the scene of his departure into verbal form—ornate, elevated language which makes a magnificent ironic contrast with the style used by the real author. His fantasies in part I, chapters 21 and 50 and his description of the battle of the flocks are brilliant pastiches, scarcely more absurd than the sort of writing that inspired them. He is repeatedly stimulated by literature. Cardenio's verses found in the Sierra Morena immediately induce in him thoughts of imitation; Cardenio's reference to Amadis occasions his disastrous interruption; the dramatized ballad of Gaiferos and Melisendra provokes him to violence.

His artistic instinct does not desert him in action, though it seldom has a chance to operate fruitfully. He takes much trouble over his preparations. Like a well-instructed writer he thinks long before he chooses names.[3] When conditions are particularly favourable, as on the occasion of the penance in the Sierra Morena, he is most attentive to detail and concerned with effect. This is art in action, if it is also madness. But the idea of bringing art into the business of living was not foreign to Cervantes' contemporaries. The lesson of Castiglione's much-read work was that the life of the perfect courtier should be a veritable work of art. It is perhaps not too fanciful to see the urge to render art in action, which may lie among the motive forces of heroism itself, as one of the distinguishing marks of the Spanish genius. It is realized in two of the most individual forms of Spanish art: the dance and the bullfight, where stylization combines with improvisation and author with actor. In the same way Don Quixote must improvise to meet the situations life offers him, without departing from the conventions laid down by his chivalresque models; and he creates, in part at least, the story of which he is the hero. The difference is that life is long and a dance is short and the world is not contained in a bullring. But the impulse which prompts the Knight to shape his life into an epic and that which puts beauty into the dancer's and the matador's every movement is the same.

Unfortunately he is a bad and a frustrated artist. He overestimates his capacities and underestimates the peculiarly intractable nature of his material, which is life itself. He executes a comic parody. But in so far as he is an artist, certain artistic principles may up to a point be applied to his behaviour. Let me say at once that I have not the least idea whether they were in Cervantes' conscious mind in this strange connexion. Probably not; but it is the privilege of books like the *Quixote* to contain far more than the author could ever have been aware of putting in. He was certainly much concerned with those principles on other occasions. Where literary fiction and 'real' experience are so curiously combined it need not surprise us to find unusual applications of literary theory. We shall note them later when they occur.

THE *QUIXOTE* IS A NOVEL of multiple perspectives. Cervantes observes the world he creates from the viewpoints of characters and reader as well as author. It is as though he were playing a game with mirrors, or prisms. By a kind of process of refraction he adds—or creates the illusion of adding—an extra dimension to the novel. He foreshadows the technique of modern novelists whereby the action is seen through the eyes of one or more of the personages involved, although Cervantes does not identify himself with his own characters in the usual sense.

What is fiction from one standpoint is 'historical fact' or 'life' from another. Cervantes pretends through his invented chronicler Benengeli that his fiction is history (though dubious history, as we shall see later). Into this history fictions of various kinds are inserted. The *novela* of the *Curioso impertinente* is one example. Another, of a different sort, is the story of Princess Micomicona, a nonsensical tale attached to the 'historical' episode of Dorotea which is part of Benengeli's 'history' of Don Quixote, contained in Cervantes' novelistic fiction *Don Quixote*. There is no need to make ourselves dizzy with more examples. Tales and histories, of course, are only the more overtly literary parts of an immense spectrum in the novel, that includes hallucinations, dreams, legends, deceptions, and misapprehensions. The presence of chimerical chivalresque figures in the book has the effect of making Quixote and Sancho and the physical world in which these two move seem more real by comparison. At one stroke Cervantes enlarged infinitely the scope of prose fiction by including in it with the world of external appearances the world of the imagination—which exists in books, as well as in minds.

If the reader adopts the point of view of any sane travelling companion of the Knight and Squire, he can see the problem of the unity of the *Quixote* in another light. The literary episodes or 'digressions' of Cardenio, Leandra, Claudia Jerónima, and others then appear as true adventures, as opposed to the fantastic ones imagined by the Knight or concocted for him by other people. To the characters they are true; to the reader outside they are things that could have happened; to both they are unusual events, adventures. On examination it becomes clear that Don Quixote's reactions to them and the degree to which he intervenes, if he does, are dictated by the nature of the episode and his state of mind together. A subtle but essential link is apparent between himself and these external events. There is a clear exception to this in the case of the *Curioso*, and another possible one in that of the Captive's tale; about both of these Cervantes himself expressed doubts.[4]

The episodes are complicated by the introduction of pastoral incidents, which, precisely because they are by their nature more bookish than the others, have a special attraction for Don Quixote, although he is never able to enter the pastoral world effectively. Cervantes rings the changes on pastoral in the stories of Grisóstomo and Marcela, the fair Leandra, Camacho's wedding, and the incident of the simulated Arcadia. They have a special place in the life–literature theme, because they represent different levels of an intermediate region which is not impossibly fabulous fiction in the way the novel of chivalry is, or part of the everyday world of innkeepers, barbers, and friars—which is a world that also includes runaway Moorish ladies, seducers, and dukes and duchesses, who are no less real, only less commonly encountered.

Cervantes' ironic vision enables him to put within the pages of *Don Quixote* things that are normally outside books automatically; and also to manipulate the story so that the principal characters are actually conscious of the world outside the covers of the book. He includes within its pages an author (supposedly *the* author), Benengeli. He brings his real self in incidentally as the man who presents Benengeli's fiction to the public. On occasion he mentions himself just as if he were a personage who existed cheek by jowl with his characters: as the author of the *Galatea* and friend of the Priest; as the soldier 'something Saavedra' whom the Captive knew in Algiers; and we are also indirectly reminded of him as the author of the *Curioso impertinente, Rinconete y Cortadillo,* and the *Numancia.* Not only this, he brings his public into the fiction. part II is full of characters who have read part I and know all about the earlier adventures of Quixote and Sancho. He even introduces into part II the sequel by his rival Avellaneda: the book itself and one of the characters who belonged to it. He makes Quixote and Sancho conscious of themselves as the literary heroes of a published work and therefore conscious of the world outside their story. The claims to reality of Avellaneda's spurious *Quixote* become in part II an issue of some moment to the protagonists.

Cervantes handles his work in such a way as to show his complete control over the creation he tries so hard to make seem independent. A curious instance of this occurs at the end of chapter 8 in the first part. He abruptly stops the action as one might cut off a cinematograph projector. Everything is arrested at a dramatic moment when Don Quixote and the Biscayan are engaged in mortal combat. They are left frozen, with their swords raised, while Cervantes interposes an account, several pages long, of how he discovered Benengeli's manuscript. He often uses the device of interruption as a way of procuring suspense and variety, just as Ercilla and other writers had done, but nowhere so graphically as here.[5] This destruction of the illusion is another typical piece of irony. It is also a piece of artistic exhibitionism displaying the power of the writer.

Nevertheless, Cervantes sometimes has difficulty in containing his novels and stories within the bounds prescribed by art and the capacities of his readers. The trouble is the vastness of his imaginative vision of life. The problem faces every fertile novelist, but life and literature are so intricately geared for Cervantes that sometimes they seem actually to interfere with each other. A couple of passages are revealing in this respect. The convict Ginés de Pasamonte has his picaresque autobiography fully planned, but even he cannot say how long it is going to be. When asked whether it is finished, he replies, 'How can it be, when my life is not finished yet?' (*DQ* I, 22). The other is from the *Persiles*. When Periandro says to Arnaldo, 'Do not be concerned for the time being. We arrived in Rome only yesterday and it is not possible that in so short a time procedures can have been devised, schemes drafted and inventions set up that will bring our actions to the happy conclusions we desire' (*Persiles* IV, 4), it is hard to avoid the suspicion that what he really means is 'Give the author time to work out the plot!' The length of Ginés' book is adjusted to the length of his life; Periandro leaves it to the author to bring his travails to their happy conclusion whenever the exigencies of the novel permit. These curious suggestions illustrate the way in which life and literary composition run *pari passu* in Cervantes.

There is artistic point to the whimsical tricks in *Don Quixote*. Those alluded to (with the exception of the interrupted combat, which is the same trick in reverse) all contribute to two major effects. They give the novel an appearance of receding depths, by comparison with which most other prose fiction is two-dimensional. They also give solidity and vividness to the figures of Quixote and Sancho and make them appear to exist independently of the book that was written about them. The comments of other characters sometimes help in this. Cardenio agrees that Don Quixote's madness is so extraordinary that he doubts whether anyone could have managed to invent the idea (I, 30). Sansón Carrasco finds Sancho in the flesh even more amusing than he had suspected from reading part I (II, 7).

The author stands well back from his own work, seeming not to be responsible for his own manipulations. They are conjuring tricks that enhance the general artistic illusion of reality. One might consider them 'improper' aesthetic procedures, if one could possibly call anything that furthers the end of art unaesthetic. They are certainly unconventional, but the illusion to which they contribute is an important constituent of the 'poetic truth' of the literary fiction. The word 'contribute' must be stressed: the effect owes more to art than to artifice in the end. But it is impossible to doubt Cervantes' single-minded purposefulness behind these tricks. He practically succeeds in making the reader say of Don Quixote what Don Quixote said of the hero who was so vividly real to him: 'I can almost say that I have seen Amadis of Gaul with my own two eyes' (II, I). And he was successful enough to deceive Unamuno and those who have judged the creation to be, in some freakish way, bigger than the mental capacity of the creator. Like conjuring tricks, however, they should not be re-sorted to too often. As Corneille said in the *Examen* of his *Illusion comique*: 'Tricks of this kind should not be chanced more than once.' Cervantes used similar devices in a few other writings, but he never again attempted feats of literary legerdemain on the same scale in a single work.

Two problems of importance to Cervantes' theory of the novel underlie these intricate manipulations of his invention. The first is the nature and limits of a work of art. The Knight's confusion of fiction and fact is an extreme case, but the author clearly shows that there is some justification for it. Not only the boundaries between what is imaginary and what is real, but those between art and life, are indeterminable. Life and art are continually in-terfering with each other. Inherent in this problem is that of the nature of artistic truth. What truth is to history, verisimilitude is to fiction. But can you by pretending fiction is history turn ver-isimilitude into something as potent as historical truth? The ques-tion is insistent throughout the *Quixote* and the *Persiles*.

The second problem concerns the effects of imaginative literature on people. Here again Don Quixote is an extreme case. But the matter was one of considerable importance in the Counter-Reformation, especially in Spain. In the century or more since the invention of printing the size of the reading public had enormously increased. The Church was naturally sensitive to the effects of literature on men's minds, and there was a wide awareness, not confined to the Church, of the power of literature and art to influence men's lives. The impact of the printed book in the sixteenth century has some analogy with that of television today, and produced some perhaps not wholly dissimilar reactions.

In Cervantes' novel, imaginative literature has affected the behaviour of many people beside the hero. What sort of a hold, for instance, has fiction on the minds of the Duke and Duchess and all those who concoct for their own amusement fantastic and elaborate situations involving Quixote and Sancho? Or on the Innkeeper, of whom Dorotea, with a significant confusion of ideas, says, 'Our host is not far from making a second Don Quixote [or *Don Quixote*]' (I, 32)? Or on the people who devise imitation Arcadias? Books affect people's lives; literature is a part of their experience; Cervantes' novel is, among other things, about books in life.

PRECEDENTS OF A SORT can be found for the way in which Cervantes treats *Don Quixote*.[6] Many of the more obvious forms of critical detachment in writing were formalized early in rhetoric as topics of apology, topics for use in the exordium, the conclusion, and so on.[7] Moral reflections and asides and even the conventional formula 'the history relates', common in the novels of chivalry, implied a measure of detachment. In renaissance prose and poetry comments on the progress of the narrative and announcements of new developments or scenes were common, a relic, probably, of oral poetic techniques. Ariosto and Ercilla regularly remind one of their presence in this way at the end of cantos. Ariosto especially takes up positions alongside his creation from time to time, in the poem yet not of it. This, and his ironical way of suggesting that the story is really controlling him, begin to remind one strongly of Cervantes' methods.[8]

The effect of literary fiction on literary characters makes itself felt in some degree in the *novelle* written after Boccaccio. The influence of the *Decameron* was so powerful that it often occurs to later *novellieri* to make their ladies and gentlemen consciously imitate those in Boccaccio's 'framework' by telling tales.[9] A member of the company may even have the *Decameron* with him, when they decide to entertain themselves in this manner.[10] The examples are slight, but to make an invented character aware of literary fiction as such is an advance in sophistication over the mere appropriation of another author's fictional characters for one's own use, as was quite commonly done.

But it was still a long way from making a character aware that he or she had a literary existence. Glimmerings of this Pirandellian idea, however, appear in one of the earliest of all novels, Heliodorus's *Ethiopic History*. 'It's just like a play!' exclaim the characters of the events in which they are participating, thus recognizing the resemblance to fiction, if not the identity with it.[11] Heliodorus's little trick of making his figures themselves draw attention to the exceptional nature of the story is strongly reminiscent of Cervantes. Another striking procedure for its time is that used in the remarkable renaissance novel *La Lozana andaluza*, by Francisco Delicado. The author introduces himself into the work, not as a character of any importance, nor yet as a mere vehicle for conveying the story, but as a sort of sixteenth-century Isherwood (an exceedingly candid camera), actively engaged in observing and recording everything the prostitute Lozana says and does. He does not exploit the possibilities of this, however, for Lozana's conduct is not influenced by knowing herself (as she does) to be the subject of Delicado's 'portrait'.[12]

The writer's personal relationship with his narrative was often very complex and its clear expression important to the understanding of the work. The distinction between Dante the author and Dante the pilgrim has been described as 'fundamental to the whole structure' of his poem.[13] In the sixteenth century, one may observe a good deal of confusion give way to a clarifying of the author's position *vis-à-vis* his own work. The *Arcadia* suffers from Sannazaro's failure to define his role within the work, and his position outside it as writer, with any clarity. The confusion over who's who in Garcilaso's *Eclogues* arises from the medley made by the poet of personal matters from his own experience, details from the lives and personalities of his intimates, and pure fiction. The chivalresque novelists, feeling the need for some sort of detachment, formally dissociated themselves from the fiction but only confused the issues. Bandello, much more clear-sighted, nevertheless raised other questions when he sought to use detachment as a moral alibi, disclaiming responsibility for the crimes and vices of his characters. A richer and less dubious complication of moral attitudes was contrived by Mateo Alemán, who used the autobiographical form habitual to picaresque novelists. He was remarkably successful in combining objectivity with autobiographical method in *Guzmán de Alfarache*. The picaroon's conversion made this possible: the reformed character could look back and write about himself as 'a different man'.

Though Alemán's method was not that of Cervantes (who for one thing never presented a prose story as happening to himself), the peculiar achievements of both novelists demanded a highly developed sense of the difference between poetic fiction and historical fact—a development which followed the diffusion of the Aristotelian poetic doctrines, which justified poetic fiction by the universal truth it contained. A heightened awareness of the relationship between life and literature made possible the unparalleled degree of autonomy enjoyed by Don Quixote and Sancho, and also permitted the author to achieve a simultaneous detachment from and involvement with his work, a highly complex operation but one that no longer brooked confusion. Confident in his freedom and power to control his work completely, he might then, like God, be both in and outside his handiwork. Cervantes, at the very end of his novel, draws away from his creation when he makes Cide Hamete—or rather, makes his pen—say: 'For me alone Don Quixote was born, and I for him; he knew how to act, and I how to write...', only to reaffirm their identity with the words 'we two are one'.[14]

In the critical thought of the sixteenth century, life and literature, though distinguished with a preciseness unknown since Antiquity, came closer together. This is exemplified in Scaliger's doctrines. He ultimately makes the matter of poetry and the matter of reality indistinguishable.[15] The poet imitates nature; Virgil alone did this perfectly; so the modern poet should imitate Virgil (thereby imitating nature) for the edification of his public. If the argument in this simplified form is hardly persuasive, the narrowing of the gap, of which this is but one illustration from the complex corpus of his theory, can be seen in this fusion of nature with a literary model. The levels of fiction were also explored. Piccolomini we find speculating upon imitations of imitations, which recall the stories within stories of *Don Quixote*:

> So being therefore inclined to think that a double imitation of this sort could well be done, I continued to reason how much further one could proceed with this reflection and multiplication [of what is imitated]: that is to say, whether one could not only duplicate, but triplicate and quadruplicate it, and go as far as one liked, finally, as it were one imitator imitating another imitator, and so on and so on. . . .
>
> And in truth, when imitating an imitator, one also in a certain fashion imitates what is true, since it is true that that imitated imitator imitates.[16]

By the early 1600s art had become thoroughly introverted. Some curious optical tricks resulted. Artists turned their glass on the working of art and made works of art out of what they saw. Lope de Vega wrote a well-known *Soneto de repente*, the subject of which is simply the writing of that very sonnet. The ironic vision made possible the 'play within the play' in *Hamlet*, Corneille's *Illusion comique*, and the incident of the puppet-show in *Don Quixote*, to mention no more. It also produced the possibilities so brilliantly exploited by Calderón in *El gran teatro del mundo* and *No hay más fortuna que Dios*.

Some of the juggling with fiction which is an integral part of *Don Quixote* continued to be popular with authors and readers.

Such is the case of all that apparatus of fictitious documents and supposedly second-hand stories dear to European novelists from the seventeenth century on; it owes much to Cervantes although he did not invent it. And some of the more tricksy devices had to wait from the seventeenth century until the nineteenth before becoming again a significant part of works by major writers. In fact, of course, the autonomous characters of Pérez Galdós, Unamuno, and above all Pirandello are anticipated by Quixote and Sancho by some three centuries. So are some of the notions of such disparate writers as André Gide and Lewis Carroll. Long before Edouard in *Les Faux-Monnayeurs*, Cervantes wrote a book about 'the struggle between facts as proposed by reality, and the ideal reality'.[17] In *Through the Looking-Glass* Alice's distressed and angry reaction to Tweedledum's provoking suggestion that she is only one of the things in the Red King's dream recalls that of Quixote and Sancho when their reality is challenged by Avellaneda's rival heroes.

But the closest analogy with the 'looking-glass game' Cervantes plays in *Don Quixote* is not in a book at all but a painting. It is roughly contemporary, a masterpiece of comparable magnitude, and the effect is similar. I mean Velasquez's *Las Meninas*.[18] It is full of tricks. There in the picture is the painter at work on his own painting, the largest figure in the scene, but dark and unobtrusive. There too is the back of the very canvas we are looking at. Arrested, half in half out of the room, and, as it were, of the picture, is the figure in the doorway. The King and Queen are seen reflected in a mirror on the far wall, which is hung with dim paintings. And the viewer realizes with a shock that he is looking at the picture from the spot, close to the watchful monarch and his wife, from which the picture was painted in effect. One all but glances over one's shoulder. Did a mirror stand there (there is some doubt), or did Velasquez, projecting himself mentally right outside his subject, paint from that spot as though he had been someone else altogether, painting—himself—at work? In either case, he has contrived to be simultaneously outside and inside his subject, and what is more, to draw the outside spectator into it too. 'But where is the frame?' exclaimed Gautier when he saw the picture. Picasso's comment was, 'There you have the true painter of reality.' 'His aim', Sir Kenneth Clark has written, 'was simply to tell the whole truth about a complete visual impression . . . maintaining, unobserved, a measureless impartiality.'[19]

They might all, no less aptly, have been speaking of Cervantes and *Don Quixote*.

Notes

1. José Ortega y Gasset first saw its importance in 'Meditación primera', *Meditaciones del Quijote* (Madrid: Revista de Occidente, 1957), 124ff. See also Américo Castro, 'Cervantes y Pirandello', *La Nación* (Buenos Aires), 16 November 1924, and *El pensamiento de Cervantes* (Madrid: Revista de Filología Hispánica, 1925), 30ff; and many observations in his later essays in *Hacia Cervantes* (Madrid: Taurus, 1957); Joaquín Casalduero, *Sentido y forma del 'Quijote'* (Madrid: Insula, 1949), *passim*; Leo Spitzer, 'Perspectivismo lingüístico en el *Quijote*', in *Lingüística e historia literaria* (Madrid: Gredos, 1955), 161–225; M. I. Gerhardt's substantial study, *'Don Quijote': La vie et les livres* (Amsterdam: Noord-Hollandsche Uitgevers Maaarschappij, 1955); R. L. Predmore, *El mundo del 'Quijote'* (Madrid: Insula, 1958); and Harry Levin's perceptive essay, 'The Example of Cervantes', in *Contexts of Criticism* (Cambridge: Harvard University Press, 1957).

2. Giuseppe Toffanin, *La fine dell'umanesimo* (Turin: Fratelli Bocca, 1920).

3. M. T. Herrick, 'Comic Theory in the Sixteenth Century', *University of Illinois Studies in Language and Literature* 34 (1950): 63, observes that Donatus, Servius, Robortelli, and Castelvetro all attached importance to the choice of appropriate names in the writing of comedy.

4. See E. C. Riley, 'Episodio, novela y aventura en *Don Quijote*', *Anales Cervantinos* (1955–56): 209–30.

5. It will be remembered that this particular scene is also reproduced as a picture, 'muy al natural', on the first page of Cide Hamete's manuscript (*DQ* I, 9; i. 285).

6. For observations on developments before and after Cervantes, see J. E. Gillet, 'The Autonomous Character in Spanish and European Literature', *Hispanic Review* 24 (1956): 179–90. For later developments, see A. Lebois, 'La Révolte des personnages, de Cervantes et Calderón à Raymond Schwab', *RLC* 23 (1949).

7. E. R. Curtius, *European Literature and the Latin Middle Ages* (New York: Harper, 1953), 408ff.; also 79–105.

8. Ariosto, *Orlando furioso* (ed. Naples–Milan: R. Ricciardi, 1954), e.g., xxxii. ii; xxxv. ii.

9. E.g. in Firenzuola's *Ragionamenti*. See L. Di Francia, *Novellistica* (Milan: F. Vallardi, 1924–5), i. 601–2.

10. Thus in Il Lasca's *Cene* (in Di Francia), *op. cit.*, i. 622.

11. *Historia etiópica de los amores de Teágenes y Cariclea*, Fernando de Mena's translation of 1587 (ed. Madrid: Aldus, 1954): cf. 183–4; also 91, 388, 424. Cervantes may have read this translation or the anonymous one of Antwerp, 1554, based on Amyot's French version.

12. A. Vilanova, whose edition of the book I have used (Barcelona, 1952), suggests that Delicado's work inspired Cervantes in this respect—'Cervantes y *La Lozana andaluza*', *Insula*, no. 77 (May 1952): 5–17. It is an extremely doubtful supposition.

13. Francis Fergusson, quoted by R. H. Green, 'Dante's "Allegory of Poets" and the mediaeval theory of Poetic Fiction', *Comparative Literature* 9 (1957): 124.

14. 'Para mí sola nació don Quijote, y yo para él: él supo obrar, y yo escribir; solos los dos somos para en uno' (*DQ* II, 74; viii. 267).

15. See B. Weinberg, 'Scaliger versus Aristotle on Poetics', *Modern Philology* 39 (1942): 348–9.

16. 'Inclinando io adunque allora a credere che così fatta doppia imitazione si potesse con ragion fare; andai discorrendo quanto oltra con questa reflessione e moltiplicazione si potesse procedere: cioè se non solo doppia si potesse fare, ma tripla, e quadrupla, e quanto si voglia finalmente com' a dire uno che imiti uno altro imitante, e così di mano in mano ...' 'Ed in vero in imitar un imitante, s'imita ancora in un certo modo il vero; essendo vero che quel tal' imitato imitante imita'. *Op cit.*, 37, 39.

17. Quoted through E. M. Forster's *Aspects of the Novel* (London: Harcourt Brace, 1927). Like so many contemporary writers on the subject, he quite forgets the first modern novel and describes the attempt to combine the two truths as 'new' (135).

18. I believe the analogy extends further and is much more fundamental than is suggested either by Ortega, *op. cit.*, 169, or H. Hatzfeld, 'Artistic Parallels in Cervantes and Velázquez', *Estudios dedicados a Menéndez Pidal* (Madrid: Patronato Marcelino Menéndez y Pelayo, 1950–7), iii. 289, who touch on the point I am making.

19. Sir Kenneth Clark, *The Sunday Times* (2 June 1957).

Don Quixote

Story or History?

BRUCE W. WARDROPPER

◆　◆　◆

ALTHOUGH TODAY WE CALL *Don Quixote* a novel, Cervantes did not. The modern Spanish word "*novela*" did not yet exist in the sense of an extended work of prose fiction; it could be applied only to the short story of Italian origin. The other family of words used to designate longer prose fiction derived from Latin "*romanice*"; in France "*roman*" covered fictional romance, but in Spain the equivalent word "*romance*" had been preempted for other purposes.[1] There was thus no appellation for the early Spanish romance or novel. The chivalric and pastoral romances were called "*libros*"; the sentimental romances, "*tratados*," or treatises; Francisco Delicado's *La lozana andaluza*, a "*retrato*," or portrait; the picaresque works, "*vidas*." On his title pages Cervantes carefully refrains from saying what his work is: "*El ingenioso hidalgo don Quijote de la Mancha*" and "*Segunda parte del ingenioso caballero don Quijote de la Mancha*." The friend who advises him, in the prologue to part I, about the preliminaries to his work calls it simply a "book." If, as the friend assumes, *Don Quixote* is essentially a parody of the *libros de caballerías*, one would think that the term designat-

141

ing the original would be the best to apply to the parody. But Cervantes seldom uses it in the body of his text. He prefers to call his book an "*historia*," by which, as we shall see, he means, not a story, but a history. We know, of course, that he is fooling us: *Don Quixote* may be a romance, or a novel, or a story, but it is certainly not a history. We have to deal, then, with a story masquerading as history, with a work claiming to be historically true within its external framework of fiction. The study of *Don Quixote*, it seems to me, must begin with this paradox.

The problem of the spurious historicity of the work is usually stated in terms of the Aristotelian principles of the universality of poetry and the particularity of history. "The difference between the historian and the poet," says Aristotle, "is not the difference between writing in verse or prose; the work of Herodotus could be put into verse, and it would be just as much a history in verse as it is in prose. The difference is that the one tells what has happened, and the other the kind of things that would happen. It follows therefore that poetry is more philosophical and of higher value than history; for poetry unifies more, whereas history agglomerates."[2] This approach to *Don Quixote*—adopted wholeheartedly in Américo Castro's *El pensamiento de Cervantes* (Madrid, 1925) and more cautiously in E. C. Riley's *Cervantes's Theory of the Novel* (Oxford, 1962)—would seem at first sight to be sound. El Pinciano, whom Cervantes had certainly read, expounded this doctrine in his *Filosofía antigua poética* (1596),[3] and Cervantes himself has his characters in *Don Quixote* discuss literature from this Aristotelian point of view.[4] In terms of sixteenth-century aesthetics it might be said that history is natural, since it narrates events as they occurred, each one emerging by the logic of nature from those which preceded it,[5] while a story is artistic—"*artificiosa*"— since in it events are made to happen in a peculiarly satisfactory way.[6] In *Don Quixote* Cervantes both manipulates the adventures to achieve an artistic end and allows each adventure to spring naturally from what has gone before. One is left with the conclusion that the work is at the same time poetry and history, that it is, to use Castro's critical imagery, a watershed from which the two slopes, the "*vertiente poética*" and the "*vertiente histó-*

rica," may be contemplated.[7] The difficulty with the Aristotelian approach is that it does not explain so much the work as some of the theory behind the work.

My own approach derives not from such theoretical considerations but from the history of literature and the history of history. This historical method, old-fashioned as it is, may be made to shed light on the form and the thematic sense of Cervantes' masterpiece.

Cervantes, then, seldom refers to his book as anything but an "historia." Does he perhaps mean by this term what we call a story? The word could, even in the early years of the seventeenth century, be used to designate fiction. Don Quixote himself uses it in this sense on one occasion: "tú has contado una de las más nuevas consejas, cuento o historia que nadie pudo pensar en el mundo" (I, xx). Against this quotation, however, one could set hundreds in which the word means what historians mean by history. This is clearly the sense in which Cervantes normally uses the word. Cervantes (or his alter ego, the fictitious historian Cide Hamete Benengeli) describes this history with a variety of adjectives: "sencilla," "grande," "curiosa," "peregrina," "apacible," "sabrosa," "moderna," "nueva," "imaginada." But the one used over and over again is "verdadera." *Don Quixote* is a true history. We tend to discount these assertions as playful irony, or we disregard them altogether as a convention of the time, like the *comedias verdaderas* that were no such thing.[8] But are we justified in ignoring even an ironic clue to the nature of the book? Some historical perspective will help us answer the question.

English, alone among the Indo-European languages, draws a clear (though not absolute) distinction between history, the narration of true events, and story, the narration of imagined events.[9] Both words have the same Greco-Latin etymon. Other tongues use a single word—*histoire, historia, storia, Geschichte*—to denote both kinds of narrations of events. A bifurcation must have occurred in the semantic development of antique *historia*, permitting the word to embrace both the actual and the fictional. The linguistic bifurcation corresponded to a development, or rather to repeated developments, in literary history. In the second and third centuries A.D., for example, the *Erotici Graeci* wrote several imaginary histories: the most famous, Heliodorus' *Historia Aethiopica*, was, despite its apparently scholarly title, one of the most far-fetched pieces of fiction the world has known. It is important to realize that the Alexandrian romance, the only considerable body of prose fiction in antiquity, emerged not from epic poetry but from historiography. Although this stepchild of history found favor, it was barely conscious of its debt to historical writing, and its false claims to be truthful irked intellectuals and scholars alike. Because the fictional history of the ancients abstained from irony, it never attained the dignity of the novel. Lucian found it necessary to parody this absurd type of romance in his ironically entitled *Vera historia*, just as in modern times Cervantes would parody ironically another kind of romance.[10] Lucian's *Vera historia* was, in some respects, the *Don Quixote* of its culture.

The same bifurcation of *historia* took place in the Romance territory of medieval and Renaissance Europe. At first the classical distinction between prose and poetry was scrupulously observed: poetry—whether epic, lyric, or dramatic—was for fiction; prose was used to expound unimaginative thought—on astrology, theology, or gemmology—but, above all, it was used for historical narrative. The rise of the novel is explained in traditional scholarship as a prosification of the epic, with important generic mutations resulting from the shift from male hearer to female reader, from market place to boudoir, from public performance to intimate reading.[11] Strictly speaking, however, this explanation covers only the idealized fiction of the romance: stories of chivalry, of Troy, of Alexander the Great, and, much later, of shepherds—in short, stories of Never-Never-Land.[12] In the meantime, the folk were telling their tales, orally and in prose. And similar, though more didactic, tales were imported from the Orient and written down in Latin or in the vernacular for the benefit of sermon-writers and others in search of edifying moral illustrations. Medieval prose fiction—if we exclude the work of an innovator like Boccaccio—consisted of romances, folktales, and *exempla*. It is confusing to relate any of these kinds of writing to the modern novel. The novel has its roots in historiography.[13]

The earliest chroniclers could not entirely suppress their imagination. Historical *lacunae* were filled with original inventions or with prosified epics, which are by definition products of the imagination.[14] It is the tragedy of historiography that the historian can never operate on a purely factual or intellectual plane: he imagines motives; he imagines conversations; he imagines what his sources neglect to tell him. To a greater or lesser degree all history merely pretends to be history.[15] And now, in the later Renaissance, we have a new factor: some works of fiction, such as the *Lazarillo de Tormes* and *Don Quixote*, also pretend to be history.

Prose writing contained thus a moral dilemma. Did an author have a right to tamper with what he believed to be true by injecting into it the fancies of his imagination? Did he, on the other hand, have a right to present the flights of his imagination as the truth? The imagination, the dimension of poetry, was the lying faculty of the mind. By the sixteenth century fiction, whether in poetry or prose, was unequivocally called lying; to the ascetic critics of the Counter-Reformation, Garcilaso and Montemayor were morally reprehensible liars who planted the seeds of error in fertile young minds.[16] The poetic mode, since it was expressly designed for this pleasant lying, at least deceived no one. Prose, however, the vehicle for legal documents, for sermons, for history, was considered to have been abused by those who made it carry the falsehood of fiction. The dangers contained in fictional prose were greater. How was the reader of prose to know when the historian, or the storyteller, was telling a truth or a lie? A reader is more easily misled when the safeguards of convention have been removed. It follows that the moral responsibility of the prose-writer is greater than that of the poet. But there is an aesthetic consequence of this analysis that is of far greater significance to us today. The problems entailed in writing prose fiction are themselves admirable subjects for prose fiction. The prosaic mode supplies a ready-made allegory for the moral dilemma of man, who must live in a world where the boundaries between truth and falsehood are imprecise.

It was the great merit of the Spanish baroque that its writers of fiction, in both prose and verse, having understood the analogy between their professional dilemma and their readers' dilemma, exploited it to the full. This continuing discussion revolved around the words *engaño* and *desengaño, verdad* and *mentira*. In the *letrillas* of Góngora, the plays of Calderón, and the *sueños* of Quevedo clear-cut answers are given to man's baffling predicament; he is handed a thread with which to make his way through the *confusión*, the *laberinto* of this world. It is as though these writers imposed their orderly artistic solution on an existential quandary. By its nature, however, history abstains from organizing and rationalizing the chaos and unreason of the world of men; it reflects faithfully the reigning confusion. Cervantes—a "historian" and a novelist—was inevitably less dogmatic than were contemporary artists, less sure of the line separating truth and error. *Don Quixote* does not disentangle the story from the history, but points its telescope at the ill-defined frontier itself. It presents the evidence for the uncertainty of truth and says to the reader: "You be the judge." "Tú, lector, pues eres prudente, juzga lo que te pareciere," says Cide Hamete Benengeli in a marginal note, after casting doubt on the authenticity of the Cave of Montesinos episode (II, xxiv). This awareness of the ill-defined frontier between history and story, between truth and lie, between reality and fiction is what constitutes Cervantes' *Don Quixote*, is what constitutes the novel as distinct from the romance. The novel is the most self-conscious, the most introverted of literary genres.[17] Unlike the Alexandrian romance, it is sensitive to its origins in historiography and aware of the need to handle its claim to historical accuracy with massive doses of irony.

Cervantes' expression of the novelistic self-consciousness is complex. Because his subject matter is fictional, he must have recourse to a variety of devices to persuade, and if possible to convince, his reader that Don Quixote actually lived and actually did those things he is reported to have done. We have already noticed the reiterated claims that the history is true. But there is more to it than this. The realism of the inns and roads of La Mancha,[18] the perfect credibility of characters like Maritornes or Don Diego de Miranda, the guaranteed historicity of the bandit Roque Guinart—such details as these captivate the reader's will to disbelieve. The references to the Annals of La Mancha and to its Archives, to the manuscript found in Toledo, to the lead box full of verses discovered during the razing of a hermitage, the intrusions of the historian Cide Hamete and of his translator amount to the creation of a vast historical apparatus which gives to each and every chapter the illusion of being historically verifiable. The questions raised by the translator about the possibly apocryphal nature of Sancho's conversation with his wife or of Don Quixote's descent into the cave only serve to impart a sense of historical accuracy to all the rest of the narrative. Finally, thanks to the providential intervention of Avellaneda, the historical truth of Cervantes' Don Quixote is vindicated against the false claims of the fictional Don Quixote who appears in Avellaneda's spurious second part.[19] The "real," the "historical" Don Quixote is made, as it were, to stand up and identify himself.[20] The reader of *Don Quixote* does not really want to believe that the story is history; the author must therefore wear down his critical resistance.

What has Cervantes accomplished in making his story pass for history? The easy, or neo-Aristotelian, answer is that he has achieved verisimilitude.[21] But he has done much more than this: he has obliterated the dividing line between the actual and the potential, the real and the imaginary, the historical and the fictional, the true and the false. To the extent that he has been successful, he has eliminated the critical scrutiny of evidence. He has written a novel, the first novel, a novel about the problem involved in writing a novel.

In just such a destruction of the critical faculty, in just such a failure to discriminate between history and story, lies the cause of Don Quixote's madness. It is not so much the reading of too many books of chivalry that drives him mad; it is the misreading, the misinterpretation of them that causes his insanity.[22] Juan de Valdés, Saint Theresa, Saint Ignatius of Loyola remained perfectly sane after devouring all the chivalrous romances they could lay their hands on.[23] Don Quixote went mad because he could not differentiate between events that actually had happened to living people and events that had happened in the imagination of some author to people who were equally figments of his imagination. Don Quixote thought that, although the Cid Ruy Díaz was a very good knight, he could not hold a candle to Amadís, the Knight of the Burning Sword.[24] He confused the factual dimension with the imaginary dimension, history with story.

Cervantes, in seeking to undermine the reader's critical faculty, is carrying mimesis to its logical end; he is trying to make his reader participate in his hero's madness. Quite apart from the moral impropriety of trying to make a fellow human being lose his wits, one might wonder whether this objective was feasible. It surely was, to a degree. Anyone who has conducted a seminar on *Don Quixote* knows that intelligent students turn a little mad when they discuss this book. This mild form of insanity, one is tempted to think, is a part of the human condition. Certainly nearly all the characters in *Don Quixote*—excepting only the Caballero del Verde Gabán, the Duke's chaplain, and a very few others—are tainted with this form of *dementia*, which consists in the inability to distinguish the fictional from the real.[25] And we have all asked ourselves at one time or another: "Did such-and-such a thing really happen or did I only imagine it?" This kind of madness is particularly prevalent among the literate.[26] Historical truth is by no means as certain as we would like it to be. Did our modern knight-errant, Lawrence of Arabia, perform the heroic deeds with which history credits him, or are his detractors right in seeing him as an impostor? Is Jean-Jacques Rousseau or literary history more to be believed in the question of whether he put his children into a foundling home? The literate man reads both history and story. Historians make their histories read like novels, and novelists make their novels read like histories. Writers—scholars and artists alike—conspire to loosen man's grip on reality, to conduct him to the fringe of madness. The intellectual, the reader of books, is bound to ask himself repeatedly: "What is reality?" or even "What is truth?" Jesting Pilate may have been more in earnest than we realize.

The illiterate man has the same problem but feels it less intensely. He too has moments when he does not know if "he dreamed it all" or if "it really happened." But, since for him the experience is not corroborated by the testimony of a thousand books, he takes this human weakness more for granted. Accordingly, he is more certain of his grasp on reality. The illiterate Sancho Panza, in part I, does not doubt that Don Quixote's armies are sheep and his giants, windmills. But with something remote from his experience, the fulling-mills pounding away in the dark, he is face to face with the noumenal; he feels the awesome fear of the unknown which the intellectual derives from his books. In part II, after having consorted intimately with the literate Don Quixote, some of the intellectual's anxieties about truth have rubbed off on him. Though, by misrepresenting an ugly peasant girl as the mistress of his master's thoughts, he has personally enchanted Dulcinea, he will be convinced by the Duchess' words and his self-flagellation that the randomly chosen wench is indeed Dulcinea. He knows the truth and yet doubts that he does.[27] Within Cervantes' fictional world he cannot distinguish between history and story, between the reality of a country girl seen with his own eyes and the lie he has told about her. The text assures us that in part II Sancho becomes as mad as his master. His madness, it should be observed, has the same cause and is of the same kind.

Cervantes' preoccupation with the problems of historical truth and its cognition was induced, I believe, by the crisis being undergone by the historian's art. If medieval chroniclers had innocently—perhaps unwittingly—blended fiction into their narrations of events, since the fifteenth century historians had been busily engaged in the deliberate falsification of history. Pedro de Corral, in the *Crónica sarracina*, which he wrote about 1430, was so inventive that his contemporary Fernán Pérez de Guzmán said that rather than a chronicle "más propiamente se puede llamar trufa o mentira paladina."[28] Modern critics, more charitably but less accurately, call the work the first Spanish historical novel.[29] The important fact is that it pretended to be history and was accepted as such by later historians. The work was printed in 1499 and ran through a large number of editions down to Cervantes' day. Pedro de Corral started a vogue for what has been called "la historia novelesca y fantaseada."[30]

This vogue drove scholars crazy. Humanistic historians like Jerónimo de Zurita (1512–80) and Ambrosio de Morales (1513–91) made a valiant attempt to sift the truth from the lie. By studying their sources carefully, doing research in archives, adducing new kinds of evidence like medals, inscriptions, and monuments, they restored to history some of its lost dignity. They paved the way for the greatest and most reliable of Golden Age historians, Father Juan de Mariana. But these conscientious efforts to ascertain the truth of history scarcely stemmed the tide of false historiography: they may even have planted new ideas in the minds of the counterfeiters.

The discovery in the Sacro Monte of Granada, between 1588 and 1595, of the so-called *Libros plúmbeos*, or Leaden Books, revealed the most monstrous attempt to rewrite history before the compilation of the *Soviet Encyclopaedia*. In Ticknor's words, these metallic plates

> when deciphered, seemed to offer materials for defending the favorite doctrine of the Spanish Church on the Immaculate Conception, and for establishing the great corner-stone of Spanish ecclesiastical history, the coming to Spain of the Apostle James, the patron saint of the country. This gross forgery was received for authentic history by Phillip II, Phillip III, and Phillip IV, each of whom, in a council of state . . . , solemnly adjudged it to be such; so that, at one period of the discussions, some persons believed the "Leaden Books" would be admitted into the Canon of the Scriptures.[31]

Another great imposture was what cultural history knows as the *falsos cronicones*, a series of fragments of chronicles circulated from 1594 in manuscript and printed in 1610.[32] They purported to have been written by Flavius Lucius Dexter, Marcus Maximus, Heleca, and other primitive Christians and contained important and wholly new statements concerning the early civil and ecclesiastical history of Spain. Flattering fictions were fitted to recognized facts, as if both rested on the same authority; new saints were given to churches inadequately provided for in this department of hagiology; a dignified origin was traced for noble families that had before been unable to boast of their founders; and a multitude of Christian conquests and achievements were hinted at or recorded, which gratified the pride of the whole nation the more because they had never till then been heard of.[33]

Belief in these forgeries was very persistent. As late as the eighteenth century some overcredulous writers were still citing the *Libros plúmbeos* and the *falsos cronicones* as authorities for alleged historical facts. The Roman church—around the middle of the seventeenth century—had indeed declared that the Leaden Books were counterfeits, and an obedient Spain had for the most part reluctantly given up accepting the story they told as history. The false chronicles were harder to dispose of. A lively controversy over their authenticity raged for the better part of a century. Their author, the Jesuit Father Higuera of Toledo, himself had the audacity to express his doubts concerning their veracity. As early as 1595 Juan Bautista Pérez, the Bishop of Segorbe, exposed the whole fraud. In spite of this, as late as 1667–75 Gregorio de Argáiz, "a man of much worthless learning,"[34] published six large folio volumes in defence of the *falsos cronicones*. The *coup de grâce* had really been given them, nevertheless, in 1652, when the great bibliographer Nicolás Antonio began his *Historias fabulosas*, a book which, although never finished, left no doubt as to the extent and nature of Father Higuera's fraud.

If scholars were baffled by the reams of imaginary history pouring from Spanish presses, what was the layman to think? If he was naïve, like the innkeeper in *Don Quixote*, he believed in the historical accuracy of the forgeries on the grounds that they had been printed by royal license. If he was skeptical, like Cervantes, he reserved judgment and pondered on the difficulty of sorting out historical fact from fictional fraud. And if, again like Cervantes, he had a free, inquiring mind—what Cervantes called "*curiosidad*"—he reflected on the human dilemma posed by the uncertain frontier separating story and history.

I like to think that some of the inspiration for *Don Quixote* may have come from yet another example of spurious history: Miguel de Luna's *Historia verdadera del rey don Rodrigo, compuesta por Albucácim*

Tárif.[35] Part I of this "true history" appeared in Granada in 1592 and part II in 1600, "tres años antes y cinco después del falso hallazgo de los libros plúmbeos que problaron de mártires fantásticos el Sacro Monte de aquella ciudad," comments Menéndez Pidal significantly.[36] Miguel de Luna, the official Arabic interpreter to Phillip II, had the gall to dedicate to his sovereign this egregious example of intellectual dishonesty. He claimed to be merely the translator of a work written in the eighth century by Albucácim Tárif, a Moor alleged to have had access to King Roderick's archives and to letters written by Florinda and Don Pelayo. To give his work an air of authenticity Luna entered into the margins the alleged Arabic original of words he had supposedly found difficult to translate.[37] Given the fraudulent nature of his undertaking, he comes perilously close to blasphemy when in his preface he has Albucácim invoke God's help: "solo Dios criador, y sumo hazedor de todas las cosas criadas en este mundo . . . , a quien humilmente suplico me dè aliento para que *sin genero de inuencion* pueda contar *con verdad clara, y abierta* la historia del sucesso de la guerra de España."[38] God is called upon to bear witness to the truth of this fake history. The new light Luna (or Albucácim) shed on the Arabic conquest of Spain served to illuminate countless histories written later by well-meaning but unwary historians.[39] I cannot, of course, prove that Cervantes saw in Albucácim the progenitor of Cide Hamete Benengeli, but the point is that, at the time he was composing *Don Quixote*, such liberties were being taken with history. Cervantes does with pleasant irony what Luna does with the deadly seriousness of a forger.[40] A whole generation had lost its respect for historical truth.

Along with this fictionalizing and falsifying of history went a fundamental change in the role of the historian. In genuine histories the author retreats modestly behind his narrative, appearing, if at all, only in the prologue, where he customarily reviews his qualifications to write the book. Fiction, even the prenovelesque romance, is more self-conscious than history; the author cannot conceal himself. In a romance of chivalry, like the *Amadis de Gaula*, the old jongleuresque parenthetical address to the listeners still shines through the chinks in the narration: "como oÿdes," "el enano que ÿstes," "que sería largo de contar." In the sentimental romance, *La cárcel de Amor*, El Autor plays an important part in the story.[41] In *La lozana andaluza* the author appears in a series of self-portraits as the painter, the transcriber of observed reality.[42] With the *Lazarillo de Tormes*, a feigned autobiography, the fictional author has become the actual subject of the history, even though the real author conceals himself behind a veil of anonymity. In the pastoral romance the author hides behind his narrative, but the narrative and the characters that people it reflect his own personal experiences and problems. Cervantes, who in *Don Quixote* is writing the first novel, must complicate enormously the role played by the author. He intervenes in the events to tell the reader what to believe, to steer him away from total madness with the phrase "y así era la verdad."[43] He invents a pseudo-historian whose credibility is alternately impugned and defended. And this pseudo-historian plays a part in the novel second only to those of the protagonists, Don Quixote and Sancho. This novel, then, is a fake history in which the historian assumes even greater importance than the author in a romance. The novel, emerging from false history, turns out to be far more self-conscious than the old-fashioned romance.

The most puzzling question is why Cervantes, in unknowingly inventing the novel, hit upon this dubious subject matter of the *falso cronicón*. One answer is that he was a satirist. If the overt target of his satire is the romances of chivalry, it can hardly be the principal one. His chief butt was man's gullibility—gullibility about alleged historical facts. But, as we have seen, he chose to satirize human credulity in a dangerous way: by encouraging, by seeking to some extent to cultivate, in his reader the very defect he was ridiculing. Why did he tread such dangerous ground? He did so, I believe, because he was—in older aesthetic terms—imitating the human dilemma. Today we would say that he was re-creating the human dilemma, casting it into artistic form. Man, notwithstanding the catechism, does not in his heart believe truth to be categorical; he resists the dualistic tendencies of ecclesiastical orthodoxy. He does not choose between good and evil, as the moralists say, but between greater and lesser goods and between greater and lesser evils. Similarly, he does not choose between truth and falsehood, but between higher and lower truths and between white and black lies. This is how Cervantes viewed man's situation. Everything in the human condition is for him a matter of nuance. We have seen how, in this respect, he differs fundamentally from the dogmatic writers of the baroque: Calderón, Quevedo,[44] Gracián. *Don Quixote* is, among other things, a tremendous protest against the moralistic assurance of Counter-Reformation Spain. It is in these terms that I would rephrase Américo Castro's brilliant insight associated with the term Cervantine hypocrisy.[45] Despite the furor[46] aroused by this unfortunately formulated catch phrase, there was some truth in it. "Ironic protest against dogmatic oversimplification" might be a better way to put it. Irony is the form Cervantes' protest against Tridentine dogmatism had to take; it was wholly appropriate to his serious sense of the complexity of the moral world which was being masked. Play with historical truth, like all play, has a serious basis.

Cervantes took such a risk—the risk of disseminating a madness he deplored—because in this common madness was the evidence for a truth about man's world, which the Counter-Reformation was suppressing. The truth, far from being simple, is complex and ultimately unascertainable in all its complexity. One cannot apprehend the whole truth; one can only get glimpses of partial truth. This is the great lesson of historiography, if not of history itself. Hence Cervantes' book is, as we say, "open." The *loco* is also *cuerdo*. Who can say when Don Quixote's lucid intervals begin and end?[47] Should we sympathize with a village priest whose good intentions, love of his friend, and desire for his cure are negated by his fondness for playacting? Should we condemn a Puritanical chaplain whose dour mien and inhuman severity make him one of the most unpleasant characters in the book, when he alone, of all the members of the Duke's household, protests against the baiting of a madman for the entertainment of the idle rich? These characters—all of Cervantes' characters—are compounds of antithetical qualities. This is the human reality he was seeking to convey. And the work itself—

a fusion of chivalric, sentimental, pastoral, picaresque fiction, of short stories and poems—reflects this many-sided makeup of man. Hybridization is the artistic means chosen to present Cervantes' sense of the complexity of truth.

Don Quixote, a compendium of all previous literary genres, implies the further elimination of ill-defined frontiers, just as it blurs the boundary between history and story. This is the primary intuition on which Cervantes constructs his novel. To understand this intuition is to see the answer to the most baffling question one can ask about the work: why is it that across the ages no two people have been able to agree on the meaning of *Don Quixote?*

Notes

1. The word meant "vernacular" or "ballad."

2. Aristotle, *On the Art of Fiction*, trans. I. J. Potts (Cambridge: Cambridge University Press, 1953), 29.

3. Alonso López Pinciano, *Philosophia antigua poetica*, ed. Alfredo Carballo Picazo (3 vols., Madrid: Consejo Superior de Investigaciones Científicas Instituto "Miguel de Cervantes," 1953), I, 203–4, 206, 265–68; III, 165–67.

4. Especially in chaps. 47 and 48 of part I. But for some reservations about the genuineness of Cervantes' Aristotelianism in these chapters see my "Cervantes' Theory of the Drama," *Modern Philology* 52 (1955): 217–21.

5. Raymond S. Willis, Jr., in his admirable structural study *The Phantom Chapters of the "Quijote"* (New York: Hispanic Institute of the United States, 1953), 98–100, argues that the phrase "dice la historia," which serves to restore fluidity to apparent dislocations of the narrative, relates to a Platonic idea of Don Quixote's history, which is mythical, perfect, and whole.

6. See my "The Pertinence of *El curioso impertinente*," *Publications of the Modern Language Association of America* 62 (1957): 587–600.

7. *El pensamiento de Cervantes*, 30. Aubrey G. F. Bell, in his *Cervantes* (Norman: University of Oklahoma Press, 1947), 88, writes: "*Don Quixote* is both true and imaginary; it is a *historia verdadera* and it is a *historia imaginada* (I, 22). Cervantes bends his whole genius to reconcile the two worlds."

8. Some authors, of course, saw nothing transcendental, nothing more than an amusing convention, in fiction's claim to historical truth.

The fictional hero of the *Estebanillo González* advises his reader that his autobiography "no es la *fingida* de Guzmán de Alfarache, ni la *fabulosa* del Lazarillo de Tormes, ni la *supuesta* del Caballero de la Tenaza, sino una relación *verdadera* (*Biblioteca de Autores Españoles* 33: 286; italics mine).

9. The distinction is clear enough for all practical purposes, but it should not be forgotten that we tend to blur it at times. A child's book may be called *The Story of Ancient Rome* (for *The History*); H. G. Wells could write a (fictional) *History of Mr. Polly*.

10. It is interesting to note that for El Pinciano the romances of chivalry are modern Milesian tales: "las ficciones que no tienen imitación y verisimilitud no son fábulas, sino disparates, como algunas de las que antiguamente llamaron Milesias, agora libros de cauallerías, los quales tienen acaescimientos fuera de toda buena imitación y semejança a verdad" (edition cited, II, 8).

11. See, e.g., Karl Vossler, "La novela en los pueblos románicos," in his *Formas literarias en los pueblos románicos* (Buenos Aires: Espasa-Calpe, 1944), 91–106.

12. I observe in this essay the distinction between romance and novel habitually drawn in the eighteenth century and redefined for ours by Northrop Frye, *Anatomy of Criticism* (Princeton: Princeton University Press, 1957), 304–7.

13. Frye sees the connection between the novel and history, but he thinks of the novel as a romance *moving toward* historiographical form: "The novel tends rather to expand into a fictional approach to history. The soundness of Fielding's instinct in calling *Tom Jones* a history is confirmed by the general rule that the larger the scheme of a novel becomes, the more obviously its historical nature appears" (*op. cit.*, 307). Philip Stevick ("Fielding and the Meaning of History," *Publications of the Modern Language Association of America* 79 [1964]: 561–68) is not concerned with the novel as history; he is interested in the intellectual history which shaped Fielding's understanding of the historical process.

14. Cf. Pero Mexía, *Historia del Emperador Carlos V*, ed. J. de Mata Carriazo (Madrid: Espasa-Calpe, 1945), 7: "Los antiguos ystoriadores que escriuieron las vidas e ystorias de los grandes principes y rreyes, todos procuraron y trauaxaron de dar linajes y deçendençias muy ilustres y altas, a las vezes fingiéndolas quando las çiertas no eran a su contento, e aprouechándose de las fábulas poéticas para este efecto, haçiendo ansimismo sus naçimientos y crianças de algunos dellos muy extrañas y llenas de misterios." It is often asserted, following Menéndez Pidal, that the Spanish epic is historically exact. Too often this assertion leads scholars to ignore its essential poetry, its dependence on the human imagi-

nation. It was left to Pedro Salinas ("La vuelta al esposo," in his *Ensayos de literatura hispánica* [Madrid, 1958], 45–57) and to Leo Spitzer ("Sobre el carácter histórico del *Cantar de Myo Cid*," in his *Romanische Literaturstudien* [Tübingen, 1959], 647–63) to rectify the erroneous conclusions drawn from Menéndez Pidal's well-known theory.

15. My colleague Richard L. Predmore (*El mundo del "Quijote"* [Madrid, 1958], p. 21) makes the excellent point that Cervantes insists on "el contraste . . . entre la vida y cualquier intento de registrarla con exactitud."

16. Cf. Pedro Malón de Chaide, prologue to *La conversión de la Madalena*: "¿que otra cosa son libros de amores, y las *Dianas* y Boscanes y Garcilasos, y los monstruosos libros y silvas de fabulosos cuentos y mentiras de los *Amadises, Floriseles y Don Belianís*, y una flota de semejantes portentos como hay escritos, puestos en manos de pocos años, sino cuchillo en poder del hombre furioso?" (*Biblioteca de Autores Españoles* 27: 279).

17. Excellent illustrations of the novel's self-awareness may be found in detective stories, which must repeat *ad nauseam* traditional formulas. For example, in Agatha Christie's *The Body in the Library*, Colonel Bantry, having been told of the crime committed in his house, assumes that his wife has imagined it as a result of her addiction to detective fiction. "Bodies," he says, "are always being found in libraries in books. I've never known a case in real life." In the same work a nine-year-old boy asks Superintendent Harper: "Do you like detective stories? I do. I read them all, and I've got autographs from Dorothy Sayers and Agatha Christie and Dickson Carr and H. C. Bailey." The mention of the author's name is, in this degenerate form of the novel, the equivalent of the appearance of "un tal Saavedra" in *Don Quixote*!

18. The roads are in fact evoked rather than described, as Flaubert pointed out: "Comme on voit ces routes d'Espagne qui ne sont nulle part décrites!"

19. Avellaneda's *Don Quixote* also purports to have been written by a pseudo-historian, Alisolán, "historiador no menos moderno que verdadero." But Avellanada, unlike Cervantes, falls into the most crass relativism in his attitude to the truth of fictional history: "En algo diferencia esta parte de la primera suya [sc. de Cervantes]; porque tengo opuesto humor también al suyo; *y en materias de opiniones en cosas de historia*, y tan auténtica como ésta, *cada cual puede echar por donde le pareciere*" (prologue; italics mine).

20. Cervantes' problem is the reverse of that of the historical novelist. The reader of a historical novel believes in the historical foundation of the plot, and accepts uncritically the unhistorical accretions.

21. It is interesting to compare the Aristotelian Canon of Toledo's

defense of *verisimilitude*—"tanto la mentira es mejor cuanto más parece verdadera"; "la verisimilitud y . . . la imitación en quien consiste la perfección de lo que se escribe" (I, xlvii)—with the "historian" Cide Hamete's passionate espousal of *truth*: "las escribió |sc. las locuras de don Quijote| de la misma manera que él las hizo, sin añadir ni quitar a la historia un átomo de la verdad, sin dársele nada por las objecciones que podían ponerle de mentiroso" (II, x). A different view of the relation of history to truth and verisimilitude appears in the *Elogio*, written by Alonso de Barros, of Mateo Alemán's *Guzmán de Alfarache*. There it is said that Alemán had, by his success in cultivating verisimilitude, earned the title of historian: "por su admirable disposición y observancia en lo verosímil de la historia, el autor ha conseguido felicísimamente el nombre y oficio de historiador" (*Biblioteca de Autores Españoles* 3: 187).

22. This explanation of Don Quixote's madness may seem to contradict Cervantes' statement that "del poco dormir y del mucho leer se le seco el celebro de manera que vino a perder el juicio" (I, 1). In fact, it is wholly consistent with both implications of the statement: (1) that the hidalgo read too much and (2) that he was physiologically prone to insanity. Other statements in the first chapter—and in the rest of the novel—add to this basic information the fact that he confused history with story.

23. Américo Castro produces evidence of the imitation of books by Saints Theresa and Ignatius ("La palabra escrita y el *Quijote*," in *Semblanzas y estudios españoles* |Princeton, N.J.: Ediciones Insula, 1956|, 259–60). But apart from the fact that the latter "vivió en su mocedad muy a tono con el espíritu de los libros de caballerías," they imitated books of devotion, not of fiction. Ignatius, in his youth, adopted the noble ideals of the fictional knights; he did not try to perform *fazañas*.

24. I, i. Another beautiful example of Don Quixote's confusing of fiction and history is given in his own confused words after he has slashed Maese Pedro's puppets: "a mí me pareció todo lo que aquí ha pasado que pasaba al pie de la letra: que Melisendra era Melisendra; don Gayferos, don Gayferos; Marsilio, Marsilio, y Carlo Magno, Carlo Magno" (II, xxvi). In each case the first mention of a name refers to the fictional character, and the second, to the historical character.

25. Almost all the literate characters (and semiliterate ones like the innkeeper) are avid readers of books of chivalry. There are many shades in their acceptance of the fictional as real. The village priest tells the innkeeper that Don Felixmarte and Don Cirongilio are imaginary: "todo es compostura y ficción de ingenios ociosos que los compusieron para

el efecto que vos decís de entretener el tiempo" (I, xxxii). For his part, the innkeeper is sure they are historical. The Canon of Toledo sometimes lets his guard down: "de mí sé decir que cuando los leo, en tanto que no pongo la imaginación en pensar que son todos mentira y liviandad, me dan algún contento" (I, xlix).

26. Leo Spitzer, while not concerned with history as such, stressed the importance of the *book* as the major issue discussed in *Don Quixote*: "a theme which informs the whole novel: the problem of the reality of literature" ("Perspectivism in *Don Quijote*," in his *Linguistics and Literary History* [Princeton: Princeton University Press, 1948], 51 [This is the next essay in this book—ED.]). See also his lecture "On the Significance of *Don Quijote*," *Modern Language Notes* 57 (1962): 113–29.

27. The parallel experience for Don Quixote is the vision of the Cave of Montesinos: he *thinks he knows* what he saw, and yet *doubts* that he does (as a result of Sancho's skepticism, Maese Pedro's monkey's equivocal oracles, etc.). This statement of the nature of truth and its cognition differs somewhat from previously enunciated theories: prismatic truth, objective truth, perspectivism. Truth is presented paradoxically or ambiguously in *Don Quixote*: one has it and at the same time does not have it. The root of the problem is historical truth, which mankind both possesses and does not possess. This paradoxical view of truth harmonizes, I believe, with the thesis so persuasively sustained by Manuel Durán in *La ambiguedad el en "Quijote"* (Xalapa: Universidad Veracruzana, 1960).

28. *Generaciones y semblanzas*, in *Biblioteca de Autores Españoles* 68: 697.

29. Cf. Marcelino Menéndez Pelayo, *Orígenes de la novela* (Buenos Aires: Glem, 1943), III, 171, and Ramón Menéndez Pidal, *Floresta de leyendas heroicas españolas* (Clásicos Castellanos), I, lxxxix.

30. Alonso Zamora Vicente, in *Diccionario de literatura española* (Madrid: Revista de Occidente, 1953), 764.

31. George Ticknor, *History of Spanish Literature* (4th ed., Boston: Houghton, Osgood and Company, 1879), 215, n15.

32. See J. Godoy Alcantara, *Historia critica de los falsos cronicones* (Madrid: Imprento de M. Rivadeneyra, 1868).

33. See Ludwig Pfandl, *Historia de la literatura nacional española en la edad de oro* (Barcelona: G. Gil, 1952), 590–92.

34. Ticknor, *loc. cit.*

35. The full title of the "septima impression" (Madrid: Melchor Sánchez [1676?]), which I consulted in the library of Duke University, follows: *Historia | verdadera | del Rey Don Rodrigo, | en la qual se trata la cavsa |*

principal de la pèrdida de España, y la conquista | que de ella hizo Miramamolin Almançor, Rey | que fuè de el Africa, y de las Arabias; | y vida del Rey Jacob Almançor. | Compvesta | Por el sabio Alcayde Albucacim Tarif, | de Nacion Arabe. | Nuevamente traducida | de Lengua Arabiga por Miguel de Luna, vezino | de Granada, Interprete [sic] de el Rey | nuestro Señor. Menéndez Pelayo (*op. cit.*, III, 185, n2) says: "Hay, por lo menos, nueve ediciones de este libro, que todavía es muy vulgar en España. Casi todos los catálogos de libros antiguos empiezan por él."

36. *Op. cit.*, II, xliii.

37. E.g., "Cetro Real llama el Arabigo, harimalmulq" (edition cited, p. 4). The marginalia also give careful consideration to dates, which are liberally translated from the hegira to the Gothic "Era de César" and to the Christian *Anno Domini*. Some marginal comments sound like the translator's comments on Cide Hamete's "history"; apropos of a letter supposedly written by Queen Anagilda to King Roderick Luna writes: "Esta carta fue traducida por Abentarique, de Lengua Castellana en Arabiga, y aora se bolviò à traducir de Arabigo en romance, y fue hallada en la Camara del Rey Don Rodrigo, en la Ciudad de Cordoua" (8).

38. Pages 1–2. Italics mine.

39. Cf. Menéndez Pelayo, *op. cit.*, III, 186: "logró . . . una celebridad escandalosa, teniéndole muchos por verdadera historia y utilizándole otros como fuente poética."

40. Cf. R. Menéndez Pidal, *op. cit.*, II, xliv: "La única preocupación de Miguel de Luna parece ser la de dar a luz un estupendo descrubrimiento que le acredite en su oficio de docto arabista. Por eso no ceja en desfigurar o contrariar siempre las tradiciones históricas más recibidas, para dar a su relato una continua novedad. Todo falsario tiene un poco de perturbado, pero Luna tiene un mucho; sus invenciones aturden y marean al lector, como las de un loco, pues desquician y contradicen sin finalidad ni fundamento todo cuanto por tradición estamos habituados a tener como cosa sabida."

41. See my "Allegory and the Role of El Autor in the *Cárcel de Amor*," *Philological Quarterly* 31 (1952): 39–44.

42. See my "La novela como retrato: el arte de Francisco Delicado," *Nueva Revista de Filología Hispánica* 7 (1953): 475–88.

43. Cf. Richard L. Predmore, "El problema de la realidad en el *Quijote*," *Nueva Revista de Filología Hispánica* 7 (1953): 489–98.

44. Evidence that the monolithic façade of conformity could on a rare occasion be pierced by an existential anguish was brilliantly adduced for the dogmatic Quevedo by Carlos Blanco Aguinaga, in "Dos sonetos

del siglo XVII: Amorlocura en Quevedo y sor Juana," *Modern Language Notes* 77 (1962): 145–62.

45. In *El pensamiento de Cervantes* Castro made the statement (which he later recanted) that "Cervantes es un hábil hipócrita" (244). A less forceful phrase on page 240 expresses the same idea more subtly and in more acceptable terms: "Cervantes era un gran disimulador, que recubrió de ironía y habilidad opiniones e ideas contrarias a las usuales."

46. Summarized by Otis H. Green, "A Critical Survey of Scholarship in the Field of Spanish Renaissance Literature, 1914–1944," *Studies in Philology* 44 (1947): 254, n120.

47. Don Diego de Miranda's poet son uses this phrase: "él es un entreverado loco, lleno de lúcidos intervalos" (II, xviii).

Linguistic Perspectivism in the *Don Quijote*

LEO SPITZER

◆   ◆   ◆

RGUMENTUM: HERE, the procedure will be to start from a particular feature of Cervantes' novel which must strike any reader: the instability and variety of the names given to certain characters (and the variety of etymological explanations offered for these names), in order to find out what may be Cervantes' psychological motive behind this polyonomasia (and polyetymologia). I see this as a deliberate refusal on the part of the author to make a final choice of one name (and one etymology): in other words, a desire to show the different aspects under which the character in question may appear to others. If this be true, then such a relativistic attitude must tinge other linguistic details in the novel; and, indeed, it is surely such an attitude that is behind the frequent debates (particularly between Quijote and Sancho), which never end conclusively, over the relative superiority of this or that word or phrase. It is as if language in general was seen by Cervantes from the angle of perspectivism. With this much settled, it will not be difficult to see (what, in fact, has been recognized by Américo Castro) that perspectivism informs the structure of the novel as a whole: we find it in Cervantes' treatment of the plot, of ideological themes, as well as in his attitude of distantiation toward the reader.

And yet, beyond this perspectivism, we may sense the presence of something which is not subject to fluctuation: the immovable, immutable principle of the divine—which, perhaps, to some extent, is reflected in the earthly *artifex* himself: the novelist who assumes a near-divine power in his mastery of the material, in his own unshaken attitude toward the phenomena of his world (and even in his aloofness from the reader). And it is in this glorification of the artist that the main historical significance of the Spanish masterpiece is to be seen.

MUCH, THOUGH NOT TOO MUCH, has been written about Cervantes' master novel. Yet, we are still far from understanding it in its general plan and in its details as well as we do, for instance, Dante's *Commedia* or Goethe's *Faust*—and we are relatively further from an understanding of the whole than of the details. The main critical works of recent years, which represent gigantic strides forward toward the understanding of the whole, are, in my opinion, Américo Castro's *El pensamiento de Cervantes,*[1] in which the themes of Cervantes' poetry of ideas are stated, and Joaquín Casalduero's article "La composición de 'El ingenioso hidalgo Don Quijote de la Mancha,' "[2] in which the artistic architecture of the novel, as based on the themes recognized by Castro, is pointed out. As for the style of the novel, Helmut Hatzfeld, in his book *Don Quijote als Wortkunstwerk,*[3] has attempted to distinguish different "styles" determined by previous literary traditions (the pastoral or chivalric styles, the style of Boccaccio, etc.)—without, however, achieving what I should call an integration of the historical styles into one Cervantine style in which the personality of the writer would manifest itself. Perhaps it is better not to break up the unity of a work of art into historical units which, in any case, are extraneous to Cervantes and, instead, to proceed according to a method by which one would seek to move from the periphery toward the center of the artistic globe—thus remaining within the work of art. Any one outward feature, when sufficiently followed up to the center, must yield us insight into the artistic whole, whose unity will thus have been respected. The choice of the particular phenomenon, then, would appear to be of secondary importance: any single one must, according to my ideology, give final results.

Accordingly, I shall choose certain linguistic phenomena (of, at first glance, slight importance for Cervantes' artistic cosmos) which I shall attempt to reduce to a common denominator, later to bring this into relationship with the "pensamiento," the *Weltanschauung* of Cervantes.

Any reader of the *Quijote* is struck by the instability of the names of the main characters of the novel: in the first chapter we are told by Cervantes that the protagonist has been called, by the sources of "this so truthful story," alternatively Quijada, Quesada, or Quijana (this last, according to Cervantes, being the best "conjecture"); from this assortment the *ingenioso hidalgo* [ingenious gentleman] chose, before starting his knightly career, the name that he was to bear in the whole book: Quijote. When, at the end, he is cured of the fever of quixotism and repudiates *Amadís de Gaula* and the rest of the novels of chivalry, he recovers his unpretentious prosaic original name (II, 74): "ya no soy don Quijote de la Mancha, sino Alonso Quijano, a quien mis costumbres me dieron renombre de *Bueno*" [I am Don Quijote of la Mancha no longer, but Alonso Quijano, called for my way of life *the Good*][4]; and the final scene of his Christian death and regeneration seems rounded out by a kind of re-baptism, as this *loco* [madman] becomes a *cuerdo* [sane man] (the change of name is thrice mentioned in this final chapter, as if the author wanted to din it into our heads that the old Adam is dead); in his will, "Quijano" calls his niece Antonia by the name "Quijana," as if to emphasize that he is now a *bourgeois rangé* to the extent of having a family bearing his own (everyday) name. The first-mentioned name, Quijada, is also used in recognition of the reasonable side of the protagonist's nature: earlier (I, 5) he was referred to, by an acquaintance who knew him in the days before his madness, as "Señor Quijada." Again, just as Quesada, Quijada, or Quijana became a Quijote when he fancied himself a knight, so, when his chivalric dreams seemed about to give way to those of pastoral life, he imagines himself to be called "el pastor Quijotiz" [the shepherd Quijotiz] (and his companion, Sancho Panza, "el pastor Pancino").[5]

In another episode, Dorotea, who plays the role of Princess Micomicona (I, 30), feigns that her presumptive rescuer is called "{si mal no me acuerdo,} don Azote o don Jigote" [{if I remember rightly,} Don Azote or Don Gigote]. And the Countess Trifaldi jocundly endows him with the superlative for which she seems to have a predilection: "Quijotísimo." As for his epithet "de la Mancha," this is coined (I, 1) after Amadís de Gaula. Later, he will be called by the name, first given him by Sancho, "el Caballero de la Triste Figura" [the Knight of the Sad Countenance], still later by "el Caballero de los Leones" [the Knight of the Lions] (in II, 27–29, this change is strongly emphasized, and a certain character is rebuked by Sancho for having disregarded the distinction).[6]

It is obviously required by chivalric decorum that whoever enters the sphere of the knight Don Quijote must also change his or her name: Aldonza Lorenzo>Dulcinea ("nombre a su parecer músico y peregrino y significativo" [a name that seemed to him musical, strange, and significant]), Tolosa>doña Tolosa, la Molinera>doña Molinera (I, 3), and the anonymous nag receives the name of Rocinante ("nombre a su parecer alto, sonoro y significativo" [a name that seemed to him grand and sonorous]: note the parallel wording appearing in the justifications for the names given to Dulcinea and to the nag); incidentally, the ass from which Sancho is inseparable is not deemed worthy of a change of name that would be indicative of a change of rank. Although Sancho Panza, the peasant squire, undergoes no change of name similar to that of his master,[7] and is resolved always to remain (governor or no governor) plain Sancho without the addition of "don" (II, 4), there is some uncertainty in regard to his name, too, since, in the text of Cide Hamete Benengeli, the Arabian chronicler whose manuscript Cervantes purports to have found at the moment when other sources gave out (I, 9), there is a picture of thick-set Sancho with "la barriga grande, el talle corto, y las zancas largas" [a big belly, a short body, and long shanks], bearing the inscription: "Sancho Zancas."

It is, however, in regard to the name of Sancho's wife that the greatest confusion obtains: Sancho calls her first "Juana Gutiérrez mi oíslo" [Juana Gutiérrez, my poppet] (I, 7); a few lines later, he ponders whether a crown would fit "la cabeza de Mari Gutiérrez" [Mary Gutiérrez's head]—which change the more intelligent commentators, seeking to avoid bringing the charge of inconsistency against Cervantes, rightly explain by the fact that *Mari* had come to represent simply a generic and interchangeable name for women. But in II, 5, Sancho's wife calls herself Teresa Cascajo; from then on she is either Teresa Panza or Teresa Sancho, "mujer de Sancho Panza" [wife of Sancho Panza]; of the name Teresa itself she says (II, 5): "Teresa me pusieron en el bautismo, nombre mondo y escueto" [Teresa they wrote me down at my baptism, pure and simple]. Evidently we have to do with a woman named Juana Teresa Gutiérrez, who becomes a Juana Panza, or Teresa Panza when called after her husband, or . . . Cascajo when called after her father. Occasionally, however, according to the mood of the situation, she may be called "Teresaina" (II, 73) or "Teresona" (II, 67: because of her "gordura" [fatness]).[8]

There are other cases, slightly different from those enumerated so far, in which the ignorance and weak memory of Sancho seem to create a "polyonomasia": here we can hardly think in terms of different traditions offered by chroniclers (as in the case of the names of Quijote), or of popular variation (as in that of the names of Sancho's wife): Sancho must multiply names simply because all the forms of names that he retains are only approximations to the real ones; they are variable because he cannot take a firm hold on them; he indulges in what linguists call "popular etymologies"—that is, he alters names according to the associations most convenient to his intellectual horizon. Sometimes he offers several variations, but even when only one alteration is involved, the effect of polyonomasia still remains because of the fact that the real name is also present in the reader's mind. Mambrino (I, 19–21), of whose helmet he speaks, becomes "Malandrino" (a "moro" [Moor]), "Malino" (=the Evil One), or "Martino" (a common first name); Fortinbras>feo Blas [ugly Blas] (I, 15), Cide Hamete Benengeli>"... Berengena" [eggplant or aubergine] (II, 2; this Sancho justifies with the remark: "los moros son amigos de berenjenas" [Moors, for the most part, are very fond of aubergines]⁹), Señora Rodriguez de Grijalva>Señora González (II, 31), Magalona>"la señora Magellanes o Magalona" (II, 41).

A similar alteration of names is practiced by the *ama* [housekeeper], who (I, 7) contends that the books which we know to have fallen prey to the *auto-da-fé* (I, 6) had been ravished by the sorcerer Muñatón: Don Quijote corrects this to "Frestón." "Never mind Frestón or Fritón," answers the *ama*, "provided it is a name ending in —*ton*": word forms that are unalterable for the learned Don Quijote are quite exchangeable in the mind of the uncultured *ama*.

The names of the Countess Trifaldi are in a class by themselves since, in addition to the instability of names conditioned by a masquerade, there are involved the alterations to which Sancho is prone: here there coexist polyonomasias of the first and second degrees. The Countess is first (II, 36) introduced to us (by her messenger Trifaldín de la Blanca Barba [Trifaldín of the White Beard]) as "la condesa Trifaldi, por otro nombre llamada la Dueña Dolorida" [the countess Trifaldi, otherwise called the Afflicted Waiting-Woman]; one of the two names is her authentic one, the other, her "name within the world of romance" (just as Don Quijote is also the "Caballero de la Triste Figura"). When she appears in the pageant (II, 38) of the *carro triunfal* [triumphal car],[10] her name "Trifaldi" is given the following explanation: "la cola, o falda, o como llamarla quisieren, era de tres puntas" [her tail or skirt, or whatever they call it, fell in three trains]; the "mathematical" (geometrical) figure of her skirt with three flounces (or trains?) is so striking that every spectator must interpret her name as "la Condesa de las Tres Faldas" [the Countess with the Three Skirts]. But the scrupulous chronicler Benengeli, who, like Cervantes, seems to care about even the minor details of the fiction-within-the-fiction, is said by Cervantes to have stated that the character was really called "la Condesa *Lobuna*"—allegedly because of the presence of wolves [*lobos*] in her domain (he adds that, according to onomastic traditions in princely houses, she would have been called "la Condesa Zorruna" if foxes [*zorros*] had been prevalent in her domain)—but that she had dropped this name in favor of the more novel one derived from the form of her skirt. Now, this etymology of the name "Trifaldi," as stated by the chronicler (and as made evident to the eye of the spectators who see the masquerade skirt), had been somewhat anticipated by Sancho's popular etymology in II, 37: "esta condesa Tres Faldas o Tres Colas (que en mi tierra faldas y colas, colas y faldas todo es uno)" [this Countess Three Skirts or Three Tails (in my country skirts and tails, tails and skirts, are all the same)]. Ultimately we are presented with an array of (possible) names for the same character: la Condesa Trifaldi, de Tres Faldas, de Tres Colas (the latter name would be due to what the modern linguist in his jargon calls "synonymic derivation"), Lobuna ("Zorruna" again being a "synonymic derivate"),[11] Dueña Dolorida—a list as impressive as that of the names of Don Quijote.

Now those commentators who, in general, take the line of emphasizing the satiric intent of Cervantes will point out that the variety of names attributed to the protagonist by Cervantes is simply an imitation of the pseudo-historical tendencies of the authors of chivalric novels who, in order to show their accurateness as historians, pretend to have resorted to different sources.[12]

In the case of the names of Sancho's wife, some commentators point out, as we have seen, that the polyonomasia is due to the onomastic habits of the period; in the alterations of the name "Mambrino" they usually see a satire on Sancho's ignorance; in the case of the Condesa Trifaldi I have seen no explanation (Rodríguez Marín's edition points out possible "historical" sources for the costume itself of "tres colas o faldas").[13] But, evidently, there must be a common pattern of thought behind all these cases, which would explain (1) the importance given to a name or change of name, (2) the etymological concern with names, (3) the polyonomasia in itself.

Now it happens that just these three features are well known to the medievalist (less, perhaps, to students of Renaissance literature): they ultimately derive from biblical studies and from ancient philology: one need only think of Saint Jerome's explanation of Hebrew names or of Isidore's "Etymologies"—and of the etymologizing habits of all great medieval poets. The names in the Bible were treated with seriousness; in the Old Testament the name, or rather the names, of God were all-important (Exodus 6: 2–3: "I am *Iahve*, and I have appeared to Abraham, Isaak and Jacob as *El Schaddai*, under the name of *Jahve* I was not known to them"; compare Exodus 3:14); the many *nomina sacra* [holy names] revealed the many aspects through which the divine might make itself felt.[14] Nor does the importance of the name decrease with the New Testamentary divinity (Christ is Immanuel). And, in the New Testament, a tendency appears which will have great influence on medieval chivalry: The change of name subsequent to baptism will be imitated by the change of name undergone by the newly dubbed knight. In all these sacred (or sacramental) names or changes of names, etymology plays a large part, because the true meaning (the etymon) may reveal eternal verities latent in the words—indeed, it was possible for many etymologies to be proposed for the same word, since God may have deposited different meanings in a single term: polyonomasia and polyetymology. Both these techniques are generally applied to a greater degree to proper names than to common nouns—because the former, "untranslatable" as they are by their nature, participate more in the mysterious aspect of human language: they are less motivated. In proper names the medieval mind could see reflected more of the multivalence of the world full of arcana. The Middle Ages were characterized by an admiration as well for the correspondence between word and thing as for the mystery which makes this correspondence unstable.

By all this I do not mean to deny that Cervantes followed the models pointed out to us by the commentators: what I do say is that, in doing so, he was also following certain accepted medieval patterns (which, however, he submitted to a new interpretation: that of his critical intelligence). It is possible, for example, in the case of the name "Trifaldi," to see on the surface a medieval imagination at work: the name is given an interpretation (*Trifaldi;*

eq tres faldas) which, from our modern linguistic or historical point of view, is evidently wrong but which would have delighted a medieval mind, ever ready to accept any interpretation offering a clarification of the mystery of words.[15]

The ancient and medieval etymologies are indeed rarely those a modern linguist would offer, trained as he is to respect the formational procedures current in human language; the aim of those etymologies was to establish the connection between a given word and other existing words as a homage to God whose wisdom may have ordained these very relationships. The etymological connections that the medieval etymologist sees are direct relationships established between words vaguely associated because of their homonymic ring—not the relationships established by "historical grammar" or those obtained by decomposition of the word into its morphological elements.[16] In other words, we are offered edifying ideal possibilities, not deterministic historical realities; Isidore will connect *sol* [sun] and *solus* [alone] because of the ideological beauty of this relationship, not *sol* and ἥλιος [helios] as the comparative grammarian of today must do.

But, if the equation *Trifaldi=tres faldas* represents a "medieval" etymology, Cervantes himself did not take too seriously his own etymologizing: he must have been perfectly well aware of the historically real explanation—that which prompted him to coin the word. *Trifaldi* is evidently a regressive form from *Trifaldín*, which name, in turn, is the farcical Italian *Truffaldino*, "the name of a low and ridiculous character of comedy"[17]; the reference to *truffare* "to cheat" is apposite, in our story, given the farcical episode intended to delude Don Quijote and Sancho. Thus the name of the messenger *Trifaldín* is (historically) not a diminutive of *Trifaldi*, as it might seem but, on the contrary, was preexistent, in Cervantes' mind, to the name of the mistress. The etymology of *tres faldas* is, historically speaking, entirely out of place. We have to face here the same para-etymological vein in which Rabelais (facetiously imitating medieval practice, while exemplifying the joyous freedom with which the Renaissance writer could play with words) explained the name *Gargantua* by *que grand tu as* {sc. *le gosier*}! [what a big one you've got {namely, the gullet}!] and

Beauce by {*je trouve*} *beau ce* {sc. *pays*} [I find this fine {namely, the country}].[18] In this story, the para-etymological play with names serves to underline the deceitfulness of outward evidence; what for Quijote and Sancho are wondrous events are, in reality, only *burlas* [jests] in a baroque world of histrionics and disingenuity.[19]

The disingenuous procedure of offering such "medieval" etymologies as would occur to his characters (for the simpleton Sancho as well as the learned Arab Benengeli are medieval primitives) is also exemplified in the case of the nag Rocinante, whose name is interpreted by Don Quijote[20] in the style of Isidore: the horse was a *rocín antes*—which may mean either "a nag before" ("previously a nag," "an erstwhile nag") or "a nag before all others": "antes de todos los rocines del mundo." Two explanations are given of one word, as was the general medieval practice— not the *one* historically true significance according to which the name was actually coined: namely, *rocin* + the noble and "literary" participial ending *–ante*. Cervantes was perfectly aware of the correct etymology but he allowed his medieval Don Quijote to offer a more "significant" one. He knew also the explanation of the name *Quijote* (=*quij–* "jaw" + the comic suffix *–ote*, derived from *jigote*, etc.), while his protagonist, who adopted this name, thought of it as patterned on *Lanzarote* [Lancelot].[21]

Thus we may conclude that, while, for the medieval world, the procedures of polyonomasia and polyetymologia amounted to a recognition of the working of the divine in the world, Cervantes used the same devices in order to reveal the multivalence which words possess for different human minds: he who has coined the names put into them other meanings than those conceived of by the characters themselves: a *Trifaldín* who is for Cervantes a *truffatore*, a cheater or practical joker, is understood by Don Quijote and Sancho to be the servant of a Countess *Trifaldi* who wears a three-flounce skirt.

Perhaps this procedure is symptomatic of something basic to the texture of our novel; perhaps a linguistic analysis of the names can carry us further toward the center, allowing us to catch a glimpse of the general attitude of the creator of the novel toward his characters. This creator must see that the world, as it is offered to man, is susceptible of many explanations, just as names are susceptible of many etymologies; individuals may be deluded by the perspectives according to which they see the world as well as by the etymological connections which they establish. Consequently, we may assume that the linguistic perspectivism of Cervantes is reflected in his invention of plot and characters; and, just as, by means of polyonomasia and polyetymologia, Cervantes makes the world of words appear different to his different characters, while he himself may have his own, the coiner's, view of these names, similarly he watches the story he narrates from his own private vantage point: the way in which the characters conceive of the situations in which they are involved may be not at all the way in which Cervantes sees them—though this latter way is not always made clear to the reader. In other words, Cervantes' perspectivism, linguistic and otherwise,[22] would allow him qua artist to stand above, and sometimes aloof from, the misconceptions of his characters. Later we will have more to say about what lies behind this attitude of Cervantes; suffice it for us here, where we are given the first opportunity to look into the working of the (linguistic) imagination of the novelist, to have summarily indicated the relationship between his linguistic ambivalences and his general perspectivism.[23]

If, now, we turn back for a moment to Sancho's mispronunciations of names—which, as we have seen, was one of the contributing factors to the polyonomasia of the novel—we will recognize a particular application of Cervantes' linguistic perspectivism at work: to Sancho's uncultured mind, "Mambrino" must appear now as "Malino," now as "Martino," etc. In this, there is no suggestion of smugness on the part of Cervantes, as there might be with modern intellectual writers who would mock the linguistic "abuses" of ignorant characters; Cervantes presents "Malino," "Martino," etc., simply as the "linguistic appearances" of what, for Don Quijote, for example, can evidently be only Mambrino.[24]

This lack of authorial criticism in the face of so much linguistic relativity tends to shake the reader's confidence in established word-usage. Of course, we are apt to rely on the correctness of

Don Quijote's use of words and names; but who knows whether the knight, who is so often mistaken in his attempts to define reality (as he is precisely in his identification of the helmet of Mambrino), has hit this time upon the right name, whether this name is not as much of a dream as are the fantastic adventures he envisions? (We are reminded of the baroque theme par excellence, "los sueños sueños son" [dreams are dreams].) Why should, then, "Mambrino" and not "Malino" or "Martino" be the name representing *reality?* The same insistence on "correctness" of word-usage, as applied to the nonexistent, occurs in the scene where Quijote listens to the *ama*'s cock-and-bull story of the theft of the books by "the sorcerer Muñatón," and finds nothing to correct therein but the name: not "Muñatón" but "Frestón": Frestón and Mambrino are names correct in irreality (in books), representing naught in reality. Evidently we are offered in Don Quijote a caricature of the humanist[25] who is versed in books and bookish names but is unconcerned as to their valid relationship to reality (he has a pendant in the *licenciado* [licentiate] to whom Don Quijote tells the fantastic story of his descent to the *cueva de Montesinos* [cave of Montesinos] and who is outspokenly qualified by Cervantes as a *humanista*).[26]

In these two incidents we have a suggestion of a theme which informs our whole novel: the problem of the reality of literature. I belong with those critics who take seriously Cervantes' statement of purpose: "derribar la máquina mal fundada de los libros de caballería" [overthrowing the ill-based fabric of these books of chivalry]; this statement, which indicts a particular literary genre, is, in fact, a recognition of the potential danger of "the book." And, in its larger sense, the *Quijote* is an indictment of the bookish side of humanism,[27] a creed in which, seventy years earlier, Rabelais had so firmly believed, and an indictment of the "word-world" in which the Renaissance had delighted without qualms. Whereas the writers of the Renaissance were able to build up their word-worlds out of sheer exuberance, free to "play" linguistically because of their basic confidence in life, with the baroque artist *desengaño* "disillusionment" is allowed to color all things of the world, including books and their words, which possess only the reality of a *sueño*. Words are no longer, as they had been in the Middle Ages, depositories of truths nor, as they had been in the Renaissance, an expansion of life: they are, like the books in which they are contained, sources of hesitation, error, deception—"dreams."

The same linguistic perspectivism is present in Cervantes' treatment of common nouns. For the most part we have to do with the confusion, or the criticism, engendered by the clash of two linguistic standards determined mainly by social status.[28]

Here, too, in this continuous give-and-take between cultured and uncultured speakers, there is given a suggestion of linguistic relativism that is willed by Cervantes. The opposition between two different ways of speech takes different forms: it may be Sancho who is interrupted and corrected by Don Quijote: in I, 32, {*hereje o*} *flemático* [heretical or phlegmatic] is corrected to *cismático* [schismatic]; in II, 7, *relucido>reducido* [concerted>converted]; II, 8, *sorbiese>asolviese* [resorb>resolve]; II, 10, *cananeas>hacaneas* [nackneys>hackneys]; II, 19, *friscal>fiscal* [cricket>critic].[29]

Particularly interesting are the cases in which the term used by Sancho and the correction offered by Quijote are in the relationship of etymological doublets (popular and learned developments of the same root): (I, 12): *cris–eclipse, estil–estéril* [clipse–eclipse, stale–sterile] (how admirably has Cervantes anticipated the discoveries of nineteenth-century linguistics!). Again, it may be a question of Sancho's reaction to the language of the knight which the squire either misunderstands (in I, 8, Quijote's *homicidios* "murders" is transposed by Sancho into the more familiar, semipopular doublet *omecillos* "feuds") or fails to understand (in II, 29, Quijote must explain the meaning of *longincuos* {"por longincuos caminos" [longinquous ways]}, which he "translates" by *apartados* [remote]). In general, Don Quijote shows more tolerance for linguistic ignorance (in regard to the *longincuos* just mentioned, he excuses Sancho with the words: "y no es maravilla que no lo entiendes, que no estás tú obligado a saber latín" [and it is no wonder you do not understand it, for you are not obliged to know Latin]) than his uncultured associates (who seem more concerned with things than with words) do for linguistic pedantry: they often blame the knight for his *jerigonza* [gibberish] (I, 2), for his *griego* [Greek] (I, 16). And, when Don Quijote reproves Sancho for his use of *abernuncio* [bernounce] instead of *abrenuncio* [renounce], the squire retorts: "Déjeme vuestra grandeza, que no estoy agora para mirar en sotilezas ni en letras más o menos" [Let me alone, Your Highness, I'm in no state now to consider a letter or two more or less] (similarly, in II, 3, when the *bachiller* [bachelor] Sansón Carrasco corrects *presonajes* [presonages] to *personajes* [personages], Sancho remarks: "¿Otro reprochador de voquibles tenemos? Pues ándense a eso y no acabaremos en toda la vida" [So we have another vocabulary-corrector! If it goes on like this we shall never be done in this life]). Sancho adopts the attitude of a Mathurin Régnier, opposing the *éplucheurs de mots* [hairsplitters]! It may happen that the same Sancho, the advocate of naturalness in language, turns purist for the moment[30] for the edification of his wife, and corrects her *revuelto* [revolved] (II, 5); but then he must hear from her lips—oh, relativity of human things!—the same reproach he was wont to administer to his master: "No os pongáis a disputar, marido, conmigo. Yo hablo como Dios es servido, y no me meto en más dibujos!" [Don't start arguing with me, husband. I speak as God would have me speak, and I don't meddle with grand words!] (here, she is referring to the language of God, Who, as Sancho himself had already claimed, is the great *Entendedor* [Understander] of all kinds of speech).[31]

Another example of the linguistic intolerance of the common people is the retort of the shepherd who has been corrected for having said *más años que sarna* [live longer than Sarna] instead of *que Sarra* [than Sarah]: "Harto vive la sarna," he answers, "y si es, señor, que me habéis de andar zahiriendo {='éplucher'} a cada paso los vocablos no acabaremos en un año" [*Sarna* (the itch) lives long enough, too. If you make me correct my words at every turn, sir, we shan't be done in a twelvemonth]. In this case Don Quijote apologizes, and admits that there is as much sense to the one as to the other expression (in other words, he is brought to recognize the wisdom of "popular etymology"). Indeed, Don Quijote the humanist is made to learn new words, popular graphic expressions unknown to him—such as terms descriptive of *naturalia turpia* [natural matters to be ashamed of] which the high-minded knight was wont to eschew in his conversation (I, 48: *hacer aguas* "to urinate"; Sancho is triumphant: "¿Es posible que no entienda vuestra merced hacer aguas mayores o menores?" [Is it possible that Your Worship doesn't understand what making big or little waters is?]), or low argot expressions (I, 22: *gurapas* [galleys], *canario* [canary], from the language of galley-slaves). And—the acme of shame for a humanist!—it may even happen that he has to be instructed in Latinisms by Sancho (with whom they appear, of course, in garbled form), as when he fails to understand his squire's remark: "quien infierno tiene *nula es retencio*" [for him that's in hell, there is no holding back] (I, 25): it is significant that Sancho the Catholic Positivist is more familiar with ecclesiastical Latin terms than is his master, the idealistic humanist. Thus, Don Quijote is shown not only as a teacher but also as a student of language; his word-usage is by no means accepted as an ideal. And the reader is allowed to suppose that, to Cervantes himself, the language of the knight was not above reproach: when, in his solemn challenges or declarations of love, Quijote indulges in archaic phonetics (*f-* instead of *h-*) and morphology (uncontracted verb forms), this is not so different from the *a Dios prazca* [may it please God] of Sancho, or the *voacé* of one of the captives.

It seems to me that Cervantes means to present the problem of the Good Language in all its possibilities, without finally establishing an absolute: on the one hand, Sancho is allowed to state his ideal of linguistic tolerance (II, 19): "Pues sabe que no me he criado en la corte ni he estudiado en Salamanca para saber si añado o quito alguna letra a mis vocablos, no hay para qué obligar al sayagués a que hable como el toledano, y toledanos puede haber que no las corten en el aire en esto del hablar polido" [You know I wasn't brought up at the Court, and never studied at Salamanca to learn whether I'm putting a letter too many or too few into my words. You mustn't expect a Sayagan to speak like a chap from Toledo, and there may be Toledans who aren't so slick at this business of speaking pretty either]. On the other, Don Quijote may assert his ideal of an "illustrated language" (in the sense of Du Bellay): when Sancho fails to understand the Latinism *erutar* [eruct] (II, 43), Don Quijote remarks: "*Erutar*, Sancho, quiere decir 'regoldar,' y este es uno de los más torpes vocablos que tiene la lengua castellana, aunque es muy significativo. La gente curiosa se ha acogido al latín, y al *regoldar* dice *erutar*, y a los *regüeldos, erutaciones*; y cuando algunos no entienden estos términos, importa poco, que el uso los irá introduciendo con el tiempo, que con facilidad se entiendan; y esto es enriquecer la lengua, sobre quien tiene poder el vulgo y el uso" [*Eruct*, Sancho, means belch, and that is one of the coarsest words in the Castilian language, though it is very expressive; and so refined people have resorted to Latin, and instead of *belch* say *eruct* and for *belches, eructations*; and if some people do not understand these terms it is of little consequence, for they will come into use in time, and they will be generally understood; for that is the way to enrich the language, which depends on custom and the common people]. Thus, Don Quijote would create a more refined word-usage—though, at the same time, he realizes that the ultimate decision as to the enrichment of the language rests with the people; and he does not deny the expressivity of the popular expressions. Sancho's principle of linguistic expressivity, which is in line with his advocacy of the natural, of that which is inborn in man, must be seen *together* with Quijote's principle of linguistic refinement—which is a reflection of his consistent advocacy of the ideal: by positing the two points of view, the one problem in question is dialectically developed. It is obvious that in the passage on *erutar* we have a plea for a cultured language—though ratification by the common people is urged. But this is not the same as saying that Cervantes himself is here pleading for linguistic refinement: rather, I believe, he takes no final stand but is mainly interested in a dialectical play, in bringing out the manifold facets of the problem involved. Sancho has a way of deciding problems trenchantly; Don Quijote is more aware of complexities; Cervantes stands above them both: to him, the two expressions *regoldar* and *erutar* serve to reveal so many perspectives of language.[32]

Within the framework of linguistic perspectivism fits also Cervantes' attitude toward dialects and jargons. Whereas, to Dante, all dialects appeared as inferior (though inferior in different degrees) realizations of a Platonic-Christian ideal pattern of language, as embodied in the *vulgare illustre*, Cervantes saw them as ways of speech which exist as individual realities and which have their justification in themselves. The basic Cervantine conception of perspectivism did not allow for the Platonic or Christian ideal of language: according to the creator of Don Quijote, dialects are simply the different reflections of reality (they are "styles," as the equally tolerant linguist of today would say), among which no one can take precedence over the other. Giuseppe Antonio Borgese, in "Il senso della letteratura italiana," speaks definitely of Dante's conception of the *vulgare illustre*: "Look at how, in the *De vulgari eloquentia*, Dante constructs an Italian language which has the character of divine perfection, which is, so to speak, a celestial language, a language of angels, of religion, of reason; so much that this language—illustrious, ancient, essential, and courtly— is not to be found anywhere by nature, and the native speech of this or that place, the dialect of this or that city, is more or less noble to the extent that it approaches that ideal, just as a color is more or less visible, more or less luminous, to the extent that it resembles white or contrasts with white. The white, the pure, the 'all-light,' the abstract ... is considered by Dante ... the supreme type of the beautiful."[33] Cervantes, on the contrary, delights in the different shades, in the particular gradations and nuances, in the gamut of colors between white and black, in the transitions between the abstract and the concrete. Hence we may explain the frequent excursions of Cervantes into what today we would call "dialectal geography" (I, 2): "un pescado qué en Castilla llaman *abadejo* y en Andalucía *bacallao* y en otras partes *curadillo*, y en otras *truchuela*" [a fish that is called *pollack* in Castile and *cod* in Andalusia, in some parts *ling* and in others *troutlet*] (in fact, a modern Catalonian linguist, Manuel de Montoliu, has been able to base his study of the synonyms for "mackerel" on this passage); I, 41: "*Tagarinos* llaman en Berbería a los moros de Aragón, y a los de Granada *mudéjares*, y en el reino de Fez llaman a los mudéjares *elches*" [In Barbary they call the Moors of Aragon *Tagarines*, and those of Granada *Mudejares*, and in the Kingdom of Fez they call the Mudejares *Elches*].[34]

In these lexicological variants, Cervantes must have seen not a striving toward the approximation of an ideal, but only the variegated phantasmagoria of human approaches to reality: each variant has its own justification, but all of them alike reflect no more than human "dreams." Don Quijote is allowed to expose the inadequacy of such chance designations, as appear in any one dialect, by punning on the word *truchuela* "mackerel": "Como hay muchas truchuelas, podrán servir de una trucha" [so long as there are plenty of troutlet they may serve me for one trout], where he interprets (or pretends to interpret) *truchuela* as "little trout." What, ultimately, is offered here is a criticism of the arbitrariness of any fixed expression in human language (*Sprachkritik*): the criticism which underlies the unspoken question, "Why should a mackerel be called a small trout?" Again, when Don Quijote hears the expression *cantor* used in reference to the galley-slaves, he asks the candid question (I, 22): "¿Por músicos y cantores van también a galeras?" [Do men go the galleys for being musicians and singers?]. Thus the literal interpretation of the expression serves to put into relief the macabre and ironic flavor of its metaphorical use {*cantar=cantar en el ansia*, "to 'sing' under torture"}. Here we witness the bewilderment of Don Quijote, who tries to hold words to a strict account; we may, perhaps, sense a criticism of Quijote's too-literal approach toward language—but this, in itself, would amount to a criticism of the ambiguity of human speech. Cervantes is satisfied, however, merely to suggest the linguistic problem, without any didactic expansion.

A masterpiece of linguistic perspectivism is offered in the transposition, by Sancho, of the high-flown jargon of love contained in Don Quijote's letter to Dulcinea, of which the squire has remembered the spirit, if not the exact words. Sancho, like most primitive persons, has an excellent acoustic memory—"toma de memoria" [he commits to memory] and "tiene en su memoria" [he holds in his memory] (in line with medieval practice, he does not "memorize")[35]—but, in attempting to cope with Don Quijote's florid language, he must necessarily "transpose," remembering what he *thinks* Quijote has said. In this way, "soberana y alta señora" [sovereign and sublime lady] becomes "alta y sobajada señora" [sublime and fondled lady]—which the barber corrects to "sobrehumana o soberana" [superhuman or sovereign]: for this single term of address we are presented with three versions, resulting in a polyonomasia, as in the case of the proper names. Again, "de punto de ausencia y el llagado de las telas del corazón" [the dart of absence and pierced to the heart's core]>"el llagado y falto de sueño y el ferido" [he that is oppressed with sleep and wakeful and wounded] (it is as though Sancho, while indulging in Isidorian etymologies, is shrewdly diagnosing his master). In such linguistic exchanges we have a parallel to the numerous dialogues between the knight and the squire which, as is well known, are inserted into the novel in order to show the different perspectives under which the same events must appear to two persons of such different backgrounds. This means that, in our novel, things are represented not for what they are in themselves, but only as things spoken about or thought about; and this involves breaking the narrative presentation into two points of view. There can be no certainty about the "unbroken" reality of the events; the only unquestionable truth on which the reader may depend is the will of the artist who chose to break up a multivalent reality into different perspectives. In other words, perspectivism suggests an Archimedean principle outside of the plot— and the Archimedes must be Cervantes himself.

In another chapter (II, 25), the nickname *los del rebuzno* [the brayers] is loaded with a double entendre: the Spanish variants of Gothamites draw on the doubtful art of braying for their proud war slogan: their banner bears the verse "no rebuznaron en balde/ el uno y otro alcalde" [They did not bray in vain,/ Our worthy bailiffs twain] (the *regidores* [aldermen] have been promoted to *alcaldes* [bailiffs] in the course of history and—evidently—thanks to the compulsion of rhyme). Here, Don Quijote is entrusted by Cervantes with exploding the vanity of such sectional patriotism: the humanistic knight, in a masterful speech which includes a series of Spanish ethnic nicknames (which take the modern philologian, Rodríguez Marín, over four full pages to explain)—"los de la Reloja, los cazoleros, berenjeneros, ballenatos, jaboneros" [the people of the Clock Town, the Heretics, the Aubergine-eaters, the Whalers, the Soap-boilers]—shows the excessive vanity, originating in the flesh, not in the spirit, in the devil, not in true Catholicism, that is underlying the townspeople's attitude of resenting nicknames, that is, of investing such trifling expressions of the language with disproportionate symbolic value. The Don Quijote who, on other occasions, is only too apt to introduce symbolism and general principles into everyday life is here inspired by Cervantes to expose the vanity of misplaced symbolizing and generalization. The epithet *los del rebuzno* is thus made to shine with the double light of a stupidity that wants to be taken seriously, of a local peculiarity that aspires to "national" importance. The reader is free to go ahead and extend this criticism to other national slogans. That here Cervantes is endorsing Don Quijote seems beyond doubt since, when the novelist introduces this incident, he, speaking in his own right, attributes the adoption of the communal slogan to the activity of "the devil who never sleeps" and who is forever building "quimeras de no nada" [chimaeras out of nothing]—we might say, to a baroque devil who delights in deluding man. The chimeric and self-deluding quality of human vanity could hardly be illustrated more effectively than in this story, where the art of braying is first inflated and then deflated before our eyes, appearing as a "special language of human vanity."[36] And we may see in Cervantes' two-fold treatment of the problem of nicknames another example of his baroque attitude (what is true, what is dream?)—this time, toward language. Is not human language, also, *vanitas vanitatum* [the vanity of vanities], is it not sometimes a "braying" of a sort? Cervantes does not outspokenly say so.

The double point of view into which Cervantes is wont to break up the reality he describes may also appear in connection with one key word, recurring throughout a given episode, upon which Cervantes casts two different lighting effects. We have a most successful example of this in the two chapters II, 25 and 27, where our interest is focused on the motif "braying like an ass." The connecting link between the two chapters is evidently "vanity": it is vanity that prompts the two *regidores* of the Mancha de Aragón to try to out-bray each other, as they search for the lost animal which they want to decoy and whose answering bray each seems to hear—only to learn, at the end, that the braying he heard was that of the other *regidor* (the ass, meanwhile, having died). It is vanity, again, that induces the townspeople—who, after this adventure, were called *los del rebuzno* by the inhabitants of neighboring villages—to sally forth to do battle with their deriders. And it is also due to vanity, on Sancho's part, that he, while deprecating, along with Don Quijote, the gift of imitating an ass, cannot refrain from showing off his own prowess in this regard before the townspeople—who straightway turn upon him in anger and beat him.

The vanity of "braying" shares with all other vanities the one characteristic that an inconsequential feature is invested with a symbolic value which it cannot, in the light of reason, deserve. Thus a duality (sham value vs. real value) offers itself to the artist for exploitation. In the first chapter, Cervantes has the two *regidores* address each other with doubtful compliments: "de vos a un asno, compadre, no hay alguna diferencía en cuanto toca al rebuznar" [in the matter of braying there's nothing to choose between you and an ass], or "{you are the} más perito rebuznador del mundo" [the most skilled brayer in the world]. In the word *rebuznador*, there is a striving after the noble ring of *campeador, emperador*—which is drowned out by the blatant voice of the unregenerate animal: an ambivalence which exposes the hollow pretense.

There is one case in which Cervantes' perspectivism has crystallized into a bifocal word-formation; in Don Quijote's remark: "eso que a ti te parece bacía de barbero me parece a mí el yelmo de Mambrino, y a otro le parecerá otra cosa" [what seems to you to be a barber's basin appears to me to be Mambrino's helmet, and to another as something else] (I, 25),[37] there is contained a *Weltanschauung* which Américo Castro has, in a masterly fashion, recognized as a philosophical criticism (typical of the Renaissance) of the senses ("el engaño a los ojos" [the deceit of the eyes]); and this vision finds its linguistic expression, highly daring for Cervantes' time, in the coinage *baciyelmo* [basic-helmet], with which the tolerant Sancho concludes the debate about the identity of the shining object—as if he were reasoning: "if a thing appears to me as *a*, to you as *b*, it may be, in reality, neither *a* nor *b*, but *a* + *b*" (a similar tolerance is shown by Don Quijote a little later in the same episode, when he remarks, in the argument about the hypothetical nature of the hypothetical Mambrino: "Así que, Sancho, deja ese caballo, o asno, o lo que quisieras que sea" [Therefore, Sancho, leave the horse, or ass, or whatever you would have it be] (I, 21); Quijote, however, does not go so far as to coin a *caballiasno*). Now, it is evident to any linguist that, when shaping *baciyelmo*, Cervantes must have had in mind an existing formation of the same type; and his pattern must have been that which furnished designations of hybrid animals—that is, of a fantastic deviation from Nature—so that this quality of the fantastic and the grotesque is automatically transferred to the coinage *baciyelmo*; such a form does not guarantee the "actual" existence of any such entity *a* + *b*. In most cases, Cervantes must obey language, though he questions it: a basin he can only call *bacía*, a helmet, only *yelmo*; with the creation of *baciyelmo*, however, he frees himself from linguistic limitations.[38] Here, as elsewhere, I would emphasize, more than Castro (whose task it was to show us the conformity to Renaissance thinking of what Cervantes himself has called his *espíritu lego* [secular spirit]), the artistic freedom conquered by Cervantes. In the predicament indicated by (the paradigmatic) ". . . o lo que quisieras que sea," the artist has asserted his own free will.

Now, from what has been said it would appear that the artist Cervantes uses linguistic perspectivism only in order to assert his own creative freedom; and this linguistic perspectivism, as I have already suggested, is only one facet of the general spirit of relativism which has been recognized by most critics as characteristic of our novel.[39]

Such perspectivism, however, had, in the age of Cervantes, to acknowledge ultimately a realm of the absolute—which was, in his case, that of Spanish Catholicism. Cervantes, while glorying in his role of the artist who can stay aloof from the *engaños a los ojos*, the *sueños* of this world, and create his own, always sees himself as overshadowed by supernal forces: the artist Cervantes never denies God, or His institutions, the King and the State. God, then, cannot be attracted into the artist's linguistic perspectivism; rather is Cervantes' God placed above the perspectives of language, He is said to be, as we have seen, the supreme *Entendedor* [Understander] of the language He has created—just as Cervantes, from his lower vantage point, seeks to be. Perhaps we may assume with Cervantes the old Neoplatonic belief in an artistic Maker who is enthroned above the manifold facets and perspectives of the world.

The story of the *Cautivo* (I, 37–42), one of the many tales interpolated into the main plot, exemplifies linguistic perspectivism made subservient to the divine. The maiden betrothed to the excaptive, who enters the stage dressed and veiled in Moorish fashion and who, without speaking a word, bows to the company in Moorish fashion, gives from the beginning the impression "que . . . debía de ser mora y que no sabía hablar cristiano" [that . . . she must certainly be a Moor and not know the Christian tongue] (note the expression *hablar cristiano* instead of *hablar castellano* [Castilian tongue] which, with its identification of "Spanish" and "Christian," anticipates the religious motif basic to the story). Dorotea is the one to ask the all-important question: "¿esta señora es cristiana o mora?" [is this lady a Christian or a Moor?]—to which the *Cautivo* answers that she is a Moor in her costume and in her body, but in her soul, a great Christian, although not yet baptized—but "Dios será servido que presto se bautice" [please God, she will soon be baptized] (again, we may see in this mention of God not only a conventional form but a suggestion of the main problem, which is the working of Divine Grace). The *Cautivo*, speaking in Arabic, asks his betrothed to lift her veil in order to show forth her enchanting beauty; when asked about her name, he gives it in the Arabic form: *lela Zoraida.* And now the Moorish girl herself speaks for the first time: "No, no Zoraida: María, María"—repeating this statement twice more (the last time half in Arabic, half in Spanish: "Sí, sí, María: Zoraida *macange* {'not at all'}"). The change of name which she claims—evidently in anticipation of the change of name which will accompany her baptism—is of deep significance; it is a profession of faith, of conversion. We will learn later that she must become a María because,

since her early childhood, she had been taken under the mantle
of the Virgin. After this first appearance of "Zoraida-María," whose two
names are nothing but the linguistic reflection of her double
nature, the episode is interrupted by Don Quijote's speech on
armas y letras (I, 38); thus, after the briefest of introductions, we
must lose sight for a while of Zoraida-María, the puzzle of whose
twofold name and Janus-like personality remains suspended in
midair. The interruption is significant: Cervantes, in the episodic
short stories, follows for the most part a technique opposed to
that of the main plot: in the latter we are always shown first the
objective reality of events, so that when they later become distorted after having passed through the alembic of Don Quijote's
mind (Sancho, in general, remains more true to the reality he
has experienced) we, from the knowledge we have previously
gained, are proof against the knight's folly. But, in the short stories, on the contrary, Cervantes' technique is to tantalize us with
glimpses into what seems an incredible situation, worthy of Quijote's own imagination (in our own story there suddenly appears
before the group of Don Quijote's friends assembled in an inn an
exotic-looking woman, dressed in outlandish gear, with her companion who has to talk for her) and with all the connotations of
the unreal; the author is careful to protract our suspense to the
utmost before giving us the solution of the initial puzzle. Thus
the interpolations of these episodic short stories, whose reality is
at least as fantastic as the most daring dreams of the mad knight,
offer another revelation of the perspectivism of Cervantes; we
have to do not only with the opposition between prosaic reality
and fantastic dreams: reality itself can be both prosaic and fantastic. If, in the main plot, Cervantes has carried out his program
of "derribar la máquina mal fundada" of the fantastic, he has
taken care to rebuild this machinery in the by-stories. And our
tale of the Captive is an excellent illustration of this rule.

When, after Don Quijote's speech, the Captive tells his story
ab ovo [from the beginning], explaining how the startling fact of a
"Zoraida-María" came to pass, we are allowed a glimpse into the
historic reality of that hybrid world of Mohammedans and Chris-

tians which was the equivalent in Cervantes' times of the *fronterizo* [frontier] milieu of the *romances*—only a more complicated variant because of the two different groups representative of the Mohammedan faith then facing the Spaniards: the Turks and the Arabs, the former the more ruthless type, the latter (to which Lela Marién and her father belong) the type more amenable to the Christian way of life. Indeed, the Arabs themselves seem to feel more akin to the Christian civilization than to the Turkish (the girl's father calls the Turks *canes* [dogs]; it is ironic that later, after he has been deeply wronged by the Christians, he must call them *perros* [dogs]).

As the Captive tells the story of the tragic events that took place against the background of the warring Turkish Empire, he embellishes his (Spanish-language) narrative with words from Turkish and Arabic, offering a linguistic mosaic that adds to the local color of his story. If we compare the Turkish words with the Arabic, we will note the sharpest of contrasts: the former are of a factual reference, narrowly descriptive, with no transcendental connotations (for the Turks are excluded from the possibility of Enlightenment by Grace): *leventes* [Turkish soldiers], *bagarinos* [Bagarine Moorish oarsmen], *baño* (wrongly offered as a Turkish word for "prison"), *pasamaques* [shoes], *zoltanis* [a type of coin], *gilecuelco* [jacket or slave's coat]; we find also the pejorative epithet *Uchalí Fartax* "que quiere decir en lengua turquesca *el renegado tiñoso,* porque lo era" [which means in Turkish "the scabby renegade," which he was] (again, the *convenientia* between names and objects!). The Arabic words, on the contrary, are nearly always connected with things religious and, more specifically, with things Christian—so that a kind of transposition (or perspectivism) is achieved: "Lela Marién" instead of "Nuestra Señora la Vírgen María"; "Alá" for the Christian God, and also the interjection *quelá* in the same reference; *nizarani* for "Christians"; *la zalá cristianesca* for "the Christian prayer," in which the adjective *cristianesco* (instead of *cristiano*), formed after *morisco* [Moorish], *turquesco* [Turkish], has something of the same transposed character, as if the Christian rites were seen from the outside. And, in addition to the linguistic medley offered the reader directly, there is a reference to the polyglot habits among the protagonists of the story. Zoraida, for example, chooses Arabic as the private language in which to talk and write to the Captive, but converses with the Christians (as also does her father) in the *lingua franca*—which language is characterized by the Captive as "lengua que en toda la Berbería, y aun en Constantinopla se habla entre cautivos y moros, que ni es morisca ni castellana ni de otra nación alguna, sino una mezcla de todas las lenguas, con la cual todos nos entendemos" [the language that is spoken between slaves and Moors all over Barbary, and even in Constantinople: it is neither Moorish nor Castilian, nor the tongue of any other country, but a mixture of every language, in which we can all understand one another], or "la bastarda lengua que . . . allí se usa" [the bastard language which . . . is in use there]: a characterization, it may be noted, which is not basically different from that offered in our times by Hugo Schuchardt ("Mischsprache," "Verkehrssprache"), the student of *lingua franca*, of the Creole languages, etc., and the advocate of an international artificial language. Castilian, Turkish, Arabic, with reminiscences of *lingua franca*: why this Babelic confusion of tongues in our story? It does not suffice to appeal to the historical fact that these languages were actually spoken at the time in the Ottoman Empire, where Cervantes himself had lived as a captive: for, in addition to the foreign phrases that might serve simply for local color, we have to do evidently with an express concern for each individual language as such—to the extent that we are always informed in which language a certain speech, letter, or dialogue was couched. It seems to me that Cervantes would point out that differences of language do not, by principle, hinder the working of Christian Grace—though he evidently grades the languages according to their penetrability by things Christian: Turkish is presented as on a lower level than Arabic, which lends itself so easily to the transposition of Christian concepts.[40]

And this linguistic transposition of things Christian into things Moorish reflects only the transposed situation of a Moor who becomes a Christian; the story of the Captive and of Zoraida-María shows Grace working toward the salvation of a disbeliever and toward the sacramental union, by a Christian marriage, of two beings of different races: above the divergence of race and language.[41] God understands the Christian longing of Zoraida for the *Alá cristiano*. It was the Virgin Mary, of whom she had learned from a Christian nurse, who inspired her to rescue the Christian soldier and to flee with him to a Christian country in order there to be baptized and married. When Zoraida speaks of Alá, everyone knows that the Christian God is meant—whose true nature shines through the linguistic disguise. The same symbol is carried out on another plane: when, from her window, Zoraida's white hand is seen, adorned with Moorish jewels (*ajorcas*), waving a Christian cross, the *ajorcas* are naturally overshadowed by the cross.[42] Again, in the case of Zoraida's letters to the prisoners, written in Arabic but adorned with the sign of the cross, it is clear that these indications of different cultural climates clearly express only one thing: her will to be a Christian. It is not the language, the gesture, the costume, or the body that matter to Him, but the meaning behind all the exterior manifestations: the soul. God, Cervantes is telling us, can recognize, behind the "perspective" of a disbeliever, His true faithful follower.

I cannot quite agree with Castro, who seems to see mainly the human side of the episode, when he says: "Love and religion (the latter as a kind of swathe of the former) bear Zoraida after her captive," and considers the story to be one of "harmony between human beings in perfect accord."[43] Rather, I should say that religion is the kernel, love the envelopment; we have here a drama of Divine Grace working against all possible handicaps and using the love between Moor and Christian as a means to an end: the conversion of Zoraida (and, incidentally, the return of a renegade[44] to the bosom of the Church); therefore Cervantes has devised his story against the background of the Spanish-Turkish wars, which ended with the victory of the Spaniards at Lepanto and in which, as Titian has represented it, Spain succors Christian faith.

I concur absolutely with Castro, however, when he goes on to say that this story of abduction is the most violent and the most tragic of all the episodes in the novel: Zoraida, in her zeal to receive holy baptism and the sacrament of Christian marriage, must cheat her father, must see him subjected by her doings to the violence of the Christians who truss him up and finally leave him marooned on a desert island, where he cries out to his daughter, alternately cursing and beseeching her. Here is a good Arab, meek and truthful to Christians, who is thrown back to the Mohammedan god by the ruthless deed of his Christian daughter. That such sins may be committed for the rescue of a soul can only be explained, Cervantes seems to tell us, by the incalculable will of Providence. Why should these sins be made corollary to the salvation of the particular soul of Zoraida—while the soul of her father becomes thereby utterly lost to salvation? What whimsicality of God! I should say that this scene exhibits not so much the "abysses of the human,"⁴⁵ as Castro has it, but rather the "abysses of the divine." No harmonious earthly marriage could be concluded on the basis of such a terrifying violation of the Fourth Commandment; but God is able to put the laws of morality out of function in order to reach His own goal.

In our story, which is the story of a great deceit, the words referring to "deceit" take on a particularly subtle double entendre. When, for example, Zoraida, in one of her letters to the Captive, says: "no te fíes de ningún moro, porque son todos *marfuzes*" [do not trust any Moor, they are all *deceitful*] of her Moslem coreligionists, she is using an originally Arabic word for "treacherous" which had come to be borrowed by the Spaniards, probably to refer, primarily, to the treachery of the Mohammedans (meaning something like "false as a Moor"); the choice of this word, which sounds rather strange when used by an Arab, must mean that Zoraida is judging the Arabs according to Christian prejudices (it is ironical that, in this story, it is the Arabs who are faithful and kind, and the Christians who are *marfuzes*—although working toward a goal presumably willed by Providence). Again, the accusation of cheating is reversed when Zoraida, speaking as a Moor to the Christian captive, in the presence of her father, remarks: "vosotros cristianos siempre mentís en cuanto decís, y os hacéis pobres por engañar a los moros" [you Christians always lie and make yourselves out poor to cheat us Moors]; here, where her judgment is, indeed, factually justified, she is actually speaking disingenuously—in order to further the stratagem planned by the Christians. The discrepancy between words and meaning, between judgment and behavior, has reached such proportions that we can view only with perplexity the "abyss of the divine" which makes it possible that such evil means are accepted to further a noble purpose; the story offers us no way out but to try to share Zoraida's belief in the beneficent intervention of Lela Marién, who has prompted the good-wicked enterprise ("¡Plega a Alá, padre mío, que Lela Marién, que ha sido la causa de que yo sea cristiana, ella re consuele en tu tristeza!" [May it please Allah, dear father, that Lela Marién, who has been the cause of my becoming a Christian, may console you in your grief]). When Zoraida, speaking to her father, states of her deed "que parece tan buena como tú, padre amado, la juzgas por mala" [which I know to be good, beloved father, though it appears wicked to you], we are offered basically the same perspectivistic pattern that we have noted in the case of the *baciyelmo*: it is implied, evidently, that Lela Marién knows of no perspectivism. There can be no doubt that what Cervantes is dealing with here is the tortuous and Jesuitic divinity that he was able to see in his time—whose decisions he accepts, while bringing out all the complications involved. Along with the submission to the divine there is instituted a tragic trial against it, a trial on moral grounds, and, on these grounds, the condemnation is unmitigated; the sacramental force of a father's curse is not entirely counterbalanced by the sacramental force of the Christian rites, the desire for which on Zoraida's part brought about the father's plight. Perhaps no writer, remaining within the boundaries of orthodox religion, has revealed more of the perplexities inherent in the theocratic order (a Nietzsche might have called this story an example of the immorality of God and have advocated the overthrow of such a God—whereas Cervantes quietly stays within the boundaries of the Christian fold). And this acme of submissive daring has been achieved by placing the divine beyond the perspectives which appear to the human eye.

Zoraida herself, for all her religious fervor, innocence, and supernatural beauty is, at the same time, capable of great wickedness. And again linguistic perspectivism is invoked in order to bring this side of her nature into relief. There is a moment when the band of fugitives passes the promontory called, after the mistress of Roderick, the last of the Gothic kings, *cabo de la Cava Rumía,* "la mala mujer cristiana" [*the Cape of the Cava Rumía,* the wicked Christian woman]; they insist, however, that to them it is not the "abrigo de mala mujer, sino puerto seguro de nuestro remedio" [wicked woman's shelter, but a secure haven of refuge]. Now, when the name of this infamous woman, who sinned for love, is brought before the reader, he cannot fail to think of Zoraida— though, in the comparison with the Arabic prostitute "por quien se perdió España" [through whom Spain was lost], the betrothed of the Captive must appear as a pure woman, who refused to live in a state of sin before her marriage. At the same time, however, Cervantes may wish us to realize how close was Zoraida to the abyss, and to see the ward of the Virgin, for a moment, under the perspective of la Cava.[46]

If we look back now over the development of this essay, we will see that we have been led from a plethora of names, words, languages—from polyonomasia, polyetymologia, and polyglottism—to the linguistic perspectivism of the artist Cervantes, who knows that the transparence of language is a fact for God alone. And, at this point, I may be allowed to repeat, as a kind of epitomizing epilogue, the final passages of a lecture on the *Quijote* which I have given at several universities—which, I trust, will serve to round out the linguistic details I have pointed out earlier and to put them into relationship with the whole of the novel: a relationship which, in the course of our linguistic discussion, has already been tentatively indicated. After explaining that the *Quijote* appeals as well to children as to adults because of its combination of imagination and criticism, and that the modern genre of the critical novel, which started with a criticism of books and of a bookish culture (a criticism of the romances of chivalry) and came to be expanded to a new integration of the critical and the imaginative, was the discovery of Cervantes, I continued thus:

It is one of the great miracles of history (which is generally regarded deterministically by professional historians, who present individual phenomena as enclosed within tight compartments) that the greatest deeds sometimes occur at a place and a time when the historian would least expect them. It is a historical miracle that, in the Spain of the Counter-Reformation, when the trend was toward the reestablishment of authoritarian discipline, an artist should have arisen who, thirty-two years before Descartes's *Discours de la méthode* (that autobiography of an independent philosophical thought, as Gustave Lanson has called it), was to give us a narrative which is simply one exaltation of the independent mind of man—and of a particularly powerful type of man: of the artist. It is not Italy, with its Ariosto and Tasso, not France with its Rabelais and Ronsard, but Spain that gave us a narrative which is a monument to the narrator qua narrator, qua artist. For, let us not be mistaken: the real protagonist of this novel is not Quijote, with his continual misrepresentation of reality, or Sancho with his skeptical half-endorsement of quixotism—and surely not any of the central figures of the illusionistic by-stories: the hero is Cervantes, the artist himself, who combines a critical and illusionistic art according to his free will. From the moment we open the book[47] to the moment we put it down, we are given to understand that an almighty overlord is directing us, who leads us where he pleases.

The prologue of the whole work shows us Cervantes in the perplexity of an author putting the final touches to his work, and we understand that the "friend" who seemingly came to his aid with a solution was only one voice within the freely fabricating poet. And, on the last page of the book when, after Quijote's Christian death, Cervantes has that Arabian historian Cide Hamete Benengeli lay away his pen, to rest forever, on the top of the cupboard in order to forestall any further spurious continuation (after the manner of Avellaneda) of the novel, we know that the reference to the Arabian pseudo-historian is only a pretext for Cervantes to reclaim for himself the relationship of real father (no longer the "stepfather," as in the prologue) to his book. Then the pen delivers itself of a long speech, culminating in the words: "For me alone Don Quijote was born and I for him; his task was to act, mine to write. For we alone are made for each other" ("Para mí sola nació Don Quijote, y yo para él; él supo

obrar, y yo escribir; solos los dos somos para en uno"). An im-
perious *alone* (*solo*[s]), which only Cervantes could have said and
in which all the Renaissance pride of the poet asserts itself: the
poet who was the traditional immortalizer of the great deeds of
historical heroes and princes. An Ariosto could have said the same
words about the Duke of Ferrara.

The function of eulogizing princes was, as is well known, the
basis of the economic situation of the Renaissance artist: he was
given sustenance by the prince in return for the immortal glory
which he bestowed upon his benefactor.[48] But Don Quijote is no
prince from whom Cervantes could expect to receive a pension,
no doer of great deeds in the outer world (his greatness lay only
in his warm heart), and not even a being who could be attested
in any historical source—however much Cervantes might pretend to such sources. Don Quijote acquired his immortality exclusively at the hands of Cervantes—as the latter well knows and
admits. Obviously, Quijote wrought only what Cervantes wrote,
and he was born for Cervantes as much as Cervantes was born
for him! In the speech of the pen of the pseudo-chronicler we
have the most discreet and the most powerful self-glorification
of the artist which has ever been written. The artist Cervantes
grows by the glory which his characters have attained; and in the
novel we see the process by which the figures of Don Quijote
and Sancho become living persons, stepping out of the novel, so
to speak, to take their places in real life—finally to become immortal historical figures. Thomas Mann, in a recent essay on the
Quijote, has said: "This is quite unique. I know of no other hero
of a novel in world literature who would equally, so to speak,
live off the glory of his own glorification" ("ein Held, . . . [der] von
dem Ruhm seines Ruhmes, von seiner Besungenheit lebte").[49] In
the second part of the novel, when the Duke and Duchess ask
to see the by now historical figures of Quijote and Panza, the
latter says to the Duchess: "I am Don Quijote's squire who is to
be found also *in the story* and who is called Sancho Panza—unless
they have changed me in the cradle—I mean to say, at the
printer's." In such passages, Cervantes willingly destroys the artistic illusion: he, the puppeteer, lets us see the strings of his

puppet show: "see, reader, this is not life, but a stage, a book: art; recognize the life-giving power of the artist as a thing distinct from life!"[50]

By multiplying his masks (the friend of the prologue, the Arabian historian, sometimes the characters who serve as his mouthpiece), Cervantes seems to strengthen his grip on that whole artistic cosmos. And the strength of the grip is enhanced by the very nature of the protagonists: Quijote is what we would call today a split personality, sometimes rational, sometimes foolish; Sancho, too, at times no less quixotic than his master, is at other times incalculably rational. In this way, the author makes it possible for himself to decide when his characters will act reasonably, when foolishly (no one is more unpredictable than a fool who pretends to wisdom). At the start of his journey with Sancho, Don Quijote promises his squire an island kingdom to be ruled over by him, just as was done in the case of numerous squires in literature. But, acting on his critical judgment (of which he is not devoid), Don Quijote promises to give it to him immediately after their conquest—instead of waiting until the squire has reached old age, as is the custom in the books of chivalry. The quixotic side of Sancho accepts this prospective kingship without questioning its possibility, but his more earthly nature visualizes—and criticizes—the actual scene of the coronation: how would his rustic spouse Juana Gutiérrez look with a crown on her head? Two examples of foolishness, two critical attitudes: none of them is the attitude of the writer, who remains above the two split personalities and the four attitudes.

With the Machiavellian principle "divide and conquer" applied to his characters, the author succeeds in making himself indispensable to the reader: while, in his prologue, Cervantes calls for a critical attitude on our part, he makes us depend all the more on his guidance through the psychological intricacies of the narrative: here, at least, he leaves us no free will. We may even infer that Cervantes rules imperiously over his own self: it was he who felt this self to be split into a critical and an illusionistic part (*desengaño* and *engaño* [disillusionment and illusion]); but in this baroque ego he made order, a precarious order, it is true, which was reached only once by Cervantes in all his works—and which was reached in Spain only by Cervantes (for Calderón, Lope, Quevedo, Gracián decided that the world is only illusion and dreams, "los sueños sueños son"). And indeed, only once in world literature has this precarious order come into being: later thinkers and artists did not stop at proclaiming the inanity of the world: they went so far as to doubt the existence of any universal order and to deny a Creator, or at least, when imitating Cervantes' perspectivism (Gide, Proust, Conrad, Joyce, Virginia Woolf, Pirandello),[51] they have failed to sense the unity behind perspectivism—so that, in their hands, the personality of the author is allowed to disintegrate.

Cervantes stands at the other pole from that modern dissolution of the personality of the narrator: what grandeur there is in his attempt—made in the last moment before the unified Christian vision of the world was to fall asunder—to restore this vision on the artistic plane, to hold before our eyes a cosmos split into two separate halves: disenchantment and illusion, which, nevertheless, by a miracle, do not fall apart! Modern anarchy checked by a classical will to equipoise (the baroque attitude)! We recognize now that it is not so much that Cervantes' nature is split in two (critic and narrator) because this is required by the nature of Don Quijote, but rather that Don Quijote is a split character because his creator was a critic-poet who felt with almost equal strength the urge of illusionary beauty and of pellucid clarity.

To modern readers the "schizophrenic" Don Quijote might seem to be a typical case of social frustration: a person whose madness is conditioned by the social insignificance into which the caste of the knights had fallen, with the beginnings of modern warfare—just as, in Flaubert's *Un coeur simple*, we are meant to see as socially conditioned the frustrations of Félicité, the domestic servant, which lead to the aberration of her imagination. I would, however, warn the reader against interpreting Cervantes in terms of Flaubert, since Cervantes himself has done nothing to encourage such a sociological approach. Don Quijote is able to recover his sanity, if only on his death-bed; and his erstwhile madness is but one reflection of that generally human lack of reason—above which the author has chosen to take his stand.[52]

High above this worldwide cosmos of his making, in which hundreds of characters, situations, vistas, themes, plots and subplots are merged, Cervantes' artistic self is enthroned, an all-embracing creative self, Nature-like, God-like, almighty, all-wise, all-good—and benign: this visibly omnipresent Maker reveals to us the secrets of his creation, he shows us the work of art in the making and the laws to which it is necessarily subjected. For this artist is God-like but not deified; far be it from us to conceive of Cervantes as attempting to dethrone God, replacing Him by the artist as a superman. On the contrary, Cervantes always bows before the supernal wisdom of God, as embodied in the teachings of the Catholic Church and the established order of the state and of society. Qua moralist, Cervantes is not at all "perspectivistic."[53]

Nor can we expect to find in Cervantes any of that romantic revolt of the artist against society. But, on the other hand, the artist Cervantes has extended, by the mere art of his narrative, the Demiurge-like, almost cosmic independence of the artist. His humor, which admits of many strata, perspectives, masks—of relativization and dialectics—bears testimony to his high position above the world. His humor is the freedom of the heights, no fate-bound Dionysiac dissolution of the individual into nothingness and night, as with Schopenhauer and Wagner, but a freedom beneath the dome of that religion which affirms the freedom of the will. There is, in the world of his creation, the bracing air with which we may fill our lungs and by which our individual senses and judgment are sharpened; and the crystalline lucidity of an artistic Maker in its manifold reflections and refractions.

Notes

1. Américo Castro, *El pensamiento de Cervantes* (Madrid: Imprenta de la Librería y Casa Editorial Hernando, 1925).

2. Joaquín Casalduero, "La composición de 'El ingenioso hidalgo Don Quijote de la Mancha,' " *Revista de filología hispánica*, 2 (1940): 323–69.
3. Helmut Hatzfeld, *Don Quijote als Wortkunstwerk* (Leipzig: B. G. Teubner, 1927).
4. Miguel de Cervantes, *The Adventures of Don Quixote*, trans. J. M. Cohen (Harmondsworth, U.K.: Penguin Books, 1981), has been used for translations throughout this essay. We have occasionally altered Cohen's translation to make clear the elements necessary to Spitzer's argument. All Spanish quotations were checked against the Aguilar edition, *El ingenioso hidalgo Don Quijote de la Mancha*, eds. Justo García Soriano and Justo García Morales (Madrid: Aguilar, 1968).—EDS.
5. And in that same pastoral game (II, 67) Sansón Carrasco would become "el pastor Sansonino" or "el pastor Carrascón" (two names!), the barber>"Nicolás Miculoso" (after *Nemoroso*, as Quijote explains), *el Cura* [the priest]>"el pastor Curiambro" (reminiscence of the giant Caraculiambro?); as for the name of Sancho's wife, however, the squire, who always pays heed to the *convenientia* of words and objects, agrees only to "Teresona" as the pastoral name for his fat Teresa. We see why he cannot agree to "Teresaina": this name, proposed by Sansón Carrasco (II, 73), is so evocative of the ethereal music of the flute (*dulzaina*) that Don Quijote must laugh at "la aplicación del nombre."
6. A pendant to Quijote, the believer in an unreal order of virtue, is Cardenio, the lover who cannot face that injustice which so often obtains in the reality of love. Thus we will not be astonished to find that the onomastic pattern, dear to the romances of chivalry, represented by "Caballero de la Triste Figura" is also applied to Cardenio: he is alternatively called (by the shepherds who tell his story) "Roto de la Mala Figura," "Caballero de la Sierra," "Caballero del Bosque" [Ragged Knight of the Sorry Countenance, Knight of the Mountains, Knight of the Wood]—before he himself is allowed to state his simple, real name: "Mi nombre es Cardenio" [My name is Cardenio].

The importance of the *name* for the Middle Ages appears here most clearly; any knight of romance, Amadis or Perceval or Yvain, is presented as undergoing an inner evolution, whose outward manifestations are the different "adventures" which mark his career; and it is by virtue of these adventures that he acquires different names, each of which is revelatory of the particular stage attained; in this way, the evolution is clearly labeled for the reader. Yvain acquires a new dignity, so to speak, when he becomes the "Chevalier au Lion"; "Orlando innamorato" is a different person from "Orlando furioso." Consequently, a mistake in names is no slight mistake: it is a sin against the law of inner evolution, which presides over the events of a heroic life. It is significant that Don Quijote speaks (I, 18) of "la ventura aquella de Amadís {de Grecia}, *cuando se llamaba el Caballero de la Ardiente Espada*, que fué una de las mejores espadas que tuvo caballero en el mundo" [It is even possible that my fortune may procure me the sword Amadis wore *when he was called the Knight of the Burning Sword*. It was one of the best ever worn by any knight in all the world]. It is precisely because this extraordinary sword distinguishes objectively one of the exemplary phrases of the evolution of the knight that the name under which he appears has a somewhat objective, temporally definable validity.

7. In II, 2, Sancho reports with pride that, though Don Quijote and his beloved are being celebrated by the historiographer Cide Hamete Berengana {sic} under their fanciful names ("El ingenioso hidalgo," "Dulcinea del Toboso"), his name has suffered no such treatment: "que me mientan . . . *con mi mesmo nombre de Sancho Panza* [I'm mentioned, too, . . . *under my own name of Sancho Panza*].

8. Again, we have evidence of the importance of nomenclature: a change of suffix, in itself, may be equivalent to a change of linguistic perspective.

In another incident (I, 22), from one of the secondary episodes, we are told that, when the guard speaks of his prisoner, Ginés de Pasamonte, as "el famoso Ginés de Pasamonte, que por otro nombre llaman Ginesillo de Parapilla" [the famous Ginés de Pasamonte, alias Ginesillo de Parapilla], the other retorts: "Señor Comisario, . . . no andemos ahora a deslindar nombres y sobrenombres. Ginés me llamo, y no Ginesillo, y Pasamonte es mi alcurnia, y no Parapilla, como voacé dice . . . algún día sabrá alguno si me llamo Ginesillo de Parapilla o no. . . . Yo haré que no me lo llamen" [Sargeant, . . . don't let us be settling names and surnames now. I am called Ginés, not Ginesillo, and Pasamonte is my surname, not Parapilla as you say . . . but one day somebody may learn whether my name is Ginesillo de Parapilla or not. . . . I'll stop them calling me that.] Again, just as in the case of Sancho's rebuke to the one who had altered Quijote's title, Cervantes takes occasion to show the natural indignation aroused by a violation of the "perspective" which the bearer of the name has chosen and under which he has a right to appear.

9. The same type of justification of a mispronunciation by the invention ad hoc of a (secondary) relationship is found in II, 3, when

Sancho, in order to explain his version of the Arabic name *Benengeli* (i.e., Berengena), refers to the Moors' predilection for *berenjenas*.

10. Spitzer has evidently confused the appearance of Merlin in II, 35, with that of Trifaldi in II, 38.—Eds.

11. Sancho offers us another example of popular "synonymic derivation": *rata* "rate, installment of payment" has been understood by him as "rat," which, with him, must lead to *gata* "cat." As a matter of fact, the procedure by which developments take place in argot is not basically different from this: *dauphin* "dolphin">"pimp" in French argot was interpreted as *dos fin* so that a *dos vert* could follow. The modern linguist would say that Sancho has the makings of an excellent subject for an inquirer such as Jules Gilliéron, who wanted to seize, on the spot, the working of the popular imagination. When faced with the problem of language, Sancho is not lazy and passive, as he is in general (and in this incessant linguistic criticism and linguistic activity, side by side with inactivity in other realms of life, he is typically Spanish): he asks himself why the Spanish battle cry is *¡Santiago y cierra España!* [St. James and close Spain!]: "¿Esta, por ventura, España abierta, y de modo, que es menester cerrarla, o qué ceremonia es esta?" [Is Spain perhaps open, that she has to be closed? Or what is this ceremony?]. Erroneously, he seeks to interpret, by contemporary patterns, a way of speech obscured by historic development. While he does not know as much historical grammar as does Antonio Rodríguez Marín, the modern commentator of the *Don Quijote*, he shows himself to be aware of the basic problem of linguistics: the opaqueness of certain ways of speech.

12. Accordingly, this variety of names would be on one level with such pseudo-historical interruptions of the narrative as we have seen in I, 2, when Cervantes pretends to hesitate about which particular adventure of his protagonist to narrate first: it seems that there are some *autores* ("authors" or "authorities") who say that the adventure of Puerto Lápice was the first; others contend the same about that of the windmills, while Cervantes, himself, has ascertained, from the annals of La Mancha . . . etc.

We shall see later, however, that the pseudo-historical device has implications much more important than the parodying of chronicles.

13. Cervantes, *El ingenioso hidalgo Don Quijote de la Mancha*, ed. Antonio Rodríguez Marín, 7 (Madrid: Ediciones Atlas, 1913), 29–30.

14. Leo Spitzer, "Dieu et ses noms (Francs les cumandent a Deu et a ses nuns, Roland, 3694)," *PMLA*, 56, no. 1 (March 1941): 13–32.

15. It is in the medieval vein that Cervantes, in the Trifaldi episode

(II, 40), has the name of the horse *Clavileño el Alígero* |Clavileño the Swift| explained as follows: "cuyo nombre conviene con el ser de leño y con la clavija que trae en la frente y con la ligereza con que camina" |which name fits him because he is wooden, because of the peg he has in his forehead, and because of the speed at which he travels|: *convenir, conveniencia* are the medieval (originally Ciceronian) expressions for "harmony"—as well as "grammatical accord," harmony between word and meaning, etc.

16. A characteristic trait of the ancient and medieval etymological procedures was to explain by compounds where the modern linguist would assume derivation: Thus English *dismal* was explained by *dies mali* instead of as a derivative from Old French *disme* "dime." |Spitzer, "Eng. 'dismal'=O. F. '*dism-al,' " *Modern Language Notes*, 57, no. 7 (Nov. 1942): 602–13.| In the same vein is the decomposition of the derivative *Truff-ald-{ino}* into the two parts *tri* + *fald*–. Compare also Sancho's decomposition (II, 3) of *gramática* into *grama* (the herb) + *tica* (the meaning of the latter word has not yet been elucidated by commentators).

17. Nicolo Tommaseo and Bernardo Bellini, *Dizionario della lingua italiana*, 9 (Turin: Unione Tipografico-editrice, 1865), 716.

18. Rabelais, *Gargantua and Pantagruel*, trans. J. M. Cohen (Harmondsworth, U.K.: Penguin Books, 1955), bk. 1, ch. 16.

19. The trick intended for the protagonists is revealed in the midst of the pageant, when the majordomo, who plays the countess, corrects himself: "a este su criado, *digo, a esta su criada*" |this is your waiting-man—*I should say, waiting-woman*|.

It may be stated that such baroque effects are on the increase in the second part of the *Quijote*, where pageants, *burlas*, and *truffe* flourish (compare "Las bodas de Camacho" |Camacho's wedding, II, 20, and II, 21|). In part I we are shown the aggressive Don Quijote and his grumbling but faithful follower Sancho challenging the outward world—meeting, in their adventures, with a flux of humanity in a series of chance encounters against the fluid background of roadsides and inns. In part II, however, the couple appears rather as being challenged than as challenging the world—and this world, the world of the big city, the world of the aristocracy, is now more formidable, more firmly constituted. The resistance of the first environment was not sufficient to bring about the necessary cure of the knight: Quijote must be brought to face the criticism of the higher spheres of society, where he is victimized with sophisticated *burlas*. The aristocrats play theater for Don Quijote and Sancho (in a way that may remind us of Shakespeare's Sly—and the "governorship" of Sancho resembles Sly's temporary courtship). And theater, like *sueño* [dream], is bound to end with an awakening from illusion. This is a baroque theme.

If Mr. Stephen Gilman is right in claiming for Avellaneda's continuation of the Quijote a baroque style, it might be apposite to add that Cervantes himself, whether prompted by his competitor or not (and I personally think, rather not), went the same path of "baroquization" in his own continuation of the story ["El falso 'Quijote': Versión barroca del 'Quijote' de Cervantes, *Revista de filología hispánica*, 5 (1943): 148–57].

20. Don Quijote himself explains words according to an Isidorian scheme: for example, when he takes it upon himself to explain *albogues* (II, 67), he begins by describing the *res* designated by the word ("albogues son unas chapas . . ." [*albogues* are thin brass plates . . .]), and follows this with the etymon: it is originally Arabic, he says, as the prefix *al–* suggests. Don Quijote cannot stop here, however; giving full rein to his associative imagination, he goes on to mention other Arabic words in Spanish likewise characterized by *al–*, and ends by including certain loan-words with a termination in *–i*.

21. The same "twofold pattern" is followed for the etymology of the (legendary, medieval) island of which Sancho is to become the ruler (II, 45): "la insula Barataria, o ya porque el lugar se llamaba Baratario o ya por el *barato* con que se la había dado el gobierno" [this was called the Isle Barataria, either because the town's name was *Baratario*, or because of the *barato*, or low price, at which he had got the government]; here, the first etymology is the formal or tautological one which Cervantes slyly proposes (in order to remain faithful to the dichotomy) as an alternative to the second—which is the historically "real" etymology.

My reason for believing that the *hidalgo* had *Lanzarote* in mind when he changed his name is found in the episode of I, 2, where Don Quijote adapts the text of the old *romance* [ballad] to his own situation, substituting his own name for that of the protagonist: "Nunca fuera caballero/ De damas tan bien servido/Como fuera don Quijote/Cuando de su aldea vino" [Never was there knight/By ladies so attended/As was Don Quixote/When he left his village]. The suffix *–ote* (as in *monigote, machacote* [dunce, bore]) has a comic ring for the reader but not, evidently, for the coiner of the name.

We have a somewhat similar bivalence in the case of the name *Rocinante*—though here, of course, it is not the suffix but the radical which provides the comic effect. The noble connotation of *–ante*, that participial ending which had dropped out of current use in Old Romance languages, is to be found, with a nuance of high distinction, in such epic names as Old French *Baligant, Tervagant*, and in common nouns such as Old French *aumirant* (Spanish *almirante* [admiral]) and Spanish *emperante* [emperor] (found along with *emperador* in the *Libro de buen amor*). Thus, our learned knight, with his "epic imagination," came naturally by his predilection for such a pattern of nomenclature.

As for the factual etymology of the word *quijote* (<Old French *cuissot*, "cuissart"), this has been established by Yakov Malkiel. Mr. Malkiel, however, confuses historical linguistics with the study of a work of art when he writes: "The etymology of this word naturally aroused the curiosity of Cervantes" ["The Etymology of Hispanic *que(i)xar*," *Language*, 21 (1945): 156]. In reality, Cervantes has not shown himself interested in the etymology of the common noun *quijote*, but in that of the proper name *Quijote*; and the latter was not, for him, derived from Old French *cuissot*, but from *Lanzarote*, and from the group *Quijada, Quijano* (whatever the origin of these may be).

22. As a nonlinguistic example of such perspectivism, we may point to the passage made famous by Hume: two kinsmen of Sancho, called upon to give their opinion of a hogshead of wine, find it excellent, in the main, except for a peculiar flavor—on which they disagree. The one insists it has a leathery taste, the other, a metallic taste. When they have finally drunk their way to the bottom of the cask, they find a rusty iron key with a leather strap attached.

23. It is not astonishing that Dostoevsky, that great absolutist who delighted in showing up the relativity in human affairs, should have imitated the polyonomasia of Cervantes: In *Crime and Punishment*, the monomaniac Raskolnikov (whose name, related to *raskolnik* "heretic," suggests his monomania) has a friend named *Razumichin* (related to *razum* "reason"), who is the flexible, optimistic, helpful, and loquacious defender of reason: his flexibility of mind is mirrored in the alterations to which his name is subjected by other characters in the novel: *Vrazumichin* (to *vrazumlyaty* "to explain") and *Rassudkin* (to *rassudok* "judgment").

24. Sancho, who appears so often as the representative of that Catholic positivism which takes the world, as it is, as God-given, without envisaging the possibility of a more ideal order, expresses his linguistic doubts about the mysterious, significant, and musical names of Quijote's making, just as he usually (though not always) suspects the *arcana* of the world of enchantment that his master visualizes (I, 18): "no eran fantasmas ni hombres encantados, como vuestra merced dice, sino hombres de carne y de hueso *como nosotros*, y todos, según los oí nombrar . . .

tenían sus nombres que el uno se llamaba Pedro Martínez y el otro Tenorio Hernández, y el Ventero oí que se llamaba Juan Palomeque el Zurdo" [they were not phantoms or enchanted, as Your Worship says, but flesh-and-blood men *like ourselves*. And they had all got names, for I heard them . . . one of them was called Pedro Martinez, another Tenorio Hernandez, and I heard them call the innkeeper Juan Palomeque, the left-handed]. When he hears from Quijote's lips the fantastic names of beings from a world he does not believe to exist, he tries to bring these names down to earth, to adapt them to his homely environment. And in I, 29, when it is explained to him that the princess Micomicona is called so after her estate Micomicón in Guiney, Sancho is happy only when he can find a parallel in the names of the common people he knows, such as Pedro de Alcalá, Juan de Úbeda, Diego de Valladolid, who are named after their birthplaces.

Evidently, the names in the world of Don Quijote must be, in opposition to the homespun names of Sancho's world, the more grandiloquent the less they cover of reality: they are of the grotesque, that is, the comically frightening kind, that distinguishes the names of Pulci's and Rabelais's giants: we find (I, 18) Caraculiambro de Malindranía; el gran emperador Alifanfarón, señor de la grande isla Trapobana [the great Emperor Alifanfaron, lord of the great island of Trapobana]; Pentapolín del Arremangado Brazo [Pentapolin of the Naked Arm]; Espartafilardo del Bosque, duque de Nerbia [Espartafilardo of the Wood, Duke of Nerbia]; and (I, 30) Pandafilando de la Fosca Vista [Pandafilando of the Frowning Eye]—which last is transposed by Sancho (in accord with the feeling he has acquired for linguistic correspondences between his master's speech and his own: *f* > *h*, *-ando* > *-ado*) into *Pandahilado*; similarly, the poetic name *Fili* becomes, with Sancho, *hilo* [thread] (I, 23): Sancho's capacity of transposition is the linguistic equivalent of his capacity for adopting the fanciful schemes of Don Quijote. Another aspect of Sancho's positivistic approach is his lack of that symbolic feeling so characteristic of his master. He gauges symbolic actions according to their "positive" or pragmatic value in actual life: when Don Quijote invites him, in order to symbolize the Christian democracy of men, to sit at his table with him and his shepherds, Sancho refuses because of the inconvenience of having to be on his best behavior at the master's table. On the other hand (for Cervantes knows always an "on-the-other-hand"), Sancho's unmystical attitude is capable of producing good results: he is, during his governorship, able to uncover the swindle involving the money concealed in the staff, precisely because he disregards the symbolic value of the staff.

25. For us to apply this label to the knight striving to revive a medieval chivalric world, in the midst of his contemporary world of mass armies employing firearms, may seem surprising to the reader. But the humanistic world was a continuation of the medieval world: and what Don Quijote seeks to revive and reenact are humanistic dreams of antiquarians. The humanist tends to revive, by the strength of his imagination, a more beautiful past, regardless of how it may fit into his time; this is the ideal strength and the weakness of any humanist, and Cervantes has described both aspects.

26. It has not been sufficiently emphasized that Cervantes, as so often happens (e.g., in the case of the diptychs Marcela–Don Quijote, Cardenio–Don Quijote, *el Cautivo–el Oidor* [the Captive–the Judge]; or in Don Quijote's speech on *armas y letras*), is proceeding by offering pendant pictures when he opposes to Don Quijote's vision in *la cueva de Montesinos* the speech of the *licenciado* on the humanistic books which he intends to write. Both turn to the past: the one seeks to relive it in the present, the other, to exhume it and transmit it through his books; both attempts, illustrating the same pattern of thought, are equally futile. Don Quijote's account of his visions is welcomed by the *licenciado* as a new "source" for his compilation of fanciful lore—while these same visions have been inspired by that same sort of lore.

27. Cervantes himself must have been vulnerable to the humanistic "book-virus": he tells us that he used to pick up every printed scrap of paper—surely not, like Saint Francis, because some sacred words might be on it, but in order to live through the printed words a vicarious existence, in the fashion of his Don Quijote, that is, as a "novel-reader."

Cervantes must also, like any humanist, have delighted in the deciphering of old documents: he tells us of the adventure of having Benengeli's Arabic deciphered for his benefit; in the story of the *Cautivo*, the Arabic letter of Lela Zoraida is puzzled out; and, in II, 39, a Syriac text is referred to: "escritas en lengua siríaca unas letras, que habiéndose declarado en la candayesca, y ahora en la castellana, encierran esta sentencia" [some characters written in the Syriac tongue, which, translated into Candayesque and then into Castilian, make up this sentence]. To be polyglot is to delight in many perspectives.

28. It could be said, of nearly every character in the *Quijote*, that he appears located at his own particular linguistic level, somewhere along

a hierarchic ladder. The duchess, for example, who is quite conscious of her social and linguistic superiority over Sancho, and who takes care to distinguish her speech from his (II, 32: "la flor de las ceremonias, o cirimonias, *como vos decís*" [the flower of ceremonies, or "cirimonies," *as you call them*]) must be shown her inferiority, at least in matters linguistic, to Don Quijote: when the latter has occasion to speak of "la retórica ciceroniana y *demostina*" [Ciceronian and *Demosthenian* rhetoric], the duchess asks about the significance of the last word, remarking "que es vocablo que no le he oído en todos los días de mi vida" [it is a word I have never heard in all the days of my life], and is taunted by her husband: "habéis andado deslumbrada en la tal pregunta" [you have shown your ignorance by asking such a question]. Thus the same character has a chance to snub and be snubbed linguistically—as well as otherwise.

On the other hand, we may ask ourselves: does Cervantes the superhumanist smile here at the reader over the head of the humanistic character Don Quijote? For the adjective *demostino* (an evidently popular haplology for *demostenino* "of Demosthenes") is incorrectly formed. Is Cervantes here revindicating again for himself a position above his protagonist by having Quijote the scholar make elementary mistakes?

Even when the characters lapse into a foreign language, there is a difference according to social classes—the standard "second language" in Cervantes' time being Italian. Don Quijote, being a Spanish humanist, must, of course, know Italian: he expressly states (II, 52) that he knows "somewhat" of Tuscan and can sing some stanzas of Ariosto; he examines a printer as to his knowledge of Italian vocabulary ("does he know that *pignatta* corresponds to the Spanish *olla* [stew]?"); and he occasionally inserts Italian forms into his facetious speeches: II, 24: "Notable *espilorchería*, como dice el italiano" [A notable *spilorceria*, as the Italians say]; II, 25: "Dígame vuestra merced, señor adivino: ¿qué peje pillamo?" [Tell me, you, Master Fortune-teller, *what fish do we catch?*]. Here we have rather farfetched idioms by which the humanist Quijote shows how conversant he is with the nuances that are better expressed in Italian than in Spanish.

We also find, in our novel, Italianisms used in the speech of the lower strata of society, where they seem to suggest the language of conviviality: the Ventero says of Maese Pedro (II, 25): "es hombre galante (como dicen in Italia) y bon compaño" [he's a gallant man, as they say in Italy, and a boon companion]; in the drinking scene between Sancho, his ex-companion Ricote, and the other pseudo-pilgrims, a *lingua franca* version of Italian is used at the height of their merriment (II, 54): "Español y tudesqui tuto uno: bon compaño"—(Sancho:) "Bon compaño, jura Di" |"Spaniard and Dutchman all one—goot gombanion," and Sancho would reply, "Goot Gombanion, I swear by Gott"]. Clemencín and Rodríguez Marín are therefore wrong when they object to a *caro patrón mío* |dear master| in the mouth of Sancho (II, 23); this is not humanistic Italian but the language of plain people indulging in exuberant gaiety.

Thus we have two types of Italianate Spanish, according to social strata.

29. Compare, for other mispronunciations of Sancho (II, 68): *troglodi- tas>tortolitas, bárbaros>barberos, antropófagos>astropajos, scitas>perritas a quien dicen cita cita* |troglodytes>ortolans, barbarians>barbers, Anthropophagi>Andrew popinjays, scythians>silly 'uns| |It should be noted that in some of these examples Cohen (see n. 4) translates freely in order to capture the effects of Sancho's humorous misuse of Castilian—EDS.|.

30. It was to be expected that when Sancho became governor he would establish a linguistic level of his own, above that of his subjects. And, in fact, he once satirizes the way of speaking of a peasant by ironically carrying further a grammatical mistake of the latter; the scene in question could not be better analyzed than in the words of Alfred Morel-Fatio: "When the peasant comes to relate his case to the governor of Barataria, he searches his memory for the juridical word which expresses decently the act he has committed |that is, *yacer*, 'to lie, to sleep with'|, and instead of 'hizo que *yoguiésemos*' |(the devil) made us lie together|, the imperfect subjunctive, a form of which he has only a vague memory, he says *yogásemos* . . . as if the infinitive were *yogar*. Sancho, who, since he has become governor, has made an effort to speak correctly, gleefully seizes the occasion to underscore a blatant grammatical error by one of his fellow peasants: 'See to it, my good man, that you never again *yogar* |couple| with anyone,' he says with a patronizing smile, lingering as he does so on the word. Here one observes a finesse which the majority of readers of *Don Quijote* must have noted |"Periodiques," *Romania*, 26 (1897): 476. (Summary of an article by R. Foulché-Delbosc, "Yogar, Yoguer, Yoguir," *Revue hispanique*, 4 |1897|: 113–19)—EDS.|. Sancho, the perpetrator of so many linguistic sins, is not insensitive to those committed by his subjects; his linguistic personality varies according to this interlocutor.

31. This idea, which is a medieval one, is clearly expressed by Sancho when his wife contends that, since the time he became a member of the knight-errantry, she is no longer able to understand him (II, 5): "Basta que me entienda Dios, mujer, que el es el entendedor de todas

cosas" [It's enough that God understands me, wife, for He's the understander of all things]. The same reliance on God appears in II, 7, when Sancho, whose remark, "yo soy tan *fócil*" [I am so *focile*] (*fócil* evidently representing a combination of *dócil* [docile]+*fácil* [simple]) has not been understood by Quijote, explains: "soy tan así" [I am so-so!]; when this does not help, he exclaims: "Pues si no me puede entender, no sé cómo lo diga; no sé más, y Dios sea conmigo" [Well, if you can't understand me, I don't know how to say it, I can't say any more, God help me]. The coinage *fócil*, however nonexistent it may be in common language, covers the reality of Sancho's inner being, which is defined simply as "being as he is," and which he trusts God may recognize.

(Don Quijote, himself, must admit [II, 20] that Sancho, in spite of his *rústicos términos* [country language], would make a good preacher; and Sancho concurs boastfully, immediately introducing a solecism: "Bien predica quien bien vive, y no sé otras *tologías*" [He preaches well that lives well, and I know no other *thologies*].)

32. The attitude of Cervantes toward the popular adages is no different from that toward popular words: Sancho is given to piling up such stereotyped word material indiscriminately; Don Quijote, who is himself prone to quote adages, admires Sancho's spontaneity and fluency in this regard, as well as the original and natural wisdom which they reveal—though he advocates more restraint in their use; Cervantes does not commit himself one way or the other.

33. Giuseppe Antonio Borgese, "Il senso della letteratura italiana," *Domani*, 1, no. 2 (1943): 111.

34. In the *entremés* "Los habladores" a character is made to accumulate synonyms in different languages: "Una criada se llama en Valencia *fadrina*, en Italia *masara*, en Francia *gaspirria*, en Alemania *filomiquia*, en la corte *sirvienta*, en Vizcaya *moscorra*, y entre pícaros *daifa*" [In Valencia a servant is called *fadrina*, in Italy *masara*, in France, *gaspirria*, in Germany *filomiquia*, in the court *sirvienta*, in Vizcaya *moscorra*, and among pícaros *daifa*]. Here we have the raw material (*copia verborum*) on which Cervantes will draw in the *Quijote*.

35. See Spitzer, "Español y portugués *decorar*: 'Aprender, recitar de memoria,'" *Revista de filología hispánica*, 6 (1944): 176–86. See especially pages 176 and 183.

36. The raw material from which Cervantes drew the first episode is, according to Rodríguez Marín, a folktale (I would say, of the *Schildbürger*-tale variety). But, obviously, the introduction therein of the baroque element is a Cervantine touch. It is also in line with this ele-

ment that the chimeric expedition of the townspeople, who are bent on conquering the whole countryside, should end in the beating administered to Sancho—a victory, which, if they had been familiar with the Greek custom, says Cervantes, they would have celebrated by raising a monument, a *trofeo*.

37. The same pattern is evident in other passages: what is the *cueva de Montesinos* for Quijote is a "pit of hell" for Sancho: " '¿Infierno de llamáis?' dijo Don Quijote" ["Hell, you call it?" said Don Quijote] (II, 22).

38. Linguistically speaking, *baciyelmo* fits into the group of *dvandva* formations |copulative compounds| designating hybrids in Spanish: *marimacho* |mannish woman|, *serpihombre* |serpentman| (Góngora); an object, like an animate being, may present a hybrid aspect, and be represented by the same pattern: *arquibanco* |a bench or seat with drawers|, *catricofre* |a folding bed| (and *baciyelmo*). As Anna Granville Hatcher will show, in a forthcoming article, this Renaissance type in Spanish word-formation goes ultimately back to Greek: ἀνδρογύνης-τραγέλαφος |androgynestragelaphos; man-woman-goat-deer|, in Latinized form: *masculo-femina* |man-woman|, *hircocervus* |goat-deer|, and *tunico-pallium* |tunic-cloak|. Thus Cervantes has expressed his perspectivistic vision in a word-formational pattern of the Renaissance reserved for hybrids.

39. Interesting, in connection with Cervantes' linguistic perspectivism, are the many puns that appear in the *Quijote*: (I, 2) Don Quijote calls the innkeeper a *castellano* |Castilian–castellan| because the inn appears to him as a *castillo* |castle| in which he will be dubbed knight, but the innkeeper thinks that he has been called a "Castilian" "por haberle parecido de los sanos {the toughs} de Castilla" |because he took him for a "worthy tough" of Castile|; (I, 3) "No se curó {'did not care'} el harriero destas razones (y fuese mejor que se curara porque fuera curarse {'be cured'} en salud)" |The carrier did not care for his speech—it would have been better if he had cared for it, for he would have been caring for his own health|; (II, 26) {someone takes money} "no para tomar el mono sino la mona" |not in order to catch the monkey but to get tipsy (literally, to catch the she-ape—EDs.)|; (II, 66) when the lackey says to Sancho, "tu amo debe de ser un loco" |this master of yours ought to be counted a madman| the squire answers: "¿Cómo debe? No debe nada a nadie; que todo lo paga, y más cuando la moneda es locura" |Why "ought"? He owes nothing to anyone, for he pays his debts, especially where madness passes for coin|.

The pun is a bifocal manner of expression which relaxes and relativizes the firmness with which language usually appears to speaking man.

Sometimes the "word-world," in Renaissance fashion, encroaches on outward reality. The word *donas* in the phrase *ni dones ni donas* is an entirely fantastic formation, without any reality behind it (since the feminine of *don* is *doña* or *dueña*): it is to be explained as an extraction from *don(es)* and susceptible of usage in connection with this word alone—just as *ínsulos* is possible only in the phrase *ni ínsulas ni ínsulos*. Such formations are intended to exclude from consideration all possible varieties of the species denoted by the radical—a tendency to be found in many languages: compare the Turkish *šapka yok mapka yok* "{I have} no cap no nothing" (*mapka* being a nonce-word patterned on *šapka*). But by the very creation of a name for that which exists only at the moment it is denied, the nonexistent entity is endowed with a certain (fantastic) reality.

40. In the story of Ana Félix, the Christian daughter of the Morisco Ricote, we see again how closely connected are language and faith: she explains (II, 63): "Tuve una madre cristiana . . . mamé la Fé católica con la leche; criéme con buenas costumbres; ni en la lengua ni en ellas jamas, a mi parecer, di señales de ser morisca" [I had a Christian mother . . . I sucked the Catholic faith with my mother's milk. I was brought up with good principles, and neither in my language nor in my customs, I think, did I show any signs that I was a Moor]. The reader should note the expression *mamar la fé con la leche*: the same expression is used in Cervantes (II, 16) of the mother tongue: "todos los poetas antiguos escribieron en la lengua que mamaron con la leche" [all of the ancients wrote in the tongues they sucked with their mother's milk]; and Castro has pointed out the origin of this metaphor (Bembo, *Della volgar lingua* [1525]: "nella latina {sc. *lingua*}essa {the Romans} tutti nascevano et quella insieme col latte dalle nutrici loro beeano" [{the Romans} were all born in Latin, and they all drank it {Latin} together with their wet nurses' milk]). Here, we are at the bottom of the concept of *Muttersprache*, *langue maternelle, mother tongue*, which ultimately goes back to an Augustinian concept: the Christian learns the name of God from his mother ("hoc nomen salvatoris mei . . . in ipso adhuc lacte matris tenerum cor meum biberat" [this name of my savior . . . my tender heart drank in the very milk of my mother]): the "name of God" is the most important and the most intimate linguistic knowledge the mother can impart to her child; thus (and this is in harmony with Christianity, which, in general, tends to present spiritual truths behind a human veil), the concept of "mother tongue" is vitally connected with that of maternal religion [Spitzer, "Muttersprache," *Monatshefte für deutschen Unterricht*, 36, no. 3 (March 1944): 113–30; see especially 120].

41. In the other Moorish story in our novel, that of the expelled Ricote who, having fled to Germany, comes back in the disguise of a German pilgrim to Spain (II, 54), the exile mixes German (¡Guelte! ¡Guelte! |Geld! Geld!|) into his Spanish—a language which he knows as well as does Sancho, whose "neighborhood shopkeeper" he had been. Cervantes describes Sancho's inability to understand the Germanate jargon of Ricote, whose identity he fails at first to recognize. Later, the pilgrim throws aside his incognito and hails Sancho "en voz alta y muy castellana" |loudly in Castilian|; "Ricote, sin tropezar nada en su lengua morisca, en la pura castellana le {to Sancho} dijo las siguientes razones" |Without once stumbling into his Moorish jargon, Ricote spoke as follows in pure Castilian|. In the ensuing drinking scene, Sancho, in his mellow tipsiness, finally ends up by speaking the esperanto of *lingua franca*. In this episode we must infer that the difficulties of linguistic understanding are all artificially contrived: here are *Ricote el morisco* and *Sancho el bueno*, who have lived side by side for many years and who are quite able to understand each other perfectly, who have the same habits of living, eating, and drinking—and who are separated from each other only by the (arbitrary) fact of the Morisco's exile.

Ricote is as good a Spaniard as is Sancho (perhaps also a more gifted one: this comes out in his ironic question, so natural with emigrants who, returning to their mother country, see themselves in a position inferior to their merits: "¿Faltaban hombres en el mundo más hábiles para gobernadores que tú eres?" |Was the world short of men more capable of being governors than you?|), and his daughter is a perfect Christian; nevertheless, as exiles, they have been the victims of an arbitrary death-blow. But, by his exile, Ricote has not only learned to say *guelte* instead of *limosna* |alms|: he has come to know religious tolerance as he saw it practiced in Augsberg, in the heart of Protestantism. No bolder words could have been written, in Counter-Reformation Spain, about religious freedom, than are expressed here by Ricote. Nevertheless, the same Ricote bows submissively before the expulsion of the Moors by the Spanish king and his minister, which has plunged him and his family into despair and misery. Cervantes seems here more interested in the dialectic play of arguments, in the facets and perspectives of the problem, than in giving a decision on the moral issue. To the Spanish subject matter of the novel, the stories of Moorish emigrants, renegades, and converts add a new perspective, that of Spain seen from the outside—a perspective of "spiritual geography."

42. The same double light is cast on the *caña*, that angling rod

dropped by Zoraida to the captives, which is first only a utensil, an astute device, and then becomes a symbol of the miracle (*milagro*) of a twofold salvation.

43. Castro, *El pensamiento*, 147.

44. In this tale, the "renegade" develops before our eyes and gradually comes to take on stature; he shows his eagerness to help in the escape of the prisoners: after his repentance, when he swears by the cross to change from a "foul" member of the Church to a true member, the Christian fugitives put themselves "en las manos de Dios y en las del renegado" [in the hands of God and the renegade] (as though God's hands used those of the renegade for His purposes). Later, it is true, his plan is abandoned for another one ("Dios, que lo ordenaba de otra manera, no dio lugar al buen deseo que nuestro Renegado tenía" [God decreed otherwise, and did not give this fellow a chance of carrying out his plans]) but, nevertheless, he is saved along with the whole party and succeeds in his desire "a reducirse por medio de la Santa Inquisición al gremio santísimo de la Iglesia" [to be reconciled to the bosom of Mother Church by means of the Holy Inquisition].

45. Castro, *El pensamiento*, 147.

46. One of the legends that explains the Muslim invasion of Spain in 711 is "that King Roderick had dishonored a Visigothic lady, Caba [*La Cava*]; her father, Count Julian, invited the Muslims to invade, as a means for avenging Caba's honor." See Jaime Vicens Vives, *Approaches to the History of Spain*, 2nd rev. ed., trans. Joan Connelly Ullman (Berkeley: University of California Press, 1972), 27n. It is to this legend that Cervantes (and Spitzer) refer.—EDS.

47. In this connection, we should consider the famous opening sentence of the novel: "En un lugar de la Mancha de cuyo nombre no quiero acordarme" [In a certain village in La Mancha, which I do not wish to name]. All the explanations hitherto offered—the silly autobiographical one (Cervantes had personal reasons for not wanting to remember the name); that based on literary history, proposed by Casalduero (Cervantes opposes his novel to the romances of chivalry, which claimed to know exactly wherefrom their heroes hailed); the folkloristic one of María Rosa Lida (the sentence is in line with the beginning of folktales)—fail to take into sufficient consideration the functional value, for the novel, of the attitude of the author expressed therein—which, in my opinion, is the glorification of the freedom of the artist. Even if, for example, Mme Lida should be right, the transfer of a sentence traditional in folktales into this particular novel of Cervantes could give

the transferred sentence a new meaning, just as certain folklorisms adopted by Goethe or Heine become more than folklorisms in the lyrical poetry of these poets. By the deliberate assertion of his free will to choose the motifs of his plot, to emphasize or disregard what detail he pleases (and *no quiero* expresses deliberate disregard), Cervantes has found that genre of "subjective storytelling" which, before him, is found at its incipient stage with Boccaccio and which, later, was to inspire Goethe (in the beginning of the *Wahlverwandtschaften* [Elective Affinities]: "Eduard— so nennen wir einen reichen Baron im besten Mannesalter—Eduard hatte . . ." [Edward—so we shall call a wealthy baron in the prime of life—Edward had . . .]), Laurence Sterne, Fielding, Melville ("Call me Ishmael"!).

In an address to the Baltimore Gothic Society, entitled "Laurence Sterne's *Tristram Shandy* and Thomas Mann's *Joseph the Provider*," Professor Oskar Seidlin [*Modern Language Quarterly*, 8 (1947): 101–18] pointed out the presence, in both these modern works, of some of the same comic devices (change of names, assumption of fictional sources, introduction of "relativizing dialogues," etc.) which I have been discussing as characteristic of Cervantine perspectivism. Since Thomas Mann himself had stated in 1942 that during the composition of his *Joseph* he had had two books as his steady companions, *Tristram Shandy* and *Faust*, the stylistic congruences between the German and the English novel are easily explained [From Thomas Mann, *The Theme of the Joseph Novels* (Washington, D.C.: U.S. Government Print Office, 1942), 16. Cited in Seidlin, "Laurence Sterne's *Tristram Shandy*," 102.—Eds.]. On the other hand, the devices of Sterne which reappear with Mann were, in turn, borrowed from Cervantes; and, in this connection, it is relevant to note that, in 1935, Thomas Mann had published his essay on the *Don Quijote* ["Meerfahrt mit Don Quijote," in his *Leiden und Grösse der Meister* (Berlin: S. Fischer, 1935), 209–70]: thus the Cervantine climate may have acted doubly upon him: directly as well as indirectly. And, though the idea expressed in *Joseph the Provider* that the world is "Jehovah's Jest" would not have occurred to Cervantes, who glorified the "artist beneath the dome of God," the great *Entendedor*, the Spanish poet could have subscribed to Mann's idea of "artistic lightness" as man's consolation: "For lightness, my friend, flippancy, the artful jest, that is God's very best gift to man, the profoundest knowledge we have of that complex, questionable thing we call life. God gave it to humanity, that life's terribly serious face might be forced to wear a smile. . . . Only in lightness can the spirit of man rise above them {the questions put to us by life}: with a laugh at being faced with the unanswerable, perhaps he can make even God Himself, the great Unanswering, to laugh" [Mann, *Joseph the Provider*. Spitzer quotes from H. T. Lowe-Porter's translation, *Joseph and His Brothers* (New York: Knopf, 1948), 1056.—EDS.].

It is interesting that Thomas Mann, who, in his *Buddenbrooks*, was still the pure representative of what Oskar Walzel has called "objective narration" (in the Spielhagen style), has from the time of his *Magic Mountain* developed consistently in the direction of Cervantine "storytelling" technique; this evolution must be due not only to the general change in literary trends that has been taking place, but also to Mann's growing consciousness of the triumphant part the artist is called upon to play in modern society.

In this connection I may cite also the opening line of E. M. Forster's novel *Howards End*: "One may as well begin with Helen's letters to her sister" [(London: E. Arnold, 1910); reprint (New York: Knopf, 1955), 3], on which Lionel Trilling remarks: "Guiding his stories according to his serious whim . . . Forster takes full and conscious responsibility for his novels, refusing to share in the increasingly dull assumption of the contemporary novelist, that the writer has nothing to do with the story he tells, and that, *mirabile dictu*, through no intention of his own, the story has chosen to tell itself through him. Like Fielding, he shapes his prose for comment and explanation. He summarizes what he is going to show, introduces new themes when and as it suits him" [*E. M. Forster* (London: The Hogarth Press, 1944; new and rev. ed., London, 1967), 11].

48. See Edgar Zilsel, *Die Entstehung des Geniebegriffes* (Tübingen: Mohr, 1926), 115–16, 123.

49. Mann, "Meerfahrt mit Don Quijote," 230.

50. I realize that this is an opinion contrary to that of the writers of the Enlightenment who, in their treatment of the *Don Quijote*, made much of Cervantes' own classicistic pronouncement that art imitates nature. Locke, for example, has written: "Of all the books of fiction, I know none that equals Cervantes's 'History of Don Quijote,' in usefulness{!}, pleasantry, and a constant decorum. And indeed no writings can be pleasant, which have not nature at the bottom, and are not drawn after copy." And Thomas Sydenham, the English Hippocrates and founder of modern clinical treatment, is reported to have advised young medical students to read the *Don Quijote* instead of books on medicine—because (as Professor Ludwig Edelstein shows ["Sydenham and Cervantes," in *Essays in the History of Medicine Presented to Professor Arthur Castiglione* . . ., Supplements to the Bulletin of the History of Medicine, no. 3

(Baltimore, Md., 1944), 55–61]), he evidently thought the Spanish novel offered a deterrent example of a person who views the world in the light of his preconceived ideas instead of that of facts—with which alone Dr. Sydenham was concerned.

Needless to say, my historical interpretation is also at the other pole from the poetic vision of an Unamuno, who believes that this story was dictated to Cervantes' pen by the suprapersonal and perennial Spanish character, by the innate Spanish will to immortality by suffering and the "sentimiento trágico de la vida" [tragic sense of life] as embodied in the figures of the quasi-saint Nuestro Señor Don Quijote de la Mancha [our Lord Don Quijote de la Mancha] and his evangelical squire. In my opinion, it is Cervantes the "artistic dictator" who dictated the story to his pen, and Cervantes, no half-Christian like Unamuno, knew how to distinguish the earthly plane from the transcendental. On the former plane he obeyed his own *sovereign reason*. He does not, then, belong to the family of Pascal and Kierkegaard, but to that of Descartes and Goethe.

51. Pirandello's perspectivism is in this respect different from that of Cervantes: with the latter, it is the *author* who looks for his characters, not the reverse.

I beg also to disagree with those critics who compare Cervantes with El Greco because of the novelist's "modern impressionism." We must be clear about the meaning of the term "impressionism." Cervantes never offers *his own* impressions of outward reality, as does the modern artist of the impressionistic school; he presents simply the impressions which his characters may have had—and, by juxtaposing these different impressions, he implicitly criticizes them all. The program of the modern impressionist, on the other hand, makes impossible the intervention of the critical sense into what he sees. As for the impressionism of El Greco, while this involves no criticism of reality, as does that of Cervantes (since the ultimate reality he portrays is the divine), it does offer the evanescent reflections of the divine—which may, of course, have prepared the public for the perception of the evanescent in this world, that is, for modern "impressionistic" perception.

52. Professor Erich Auerbach, in his book *Mimesis* [(Bern: A. Francke, 1946), 319], states the lack in the *Don Quijote* (as in the whole literature of the siglo de oro [Golden Age]) of any "problematic study of contemporary reality," of any "movement in the depths of life," of any search into the social motivations of Don Quijote's madness, and of the life of his age—the underlying idea being that the "real" motivations of life

are those of sociology, not of morality, on which Cervantes has based his novel (though, as we have said, he offers us the conflict between different moral standards). The attitude of this critic, which seems to abound in the sense of Carl Becker ("the historian has become the successor of the theologian"), is, in my opinion, contingent on the presupposition that moral values are obsolete in a modern world given to the sociological explanation of history.

53. It should perhaps be pointed out here that "perspectivism" is inherent in Christian thought itself. The pair Don Quixote–Sancho Panza is, after all, a Cervantine replica of the medieval characters Solomon and Marcolf, in whom the wisdom of the sage and that of the common man are contrasted (we may also see in Sancho Panza's *refranes* [sayings] a later version of the *proverbes au vilain* [simple proverbs]). Such an exemplary contrast is derived from the evangelic truth that the common man has access to wisdom, as well as the learned man; that the spirit, if not the letter, of the law can be understood by anyone. Here, we have an example of "medieval gradualism," according to which the social or mental level of Christ's followers is ultimately irrelevant. It is for this reason that, in medieval mystery plays, lofty scenes treating the life of Christ may alternate with scurrilous scenes in which shepherds or clowns are allowed to express their "point of view" on the august events in question, in their own unregenerate rustic speech. In this "gradualism," perspectivism is implied; and, to the perspectivism which Cervantes found in the medieval tradition, he added only the artistic aloofness of a renaissance thinker.

Don Quixote

Crossed Eyes and Vision

ROBERTO GONZÁLEZ ECHEVARRÍA

◆ ◆ ◆

IT IS WELL KNOWN that Alonso Quijano's brain dried up from reading too many chivalric romances, but what is much more remarkable is that this fifty-plus-year-old man, who read every night from dusk to dawn, probably by the dim light of a candle, did not actually go blind. In a novel in which the characters, above all the bruised and battered hero, suffer countless injuries and illnesses, it is never once mentioned that Don Quijote might have experienced even the slightest decline in his vision. The knight's bodily integrity diminishes gradually over the course of his adventures: He loses various molars and part of an ear, his ribs are broken, his wrists chafed, his face scratched; he sustains contusions that leave him unconscious and suffers stomach cramps and debilitating bouts of vomiting. But his eyes remain intact until death closes them. This compulsive reader can see across great distances those who bring him grace and disgrace, and he reads from a book that he finds in an abandoned suitcase while on horseback in the midst of the Sierra Morena.

Don Quixote is a novel about the vision and visions of its protagonist. Countless adventures begin when the knight and his squire see someone or something approaching and they culminate when each of them sees something different. The most comical adventures occur when intentions and identities get confused in the darkness of the inn, which contrasts with the brightness of the roads, and as a result, things and people become ill-defined and difficult to recognize. The power to see, or not to see, correctly, and to be seen or not accurately by others, determines the knight's fortunes, and these problems of vision and perception very quickly become one of the novel's central themes. For instance, during the night-long vigil he spent over his arms, on Don Quijote's very first night out, the moon was "so bright that it competed with the source of its brightness, and every action of the novice knight could be clearly observed by all" (I, 3, p. 38).[1] Even darkness turns bright to make the hidalgo's antics and strange appearance eerily visible, to which one could add that the moon's glow is a slightly ironic allusion to his madness—to his lunacy.

Almost all of *Don Quixote*, but part I in particular, is set in the luminous, sun-drenched landscape of Castile, with its clear skies, dry air, and a sun so bright that it outlines mercilessly the true shape of things. It rains only once during the entire novel, and then the water lends such a sparkle to the basin the barber had put on his head, for lack of a better cover, that Don Quijote believes it to be Mambrino's famous helmet. It is as if Cervantes had decided to place the novel's action in a setting ideal for testing knowledge and theories about optics, refraction, and the anatomy of the human visual apparatus. He did live, after all, at the time when decisive developments in science, such as the invention of the telescope, were radically expanding the range of human vision, and when the discipline of ophthalmology was making great advances.[2] Cervantes, of course, does not always set his fictions in diaphanous landscapes such as the ones in *Don Quixote*; he was not driven by a clumsy determinism that would compel him only to represent the light of his native land. In *The Trials of Persiles and Sigismunda*, for instance, there are numerous dark and foggy scenes in which it is almost impossible for the characters to see anything at all. But looking and seeing are actions specific mainly to *Don Quixote*; they are related to everything that gives the novel originality and significance on the intellectual and artistic map of its time and beyond. They are also actions peculiar to this novel because the issue of reading—an activity so dependent on seeing—and the effects of the sheer abundance of books made possible by the printing press are among the fundamental questions that it raises. Don Quijote did read, by the light of that candle, a hundred such volumes.

I am interested in sight and the gaze in their most concrete, tangible, and physical aspects, which gives my own inquiry—which cannot claim such concreteness except in a metaphoric sense—an ironic and self-critical approach. I would like to confront the mute materiality of things and the hieratic silence of actions as they are represented in the novel, running the risk of failure and even ridicule that Don Quijote faces in similar cases, when the inevitable knocks and falls generate more laughter than enlightenment. I do not just privilege this approximation over others already mired in rhetorical figures: vision and gaze as syntheses of opinions, points of view, ways of being, really pronouns of a sort that represent individuals who then assume roles in a play of perspectives, with each one seeing things his or her way. Such commonplaces are always conjured up when it comes to Cervantes. I would also like to return to their origins, to step back to a prefigurative moment or space that might reveal something fresh about Cervantine phenomenology, aesthetics, and even ontology. And if I fail in my attempt to reach all the way back to the concrete, at least the exercise of putting up the scaffolding to look at the question from this angle might prove valuable. My struggle against hasty conceptualization and facile or trite metaphors, which already got the best of me in the previous sentence, could be instructive, even if my wooden horse never lifts itself so much as a fraction of an inch off the ground to help me gain my new perspective. How do the characters in *Don Quixote* see? With what kind of eyes do they look? And what might this reveal about literary creation?

It should be obvious that both gaze and vision in Cervantes

are not only fundamental to his conceptions of being and perception but also crucial to the question that seems to have obsessed him: that of representation. How do objects and beings appear, and how can they be represented? Ambiguity and perspectivism have to first be approached as problems of perception in the most literal sense. One can see nothing in the inn's unforgiving darkness, and Don Quijote, whose sense of smell seems not to have been as keen as his sense of sight, takes Maritornes for a love-stricken damsel. The characters look and look at each other and what they see and how they see it determines their actions and reveals them to the readers and to themselves.

How the characters see each other and look at themselves is particularly interesting when physical deformities intervene. This is another issue that appears to have obsessed Cervantes and many of his contemporaries and which may be a medieval retention, even if not, in his specific case, a reflection of his own condition as a partial cripple. Misshapen individuals are compelling to the likes of Velázquez, for instance, precisely because their abnormalities make them distinct and even unique. But malformation of the visual apparatus itself is of special significance. The eyes are the windows of the soul, as the commonplace has it, and to see, according to neo-Platonist doctrine, was a means of making the soul reveal itself. But when it comes to those who are cross-eyed, blind in one eye, or have eyes that are too deeply set or close together, or that are bleary or teary, those windows are fogged over in most suggestive, if not exactly appealing, ways. The deformed person and its representations pose a challenge to mimesis and to the idealized forms of renaissance aesthetics that the Baroque revised, or better, re-formed. Its emblematic figure is that of the monster, as I have explored elsewhere.[3] The defects of sight, above all when they are themselves visible deformities and not merely functional impairments, are a sort of monstrosity—something whose display calls attention to itself but also resists representation.

In the most general terms, I would like to argue that, at a point in history that tended toward a modern idea of seeing in relation to thinking and being, as is paradigmatically manifest in

Descartes, Cervantes doubts Cartesian doubt itself by turning his novel toward the difficulties of perception and representation. (I have in mind here Descartes' treatise on optics, where it is evident that the author of the *Discourse on Method* had found a science that could reduce the relationship between being and reality to geometric terms and thus regularize perception—he therefore relegated all irregularities of vision to the realm of medicine.) Cervantes was not heir to the whole theology of vision and of seeing that originated in the Middle Ages, although he retained certain of its ideas that had become part of popular wisdom. His skepticism about vision is not backward but forward looking; it is not a defensive reaction and retrenchment into the past but an announcement of problems that the best insights that science could produce would later have to raise and address. One should remember again that Cervantes lived at a time of notable advancements in the field of optics, ophthalmology, and even artillery, in which sighting calculations were crucial. Kepler and Galileo are the names most notably associated with these advances, though they are not the only ones. But, however much one perfected tools to improve, study, or correct human vision—telescopes, magnifying lenses, eyeglasses—that vision continued to be limited, and it was even beset by congenital or accidental flaws of the human visual organs, including the vexations raised by our binocular vision (having two eyes), which binds us to a kind of double vision. We can be of one mind, but we will always be (unless an accident intervenes) of two eyes. Physical impediments, along with conceptual ones, made it difficult to reconcile eyesight, vision, reason, and a sense of being. It is not just that Don Quijote imposes on reality a preconceived vision derived from the chivalric romances he has devoured through his eyes but also that the very act of seeing, in its physiological dimension and in terms of the new physics, made it increasingly problematic to formulate a concept of what "vision" might be. Not "I think, therefore I am," but instead "I see—poorly at that—therefore I am, and in a rather vague, precarious and even perilous sense, by the way." (Perhaps the ambiguity in the *Don Quixote*, to recall the title of Manuel Durán's notable book, is, after all, a matter of ophthalmology.)⁴ Did Cervantes resist the emerging modern science—which, half a century later, would culminate in Newton—or did he really anticipate its ambivalent effects on the arts, law, literature, and philosophy? The paradox that *Don Quixote* intimates is that the more progress was made in understanding perception, the greater the doubts became about perception's epistemological and conceptual effectiveness.

Perhaps visual impediments in Cervantes derive from the fact that, in his fiction, looking is also, with some frequency, a form of expression, not just of perceiving reality. This at once opens up the problem of the dialectic between interlocutors—or "interlookers," to coin a term—the intention to influence each other that they demonstrate, not to mention the projection of an anxious inner self that does not exactly match the abstract soul Descartes imagined. In this respect, the problems of vision in Cervantes are closely related to what can be observed in Velázquez's paintings, as more than one commentator has noted. Velázquez's subjects seem to exist in a world separated from ours by a transparent, yet impenetrable, barrier that prevents them from communicating with us. But what is disturbing, and even moving, is that they appear to want to do so, and that they convey that desire and urgency with their eyes. The gaze of Velázquez's subjects becomes real in our world; it pierces the translucent wall that divides them from us and makes us part of a dialogue of eyes, a meaningful exchange of looks. Some of those looks are so penetrating that it is hard to hold them for very long, like that of Góngora, or the Conde Duque de Olivares, or of Velázquez himself in "Las Meninas." Velázquez violates the boundaries of the artistic realm with the expression of his subject's eyes. Each look has or suggests a meaning, an attitude, or a moral action to the beholder, who is therefore transformed into the one being observed. In "Las Meninas," as is well known, once we place ourselves at the correct angle, we fall under the spell of Velázquez's gaze. He looks upon us as if we were the models for his painting but also as if he wanted to tell us something. In "The Triumph of Bacchus" we find ourselves eye to eye with the drunken man at the center of the painting; his grim gaze—a mixture of impudence and stupefaction—contemplates us from eyes set above flushed cheeks. Given the difference between painting and literature, gazes in Cervantes cannot be concrete and actually visible, but they are no less expressive and unsettling.

Like Velázquez, Cervantes often took note of physical peculiarities—not only defects—in his characterizations, the significance of which he usually drew from folk beliefs or from the medicine of his times (there is really very little difference between the two, because both relied heavily on rudimentary observations of the human body). Sancho is robustly fat, and Don Quijote is gauntly thin, and the weight of each seems to determine his character as either phlegmatic or energetic. Monipodio has heavy eyebrows and is hairy, which marks him as sexually driven. Not all physical traits have negative connotations. One should note that Gitanilla has a dimple on her chin that makes her particularly attractive. As another gypsy says: "Oh, what a dimple! Any man who looks upon her will fall into the abyss."[5] The specific detail individualizes the character, snatches her from the idealized models of beauty inherited renaissance tradition, and installs her in the here and now where accidents occur. In the case of criminals, not only did specific physical features reveal traits of their character but their observation and recording were developed by the authorities to identify and apprehend them, a practice that left its mark in picaresque fiction and Cervantes, as I have argued in my *Love and the Law in Cervantes.*[6] Often, the particularizing physical attribute involves the eyes.

Details of this sort abound in *Don Quixote*, but it is the description of Ginés de Pasamonte that I want to single out: "After all these [the other prisoners], came a man of good mien, who squinted so horribly that his eyes seemed to look at each other" (I, 22, p. 157). Smollet is grappling with the original—"al mirar metía el un ojo en el otro un poco"—which more literally means that one of his eyes moved inward, crossing its line of sight with that of the other." Ginés is, in short, cross-eyed, in the same way that Maritornes is "blind in one eye, and bleared in the other" (I, 16, p. 99). In the original Cervantes had simply said, "del otro no muy sana," with a coy understatement that Smollet turns into the more specific "bleared." But what in the case of the wench is possibly just a grotesque feature (but perhaps not, as shall be seen) is complicated in Ginés' by the possibility that this character represents in *Don Quixote* the modern author, the one who breaks with the classical tradition to write a novel about himself and compete with the new genres emerging in Spain at the time, especially with the Picaresque in part I and with the theater in part II.[7] One must also note that Cervantes identifies with Ginés in an most touching way, as can be observed in the prisoner's melancholic retort when Don Quijote tells him that he seems to be "an ingenious fellow": " 'And unfortunate,' answered Ginés; 'for, genius is always attended by evil fortune' " (I, 22, p. 158). When examining Don Quijote's books, the priest says that Cervantes, mentioned as the author of *La Galatea*, is "more conversant with misfortune than with poetry" (I, 6, p. 38). Ginés' authorial role and the possibility that he is a Cervantine self-portrait are factors that should be taken seriously because of what his traits and actions suggest about the process of writing. As projections of himself, Cervantes' internal authors are not usually very flattering. They tend to reveal his own deep alienation from the world in which he lived, his truly wrenching uncertainties about literary creation, and his insecurities about the worth of his work.

If one can agree that Ginés is a figure of the modern author, then his being cross-eyed is extremely suggestive. It is first necessary to take notice of what those eyes tell about Ginés' character, the bad look (as it were) that this defect gives him. Ginés cannot look straight at his interlocutor; his crossed eyes make him appear devious, a liar, dishonest, even if he is good looking, as the narrator says he is. Being cross-eyed gives him a criminal appearance, or at least gives an impression of him as being dangerous and untrustworthy. In cosmetic terms his flaw is slight when compared with Maritornes'. But it marks him indelibly and determines both the way in which he looks at the world and how he is seen by others. Ginés' face is the very image of dissimulation and his identity changes (prisoner, gypsy, puppet-master) correspond to the relentlessly dynamic condition of his being.

Ginés looks shifty, like someone whose position, literally and figuratively, is difficult to establish. In an exchange of glances it would be impossible to meet his eyes squarely to determine the exact point from which his gaze issues. As "interlooker," in short, he makes for a breakdown in communications. Janus-like, Ginés is different if seen from one side or the other, because the visible eye's direction changes in each case. He is congenitally two-faced.

Ginés' visual defect reveals yet more about his personality once that of another character in *Don Quixote* is examined for the sake of comparison. I am referring to the character, or metacharacter, given that he is an invention of the book's other characters, of the Giant Pandafilando of the Gloomy Aspect, as Smollet calls him—in the original "de la Fosca Vista," or, literally, "Of the Menacing or Scowling Gaze." In the complicated history of Princess Micomicona, Pandafilando is the one who presumably wants to make her his victim, which requires an intervention on the part of Don Quijote, so that the hidalgo can be tricked into returning home by the priest and barber. Dorotea, dressed as Princess Micomicona, has this to say:

> But this consideration, he [my father Tinacrio the Sage] said, did not give him so much pain and confusion as certain foreknowledge that a monstrous giant, lord of a great island that bordered on our kingdom, called Pandafilando Of The Gloomy Aspect (for, it is affirmed, that although his eyes are, like any other person's, placed in the middle of his face, he always looks askance, as if he squinted; and this obliquity the malicious tyrant practices in order to surprise and intimidate those who behold him). I say, that my father foresaw by his art that this giant, informed of my being an orphan, would invade me with a great army and deprive me of my whole kingdom, without leaving so much as a village for my retreat, and that nothing could prevent this ruin and misfortune unless I would consent to marry him. (I, 30, pp. 243–44)

Javier Herrero, in a superb piece about this episode, has emphasized that Pandafilando represents the wanton passion that his name proclaims (Pan-Philanderer), but I want to draw attention to the giant's eyes.[8] "Fosca Vista" is an archaism, like the many Cervantes uses, mostly in Don Quijote's speech, when he wants to evoke the world of chivalry. But the adjective was already "hosco-a" in his time, as it is still today. In his 1611 *Tesoro de la lengua castellana o española*, Sebastián de Covarrubias writes about "Hosco": "It means something like beclouded by a frown or scowl. Bulls are called gloomy or sullen when they have dark and menacing brows which make one afraid. . . ."[9] Through eyes overshadowed by bushy brows, Pandafilando's menacing gaze projects his unbridled licentious desire. Defective eyes, capable of projecting a threatening look, are a sign of lust, as in the case of Maritornes, who is, after all, a prostitute. But what of Pandafilando's crossed eyes? What does it mean to look crookedly, or as the Spanish says, "mirar al revés"?

It is worth remembering that this is the world of pure fiction, or metafiction, and that Dorotea is another one of the authorial figures in *Don Quixote*, perhaps the most audacious one for her imaginative boldness. There are elements in the story that she concocts that transgress the conventions of a realistic account, as the other characters do not fail to observe about her geographic imprecisions. "Al revés," as the indefatigable Rodríguez Marín reports in a note to his massive critical edition, means "the contrary or inverse of the normal order . . . that which is opposed to what is right or straight."[10] "To look for askance"—crookedly—perhaps only means this, or to look in a twisted, devious, and intimidating way, but it also means to look backwards. What is essential in Pandafilando is not the fixed spot from which he sees but that his point of view—like that of Ginés—is movable and dynamic, that it is not a set perspective determined by the position of his body in space, which would in turn represent a unified, coherent, and individual self. One can easily imagine one of his eyes leaving its normal axis and moving back and forth toward that of the other as the giant gazes about him, or more menacingly, when he looks at someone. His condition suggests that a cross-eyed person can see things outside of their normal shapes and contexts, a sort of congenital anamorphosis. I avail myself here of my late

friend Severo Sarduy's work, who (via Lacan) referred to anamorphosis as typical of a "frenzied [furious] baroque."¹¹ The
dictionary of the Spanish Academy defines "anamorphosis" as "a
painting or drawing that shows an image that is confused or
perfectly normal depending from where it is seen." As if to stress
the play of mutual reflections between deformed vision and the
deformity of the look, Pandafilando himself, because of his enormous size, is a disproportionate and thus deformed being, as if
seen out of perspective. He is "anamorphic." Being cross-eyed is
part of his monstrosity, and his twisted gaze reflects his no less
twisted desires. But it also affords him a bold and unique purchase
on reality, one that by extension or analogy would be that of the
modern author. It does not take a great leap of the imagination
to think of Pandafilando as having a Picasso look, like that of one
of the many bulls he painted—a look that would not be just his
appearance but his way of seeing. What, then, does all this suggest
about Ginés de Pasamonte?

Because Ginés is cross-eyed in a way that is both monocular
and convergent (one eye looking inward), he cannot perceive the
world around him clearly, and this condemns him to represent
it aslant, as seen through the conflicting angles of his superimposed visual axes. His is a sort of innate or internal perspectivism,
necessarily prior to our common conception of the term as the
contrast among the visions of different characters which, when
reconciled in the end, produce the truth, or at least a truth.
Perspectivism thus defined in Cervantes implies that each individual has a unified, harmonious, and coherent vision consonant
with his being, and that each person expresses that vision to project an opinion and sense of individuality. Everyone sees things
in a different way; the truth would be the sum and synthesis of
these divergent visions. But Ginés' cross-eyed gaze implies that
such an individual point of view is but a hypothesis buttressed by
grammar and rhetoric—a subject possesses and is defined by a
"vision." Such a concept or conceit bypasses the literal contingencies of point of view, such as the anatomy of the visual apparatus in general and the specificity of each individual's eyes, or
of his or her particular look. I use "look" here, of course, both

as gaze and as appearance, for it has already been observed that seeing and being seen work together, if not necessarily in synchrony. One of Ginés' eyes sees in one way, the other in another, before the discrepancy between the eyes is noticeable to another character—when it is, he looks "shifty." The vision of individuals like Ginés is the discordant sum of disparate images produced by visual axes that never fully focus together; that converge at the wrong point in space and time. It is a kind of double vision, in which the lack of a common perspective makes it impossible for divergent images to be joined together. Being cross-eyed, then, may be called the modern condition of artistic or literary vision: double, distorting, anamorphic, in that it depends on the movement of one eye being independent of the other. It is the new model for being, in conflict with and within itself, capable of seeing up close and afar at the same time, like a dialogue of interior visions that cannot be resolved or harmonized. It is, moreover—and this is suggested by the physical deformities that are aggressive—a being driven by desire. Pandafilando wants to invade both Micomicona's kingdom and Micomicona herself. Ginés' desire is more narcissistic—he writes about himself—hence more artistic.

The modern writer, always being a reader before a writer, is a congenital dyslexic able to see and read "askew" (or in reverse, *al revés*), in the same way that Pandafilando and Ginés can. Ginés' famous reply to the question of whether he has already completed his picaresque autobiography—"How can I be finished . . . when my natural life is not yet concluded?" (I, 22, p. 158)—is an error in perspective in a much more literal way than critics (including myself) have thought. The end of his life is the distant vanishing point that he can see with one eye; the present from which he is speaking is the medium-range or closer distance which he sees with his other eye. His double vision does not allow him to join these two planes of perception; the book will never be finished and will forever be suspended between these two conflicting gazes. The interval or gap between them is that of fiction.

Ginés' double perspective is underlined in the same episode with the galley slaves in very concrete fashion. In this instance his defect ironically gives him an advantage over the guards from whom he flees. This is one of those typically Cervantine episodes in which something of potentially great insight and philosophical subtlety is reduced to the most brutal, tangible, and literal level. Don Quijote charges the commissary with his lance after a bitter exchange of words, throwing him wounded from his mount, at which point:

> Ginés de Pasamonte, who being the first that leapt free and disencumbered on the plain, attacked the wounded commissary, and robbed him of his sword and musket, with which, pointing at one and taking aim at the other, without firing, however, in a trice, there was not one of the guards to be seen; for they made the best of their way, not only from Pasamonte's firelock, but from the shower of stones which was rained upon them by the rest of the slaves, who had by this time disengaged themselves." (I, 22, p. 160)

Ginés can see—Argus like—in both directions at once, brandishing and aiming different weapons with each hand and each eye, a feat made possible presumably by his being cross-eyed. It is also significant that, at the end of the adventure, when he refuses to go to El Toboso at Don Quijote's behest, Ginés signals to his companions to let go with the stones by winking an eye: "finding himself treated by him [Don Quijote] in this haughty manner [Ginés] winked to his companions, who retiring with him at a little distance, began to shower such a number of stones upon their deliverer" (I, 22, p. 161). This wink is not as innocent as it may appear, or as it would be were Ginés not cross-eyed. Because of each eye's independence from the other he can express conflicting or autonomous intentions with each. The wink is a partial and sly gesture—involving only one half of the face—as all of his actions seem to be. The language of Ginés' eyes is one of deception and duplicity, as is that which he sees through them, and most certainly what he has written in that long-winded tome recounting his life.

(Is Ginés' double vision like that in Velazquez's paintings? Take, for instance "The Spinners," where images from different and independent planes are superimposed upon one another. In this painting, as in the one with the drunkard I already mentioned, one image is mythological and idealized, while the other shows the present in all its sordid specificity. Is it possible, then, to extend Ginés' doubled and cross-eyed vision allegorically to all the binary oppositions that *Don Quixote*'s critics have noticed or read into the book, such as reality versus fiction and idealism versus realism? But let me dispense with allegories and return to more concrete matters.)

In part II of *Don Quixote*, Ginés appears blind in one eye, or better yet, he passes himself off as one-eyed by covering part of his face so as not to be recognized by the authorities: "We almost forgot to observe that the left eye, and the cheek of this Maese Peter was covered with a patch of green silk, from whence it was supposed all that side of the face labored under some infirmity" (II, 25, p. 620). What Ginés covers up here is precisely that which can identify him: his crossed eyes, the sign of his identity, his signature. Without them, Ginés is no more than "a man of good mien about thirty years of age" (I, 22, p. 157). His crossed eyes reveal his furtive and dangerous character, which puts him at risk of being discovered by the agents of the Holy Brotherhood, who are surely on his trail. But seeing with a single eye, even though it pinpoints his vision—he now has only one visual axis—does not improve it. To eliminate one of the eyes is a rather brutal way of curing Ginés' convergent strabismus and of resolving ambiguities of vision by reducing the point of view to only one. The Hindu divinity Shiva solves this problem by having a third eye in the middle of the forehead that gives him a true, unified vision. And Descartes attributes extraordinary faculties to the pineal gland, a kind of blind eye, a vestige perhaps of a third eye also in the center of the forehead, where common sense as well as the imagination are presumed to be located, because it reduces to one the images coming from both eyes. He writes in *The Passions of the Soul*:

> Apart from this gland [the pineal], there cannot be any other place in the whole body where the soul directly exercises its

functions. I am convinced of this by the observation that all the other parts of our brain are double, as also are the organs of our external senses—eyes, hands, ears and so on. But insofar as we have only one simple thought about a given object at any one time, there must necessarily be some place where the two images coming through the two eyes, or the two impressions coming from a single object through the double organs of any other sense, can come together in a single image or impression before reaching the soul, so that they do not present to it two objects instead of one. We can easily understand that these images or other impressions are unified in this gland by means of the spirits which fill the cavities of the brain. But they cannot exist united in this way in any other place in the body except as a result of their being united in this gland.[12]

One-eyed, Ginés is the very image of the man with imagination, with the ability to singularize and synthesize the images he perceives. He has, then, sacrificed half of the visual field to conceal himself by having a different look and at the same time having acquired a different way of looking. But there is some loss as well as profit. With his left eye covered, he cannot see from this side and has no depth perception—perspective. One has to remember that Ginés only feigns being one-eyed, that this condition is provisional and temporary, and that he continues to be cross-eyed. (It is typical of Cervantine precision that Ginés' simulation is only partial, that his mask covers only half of his face, so that one might say that he is only half deformed and has exchanged one way of being two-faced for another.) However, I believe that it can be assumed that the eye that wanders out of line is the one that Ginés covers so as not to give himself away, by which he also in a certain way augments an already existing condition that is very much his own—that of having a distorted view of reality, now because it lacks depth. Being one-eyed, if only in make-believe, he has also unwittingly increased his menacing look, his *fosca vista*, for *tuertos*, or one-eyed men were thought to be "bellacos," according to the recent edition of *Don Quixote* coordinated by Francisco Rico.[13] "Bellaco" means rascal, but Corominas explains in his marvelous etymological dictionary that during the

evolution of the word it sometimes meant someone sexually motivated, or who engaged in activities, such as that of procurer,
that involved illicit sexual commerce.[14] Here Ginés, Pandafilando,
and Maritornes meet.

Ginés' fragmented and imperfect vision also has an effect on
his role as puppeteer, his primary one in this episode. Ginés is
not only the author of a picaresque autobiography but also the
author of comedies, even if diminutive ones—scaled-down models of those represented on the stage of the corrales, or playhouses
of the time. Miniaturization depends on bypassing perspective, a
process that is so consistent with Ginés' lack of depth perception
as to be comical. The episode is in fact filled with games of perspective involving vision.

There is no need to belabor the point that the entire puppet
show episode, in addition to being a critique of Lope de Vega and
the new theater that he represented, is a sort of laboratory for
mimesis, and not only in terms of literature but of art in general.[15]
The roles played by Maese Pedro and his young helper are of a
complexity worthy of Velázquez.[16] To begin with, the performance
by itself is insufficient as narrative; Maese Pedro's changing stage
sets require a supplementary verbal commentary from his youthful assistant. The boy is not only another one of Ginés' masks;
he is also his voice, in a sort of literal *reductio ad absurdum* of pro-
sopopeia. The clay figures are lent a voice but one that has already
been lent to the speaker by an author who is present yet silent.
But the verbal and visual representations neither work together
harmoniously nor are synchronized satisfactorily, and both Don
Quijote and Ginés have to scold the young barker for his errors.
Don Quijote's corrective is suggestively made in the language of
plane geometry: " 'Boy, boy, follow your story in a straight line,
without swerving into curves and transverse angles, for there is
not so much proof and counter-proof required to bring truth to
light' " (II, 26, p. 626). What might seem like mere rhetorical em-
broidery on the part of the knight is, on the contrary, surprisingly
appropriate in the context of this episode because the puppet stage
set depends for its theatrical illusion upon a *trompe l'oeil* based on
perspective. Ginés himself agrees with Don Quijote, and in his

own reproach to the boy he also seeks recourse in the language of geometry and of painting: " 'Boy, don't get into any flourishes [*dibujos*, drawings], but follow that gentleman's counsel, which is good and wholesome' " (II, 26, p. 626). Notice the irony that geometrical corrections are applied to the verbal representation, not to the material one staged in the puppet theater. What both Ginés and Don Quijote say means much more than they intend, as is often the case in Cervantes.

The puppet theater's illusion is a matter of perspective and proportion, and it has to do with the "straight line" that Don Quijote urges the lad to follow, without much success, and with the fact that Maese Pedro covers one of his eyes and thus has no depth perception. These are concepts that go back to Leon Battista Alberti's ground-breaking treatise on painting, which laid out the rules of perspective for renaissance art, regarding the proper size of objects in relation to the angle and distance from which they are seen.[17] Because the audience looks at the scene or succession of scenes straight on as it faces Maese Pedro's contraption, it has to overlook the fact that, at such a close distance, the human figures, horses, and buildings appear as small as if viewed from afar. The storyteller has to make the spectators swerve "into curves and transverse angles," diverting their gaze, as it were, to suspend their disbelief. Ginés cannot change the dimensions of the figures as they move away from or come closer to the audience, which mirrors his own lack of perspective as a one-eyed observer. To maintain the illusion, the barker has to appeal not only to geometrical figures—bends and side roads—but also to the rhetoric of vision. This rhetoric is a call not to see reality as such but to behold something unusual and marvelous. As in a mantra, the young man repeats "Observe . . . Observe . . . Observe . . . Behold . . . ," which is also like saying "but don't see only what's before you . . . but don't see only what's before you . . . but don't see only what's before you."

There is also within the tableau's own illusory space, as in a further game of mirrors, a literal display of the matter of perspective and the vanishing point. It is the dazzling combination of a visual and a verbal pun. Melisendra and Don Gaiferos flee on horseback toward "the road to Paris" (II, 26, p. 627), making all gazes converge at the back of the miniature stage, the virtual vanishing point. Only in this case it is doubly so because the lovers flee toward it with the intention of disappearing. In Spanish the pun is even more striking because vanishing point is "punto de fuga." The rhythmic chant and the geometric contrivance confuse Don Quijote who—predictably—throws himself into the action, entangled in the net of rhetorical and geometrical figures that deceive his mind and senses, not letting him take note of the difference in size between his own body and those of his Lilliputian foes.

Being one-eyed, Ginés rids himself of the ambiguity of binocular vision, above all because he knows that in his own case it is defective. With a single eye he would presumably and in the abstract be able to see straight. But this is not so in reality because to compensate for the loss of half of the visual field, Ginés has to turn his head. Glancing sideways to see straight would make him look as devious as being cross-eyed did. As with being cross-eyed, the new flaw in sight makes necessary movement at the site from which looking takes place. The head, and with it the face, which is the body's identifying, individualizing part, the one that reflects and guarantees selfhood, has to swivel, making it a shifting and shifty point of view. This means that seeing cannot be an action that is ideal, fixed, centered, and capable of providing a unifying perspective, one that by creating the illusion of depth can yield a "realistic" representation. But there is yet another significant detail. Ginés has placed a patch over his left eye, possibly because it is the crossed one, as suggested. But the left eye is also the "canonical eye," the eye of reading. Church law debated the advisability of ordaining priests blind in this eye because of the unusual posture they would have to assume when reading the canon before the congregation.[18] It is no coincidence that Ginés the author has a blind eye for the canon—the Western canon?—because, to create his work, he has to be blind, or at least read aslant, the received literary tradition. He does this with the story of Melisendra and Don Gaiferos, in the same way that

Cervantes rereads obliquely all the literature that precedes *Don Quixote.* Cross-eyed or one-eyed, the modern writer does not read straight and is incapable of conceiving of a gaze that is not intersected by multiple, nonconvergent angles of sight. For this reason, the texts he produces are variegated and of undetermined origin—translations, the baseless inventions of an Arabic historian prone to lying, and so forth. Only Alonso Quijano, that ideal reader who instead of writing a new chivalric romance insists on acting one out in the flesh, can see clearly in the darkness of his library. This is the reason (one of many) why one must not identify Cervantes with Don Quijote but rather instead with Ginés. I would do this brandishing all the available caveats, of course, avoiding the folly of affixing too firmly the origin of the gaze at a given point, something against which the novel warns. But neither can I submit to the sterilizing scrupulousness of a logic of vision—impersonal or collective—that can soon be turned into a dogma and eventually into an inquisition. Cervantes was not in real life cross-eyed, as far as is known; nor was he devious and criminal like Ginés, also as far as is known. But, like Ginés, he had a split point of view in a world where the clarity of vision and of reason seemed to be making increasingly remote certainty in all orders, including the moral one. The more one knew, aided by science and its instruments, the more one knew one did not know. In the darkness of the inn, Cervantes the author manages, with Don Quijote's aid, to fuse all the narrative strands that converge there after the episodes in the Sierra Morena. By ripping the wine skins, the knight slays Pandafilando, and his feat brings Fernando, whom the giant represents (an association that the rhyme suggestively carries), to the fold. All conflicts are resolved as Pandafilando's menacing gaze is (at least temporarily) suspended. It is this ability to combine conflicting images without canceling their differences that defines Cervantes as a modern writer, perhaps the modern writer. His felicitous (if virtual) cross-eyedness enables him to superimpose these different images upon one another in an imaginative order that triumphs over spatial and temporal discrepancies without entirely abolishing them. If vision's origin is double, irony is intrinsic to the creative act, and representation has to accommodate the moving and multiple points from which one (who is always more than one) perceives. Literature is the mad attempt—whose success is always deferred but never relinquished—to achieve a reconciliation of visions. Modern literature, Cervantes seems to be suggesting in *Don Quixote*, is resigned to settling for this madness. It is for this reason that when Leo Spitzer, in his powerful essay on "Linguistic Perspectivism in the *Don Quijote*" (included in this book), argues that the games of authorial attribution in the novel lead back to Cervantes, I beg to differ and defer to Cervantes himself, who in my view would not have accepted that responsibility in life any more than he did in fiction. The image of the author he left in Ginés de Pasamonte should be taken seriously before assigning to his creator a "vision" that would represent him like a pronoun and determine the whole book.

Don Quijote's madness is inscribed in his good eyesight. He can see straight and clearly because he rarely has doubts about the nature of the things he sees. He is not an author, he is the object of an author's vision, strange to the sight of others but seeing others exactly as what he believes them to be. There is no split self within him; he is alternatively Alonso Quijano or Don Quijote de la Mancha, never simultaneously both. As the latter, he sees giants where there are windmills and the contusions that he suffers as the result of his error fail to convince him otherwise. Don Quijote does not write literature or even read it as such: He lives it. The authors in *Don Quixote*, however, suffer a madness that does not allow them to live or write literature alternatively but concomitantly, never sure of which is which: The symptom of that madness is their defective eyesight.

Notes

1. I am quoting from Miguel de Cervantes Saavedra, *The History and Adventures of the Renowned Don Quixote*, trans. Tobias Smollett, with an in-

troduction by Keith Whitlock (Hertfordshire: Wordsworth Editions, 1998). I have chosen Smollett's translation because it is the most literary, but I have made changes to modernize, correct, or help me make my point.

2. See *El libro del Licenciado Benito Daza de Valdés Uso de los antojos, y comentarios a propósito del mismo*, por el Dr. Manuel Márquez (Madrid: Imprenta y Encuadernación de Julio Cosano, 1923). Daza de Valdés' book was published originally in 1623. The work of Jacques Lacan on the gaze, illuminating in some respects when readable, has become the faddish way to approach the topic. I agree with the divergence of the eye and the gaze as a harmonious dialogue between subject and object. James F. Burke provides much useful historical background on seeing and looking in his *Vision, the Gaze, and the Function of the Senses in Celestina* (University Park: Pennsylvania State University Press, 2000).

3. *Celestina's Brood: Continuities of the Baroque in Spanish and Latin American Literature* (Durham, N.C.: Duke University Press, 1993).

4. Manuel Durán, *La ambigüedad en el Quijote* (Xalapa: Universidad Veracruzana, 1960).

5. Cervantes, *Exemplary Stories*, trans. Lesley Lipson (New York: Oxford University Press, 1998), 19.

6. *Love and the Law in Cervantes* (New Haven: Yale University Press, 2005).

7. Claudio Guillén has written about Ginés and his relationship to the picaresque in "Luis Sanchez, Ginés de Pasamonte y los inventores del género picaresco," in *Homenaje a Antonio Rodríguez Moñino* (Madrid: Castalia, 1966), I, 227–31. See also George Haley, "The Narrator in *Don Quixote*: Maese Pedro's Puppet Show," *Modern Language Notes* 80 (1965): 145–65; Guillermo Díaz Plaja, "El retablo de Maese Pedro," *Insula*, 18, no. 204 (1963): 1–12; Helena Percas de Ponseti, *Cervantes y su concepto del arte: estudio crítico de algunos aspectos y episodios del Quijote* (Madrid: Gredos, 1975); Ann E. Wiltrout, "Ginés de Pasamonte: The 'picaro' and his Art" *Anales cervantinos* 17 (1978): 1–7; Manual Durán, "El *Quijote* visto desde el Retablo de Maese Pedro," *Anthropos*, nos. 98–99 (special issue on Cervantes) (July–August 1989); Roberto González Echevarría, "On Cipion's Life and Adventures: Cervantes and the Picaresque," *Diacritics* 10. 3 (1980): 15–26, reprinted in *Cervantes*, ed. Harold Bloom (New York: Chelsea House, 1986), 99–114; corrected and expanded in my *Celestina's Brood*, 45–65.

8. "Sierra Morena as Labyrinth: From Wildness to Christian Knighthood," *Modern Language Studies* 17, no. 1 (1981): 55–57.

9. *Tesoro de la lengua castellana o española*, ed. Martín de Riquer (Barcelona: Editorial Alta Fulla, 1987), 701.

10. Miguel de Cervantes Saavedra, *El ingenioso hidalgo don Quijote de la Mancha*, ed. Francisco Rodríguez Marín (Madrid: Ediciones Atlas, 1947), II, 397.

11. "Barroco Furioso," *Guadalimar* (Barcelona), año 3, no. 26 (1977): 40–41. There is more on anamorphosis in Sarduy's book *La simulación* (Caracas: Monte Avila, 1982), 21–33.

12. *The Philosophical Writings of Descartes*, trans. John Cottingham, Robert Stoothoff, and Dugald Murdoch (Cambridge: Cambridge University Press, 1985), I, 340.

13. Miguel de Cervantes, *Don Quijote de la Mancha*, edición de Instituto Cervantes, dirigida por Francisco Rico (Barcelona: Instituto Cervantes, 1998), 840, n. 24. It is suggestive that "tuerto" means literally "twisted," perhaps because of the way one-eyed persons see, or also because they have to twist their neck to be able to see. It also means "tort" in the legal sense and shares with the English word the same etymological root.

14. *Diccionario crítico etimológico castellano e hispánico* (Madrid: Gredos, 1991), I, 559–61. The word retains a sexual connotation in certain parts of the Hispanic world. In Puerto Rico, for instance, "bellaco" as adjective means "horny."

15. The burlesque emblem of all this is the fortune-telling monkey, because the monkey is the mimetic animal par excellence—"monkey see, monkey do." One should also notice that Dorotea's name, in the metafictional episode I mentioned above, is Micomicona, "Big Double Monkey," one could say, as "mico" means monkey in Spanish. If Ginés is a ridiculous author, the monkey is a sort of hairy philosopher who pretends to know and to speak. Don Quijote offers a theological explanation of the simian's abilities, asserting that Ginés has made a pact with the devil.

16. For details about what sort of puppet show Maese Pedro's is see J. E. Varey, *Historia de los títeres en España (desde su origen hasta mediados del siglo XVIII)* (Madrid: Revista de Occidente, 1957). Varey is unsure if the puppets in this episode of *Don Quixote* are marionettes or mechanical figures.

17. Leon Battista Alberti, *On Painting*, trans. Cecial Grasyson, with an introduction and notes by Martin Kemp (London: Penguin Books, 1991). The original is from 1435.

18. "Utrum autem, qui caret visu oculi sinistri, quem Stylus Romanus *Oculum Canonis* appellat, eo quod necesse sit videre eo, ut quis Canonem Missae sine indecora, & nimia faciei conversione legere possit,

sit irregularis, variant Doctores." I quote from the compilation and commentary by Anacleto Reiffenstuel, *Jus canonicum universum, clara methodo juxta titulos quinque librorum decretalium in questiones distibutum* (The Hague, Netherlands: Johannis Andrea, 1739), I, 438. The text is topic 18, Title 20, "De corporis vitiates ordinandis, vel non."

The Narrator in *Don Quijote*

Maese Pedro's Puppet Show

GEORGE HALEY

◆ ◆ ◆

IN THE CHIVALRIC ROMANCES, Cervantes found a subject ripe for parody and, with it, a way of telling stories that called for the same treatment. He made them both serve the ends of comic enjoyment and instruction in *Don Quijote*. But in the course of poking fun at the narrative technique of the chivalric novelists, Cervantes used and enlarged it with such skill that, in his hands, the overworked devices became expressive instruments once more. Through his ingenious manipulation of one of the chivalric novelist's favorite devices, the fictitious author, Cervantes was able to set before the reader a novel viewed in the round and depicted in the process of becoming: the dynamic interplay of a story, its dramatized tellers and its dramatized readers. It is this aspect of *Don Quijote* that I should like to consider.

Alongside the supposed history of Don Quijote's adventures, Cervantes' novel presents a supplementary story with a different set of characters and something of a development of its own. This is the story of how Don Quijote's adventures came to be known and set down, a record of the written stages through which it is claimed they have passed on their way to Cervantes' book. It traces the way in which a fragment becomes a complete story, a process that most novelists follow, if at all, in separate notebooks or diaries. But in *Don Quijote*, this process brought to light has become an integral part of the finished novel. As it unfolds in the margin of Don Quijote's adventures, this secondary tale develops its own entanglements and moments of suspense that have little to do with Don Quijote's insane understanding but everything to do with whether the account of it will be completed and become a book.

The characters in this corollary tale are all involved in the mechanics of telling and transmitting Don Quijote's story. Their adventures, not as violent as Don Quijote's but no less exciting for that, are the search for source materials in Manchegan archives, the creation of a continuous narrative from fragmentary and sometimes overlapping sources, the translation of the continuous narrative from Arabic to Castilian, the recasting of the translation and the publication of the revision, with intrusive commentary at every stage.

There is, first, the unidentified "I" who begins the narrative and introduces Don Quijote, only to confess at the end of the eighth chapter that he must surrender his office and leave Don Quijote with his sword poised in the air because his sources have given out. He is followed by a "segundo autor" who takes over the "I" and the narrative with a description of his experience as a frustrated reader of the first eight chapters who was left impatient to know how the story ends. He did not wait long, he tells us, for chance led him to the original Arabic manuscript of Don Quijote's story in the market at Toledo. But the discovery creates a new problem and another moment of suspense: how to read the manuscript. This difficulty is also soon resolved after he calls in a Morisco to render the text into Castilian. Don Quijote's adventures can now proceed.

At the point where the second author concludes this autobiographical detective story and returns to Don Quijote with his sword still poised in the air, what he offers the reader is his rendition of the Morisco translator's version of the Arabic original. It is here that the author of the original manuscript appears: Cide Hamete Benengeli, Moor and chronicler in the first instance of Don Quijote's high deeds. Cide Hamete is a contradictory figure, as E. C. Riley has clearly shown. He is part wizard because of his omniscience, which does not keep him from using documentary sources; part historian because of his devotion to the truth as he sees it, though he is a Moor and therefore a liar by definition, according to the Christian second author; and he is part poet because of his expressed concern with artistic selection, invention and adornment.

With the appearance of the Moorish chronicler, the focus shifts from the hunt for sources to the labor of composition, and the story of the narration of *Don Quijote* becomes essentially the story of Cide Hamete's telling, with numerous overt reminders of the refracting presence of the other intermediaries. It may be pieced together from Cide Hamete's comments to the reader: his evaluation of Don Quijote's behavior, his professional confidences concerning the task of narration with its pitfalls and satisfactions, his personal revelations.

As the novel progresses, Cide Hamete's narrative task turns into a mission as militant as the knightly career of his hero. Before the novel is done, an adversary befitting a man of letters will take up the challenge issued in Ariosto's words at the end of part I: "Forse altri canterà con miglior plettro." This adversary was Avellaneda, who published a spurious continuation of *Don Quijote* while Cervantes was still at work on his own second part. Cide Hamete duly takes notice of this effrontery in the novel, brandishes his pen and engages the challenger in a duel of words.

Cide Hamete's story comes to an end when, after describing Don Quijote's death, he turns his attention away from both his subject and his reader, who have shared it until then, to bid farewell to his pen. In putting aside his writer's instrument, which has also served as a weapon, he provides an appropriate sequel to the hero's surrender of the sword as arms and letters meet for the last time in the work. The parody of this ritual act is a suitable valediction to the story of Don Quijote, in which has been told the story of how it came to be written. But while Don Quijote's mission has given way to defeat and disillusionment, the chronicler's toil ends in triumph, the distinctly literary triumph of a narrative brought successfully to completion.

One intermediary remains. This is the agent overlooked by those who like to equate the second author with Cervantes. He is the shadowy figure who materializes at the end of chapter 8 to join the first author's fragment to the second author's contribution and appears again in the final chapter of part I to supply the concluding remarks. He is the intermediary furthest removed from Don Quijote's adventures and at the same time closest both to the book and to the reader. It is this intermediary, in fact, who formulates the relationship between the implied author and the ideal reader when he transmits the second author's request that the reader give the story "el mesmo crédito que suelen dar los discretos a los libros de caballerías, que tan validos andan en el mundo . . ." (I, lii).

The virtuoso display of this palimpsest reveals Cervantes' interest in experimenting with the techniques of telling in ways that only an artist sure of his power would dare. Consummate rhetorician that he is, Cervantes demonstrates a complementary concern with the effect of a story upon its readers, which leads him to dramatize the act of reading as well. Each of the intermediaries who work at telling and transmitting Don Quijote's story functions, at the same time, as a critical reader of a previous version of that story. In all of these cases, narration is conceived of as much in terms of the writer's preparation, reading critically and selecting, as in terms of the telling. Yet none of the intermediaries forgets the reader who follows him in the series. Cide Hamete, in the first instance, addresses himself to a hypothetical reader. The translator is that reader made explicit within the novel, and he in turn directs his translation and comments to his reader, the second author who hired him to execute the translation. The second author is a fusion of both Cide Hamete's hypothetical reader and the translator's actual reader, and he likewise addresses himself to a hypothetical reader in his adaptation. Through the good offices of the last intermediary, the second author's hypothetical reader becomes the hypothetical reader of

Cervantes' book, who would seem to subsume all of the others except for one difficulty. All of the intermediaries foreshadow coming events. They have read the story before they begin to recount it. They are second-time readers. The reader postulated by Cervantes' book, on the other hand, is a first-time reader for whom the effects that depend upon progressive inference are expressly designed, as we shall soon see.

Within the story of Don Quijote's adventures, the interplay of story, teller and reader is repeated on a smaller scale and in a different mode with countless variations. I should now like to examine one such variation which provides perhaps the most vivid illustration of this interplay in action, for in it, teller and story and listener are all literally dramatized. This is the episode of Maese Pedro's puppet show, for which folk tradition supplied the original legend and determined the basic features of its treatment as a puppet play. Cervantes had already transformed this popular art form into an examination of illusionism in the *Entremés del retablo de las maravillas*. In Maese Pedro's puppet show, Cervantes probes the same aesthetic problem more deeply from another angle of vision.

Maese Pedro arrives at the inn with his "talking" ape and puppet show just as the lance-carrier concludes his story of the two aldermen who search the woods for a lost donkey. The aldermen bray antiphonally with such skill that they confuse each other's imitation with the real thing and repeatedly mistake one another, not without reason, for the donkey. The stranger's unusual narrative will later have a sequel in which Don Quijote and Sancho Panza participate. But for the moment, it serves the more immediate purpose of preparing the company gathered at the inn for Maese Pedro's equally unusual display. After hearing the lance-carrier tell of the marvels of the braying aldermen, Don Quijote and the rest of the "senate and audience" shift effortlessly to the first part of Maese Pedro's show, which offers a reverse parallel in the form of a talking ape.

The story of the donkey-like aldermen and the demonstration of the man-like ape together constitute a carefully graduated introduction to Maese Pedro's puppet show. These complementary cases of mimicry mark successive stages in a process of dehumanization that culminates in the representation of the legend of Gaiferos and Melisendra by inanimate dolls made of paste. They constitute, at the same time, stages of increasing elaborateness in a gradual progression from simple mimicry to a more complex kind of imitation presented in a rudimentary work of art. That Cervantes intended Maese Pedro's puppet show to be seen as the climax of such a progression becomes even more clear later, when the reader learns that only on this one occasion does Maese Pedro observe this order of performance ("lo primero que hacía era mostrar su retablo, el cual unas veces era de una historia y otras de otra, pero todas alegres, y regocijadas, y conocidas. Acabada la muestra, proponía las habilidades de su mono . . ." [II, xxvii]).

The audience that begins by listening to the story of the braying aldermen's innocent mutual deception based on mimicry and then allows itself to be partially taken in by the more elaborately mounted fraud of the talking ape is thus in a proper frame of mind for a more highly articulated mimetic illusion when the puppet play begins. Having been desensitized by a charlatan's mummery, it is now fully primed for an artist's magic.

The candles on the puppet stage are blazing. They outline what Ortega calls the "frontera de dos continentes espirituales." Maese Pedro takes his place behind the scenes. His assistant, pointer in hand, stations himself alongside the stage. Don Quijote, Sancho, and the rest of the audience are waiting expectantly. The assistant begins to speak, but no sound comes forth. His speech has been suspended by Cide Hamete, who intervenes at this moment and thus reminds us that we are reading a story he is telling, that we are gazing at the spectacle of another audience gazing at a spectacle. We are promised that what the assistant tells will be both heard and seen either by the one who hears the assistant, the spectator at the inn, or by the one who sees the next chapter, the reader of the book: "lo que oirá y verá el que le oyere, o viere el capítulo siguiente." The ironic "or" here has the force of "and." The audience seated in the room at the inn has been subtly expanded to encompass the reader explicitly, even though that audience forms part of the show in the reader's more comprehensive view.

There is a further delay, for a chapter ends, again reminding the reader that this is not only a story but also a book. A new chapter begins with a verse, like the novel itself, but this one is a composite quotation from Vergil: " 'Callaron todos, tirios y troyanos.' " This audience, no less heterogeneous than the one that heard Aeneas relate the fall of Troy, is composed of a would-be knight-errant, his squire, an innkeeper, a page, someone's cousin, others. It is composed not only of characters in a story but of readers of a book, and it is still waiting in silence for a puppet play that will suggest more than one parallel with the destruction of Troy before it is over. Trumpets and artillery sound. The assistant again begins to speak. This time there is no interference. His words now begin to flow and the story unfolds before characters and reader alike.

That story is the legend of Gaiferos and Melisendra, drawn from Spanish ballads of the pseudo-Carolingian cycle. Although the puppet play has no formal title, it is more than once described as the "libertad de Melisendra" in deference to its traditional ending, which is altered in a curious way in this performance. According to the assistant, the Liberation of Melisendra is a true history with a pedigree that can be traced through Spanish ballads back to French chronicles. The assistant alludes to certain authors who have had a hand in the compilation of this "true" history, but he mentions none of them by name and offers only ballad quotations as proof of the historicity of his account.

The story is a simple one. It begins in the middle of things, which is not surprising. In this performance, it ends in the same fashion, which is surprising or at least worthy of note. The peerless Melisendra, wife of Gaiferos, is held captive by the Moors in Spain. Urged on by Carlo Magno, Melisendra's "padre putativo," Gaiferos travels to Spain incognito and manages to communicate with Melisendra in her tower. Melisendra finally recognizes her husband and together they escape, pursued by the Moors. While the original legend follows them through Gaiferos' defeat of the

Moorish pursuers to a triumphant arrival in Paris, Maese Pedro's version of the "true" history comes to an abrupt end just as the Moors begin the chase.

Maese Pedro's assistant has no name. He is simply the "muchacho" or the "criado" until it is time for the puppet show, when three different yet related terms are used to designate his various functions in the spectacle: *intérprete, declarador, trujamán*. He is, etymologically as well as functionally, a mediator, a clarifier, a translator. The assistant stands alongside the stage, yet he is a central figure in the spectacle. His physical position shows that he is not part of the play, yet the operation he performs from the sidelines is essential to it. The pointer he holds calls attention in a graphic way not only to the puppets as they enter but also to his office as "interpreter and declarer." Since the puppets he points out enact the "misterios de tal retablo" (note the reminder, rich in connotations here, of the ecclesiastical origin of the name for the puppet stage), there is even the suggestion that his use of the wand will involve magic of a sort. And indeed it does, for the pointer enables him to cross over the footlights vicariously while he stands in the offstage world. Most narrators are Janus-like creatures. The assistant epitomizes this double nature as he watches the physical movements of the puppets and translates them into words at the same time as he gauges the effect of both movements and words upon the audience.

The most striking feature of Maese Pedro's puppet show is its hybrid form. As the story is acted out by puppets, it is being narrated by the assistant. Telling and showing are simultaneous here, and the puppet play is both a narrative act and a dramatic spectacle at the same time. The talking ape needed an interpreter to translate its soundless mimicry into oracular speech. The deciding factor of the illusion's power was words, which made credible what the spectators had seen the moment after they had seen it: an ape supposedly talking. So it is with the puppet's gestures too, despite Maese Pedro's injunction just before the show: " '*operibus credite, et non verbis.*' " Cervantes' reader has no choice but to depend upon the words.

Yet the words themselves of the puppet play are not in the

dramatic mode that even puppet plays require. The puppets do not have voices, let alone individual voices, supplied by the puppeteer. They do not even speak in the whistles which were commonly used for puppet speech in Cervantes' time, as J. E. Varey tells us. There is no dialogue in this play, which offers only two utterances supposedly issuing from the puppet characters. Both examples are quotations from ballads in which the characters do speak for themselves. But in this context, even these examples of direct discourse are so overladen with narrative preface—"dicen que le dijo," "con quien pasó todas aquellas razones y coloquios de aquel romance que dicen:...las cuales no digo yo ahora, porque de la prolijidad se suele engendrar el fastidio"—that the dramatic nature of this speech is, if not lost, greatly overshadowed by the teller's narrative style.

The assistant's temporal confusion shows the same thing in a different way, recalling once more the ballads, in which it occurs for different reasons. He begins his narrative of the events unfolding on the puppet stage in the present, the tense of all drama. But as the play proceeds, the assistant occasionally shifts into the imperfect, usually used to describe events evolving in the past and here a sign that narrative style is asserting itself over drama. Though the play is still in progress, the assistant sometimes even lapses into the preterit, the tense of completed history or of legend, but certainly not of a dramatic performance in the act of taking place.

The assistant's contant exhortations—"vean vuesas mercedes alli," "Miren vuesas mercedes," "Vuelvan vuesas mercedes los ojos"—do call attention to the visible activity on the stage, but they also remind the audience that it is being directed in its theatrical experience by a figure who does not ordinarily appear in a dramatic performance unless it be this most special kind: a narrator external to the events being enacted. So that even for the audience at the inn, who can "see" what Cervantes' reader must infer, the spectacle is at least as much a narrative experience as it is a dramatic one.

The assistant is a relentlessly minute narrator who leaves various important questions unanswered but revels in explaining the obvious. In his search for the illusion of history, he dwells, as the balladeers had sometimes done, on domestic and unheroic trivia. This gives an irreverent, not to say plebeian, view of the story of an emperor's daughter and her no less noble knight: the quarrel between father-in-law Carlo Magno and son-in-law Gaiferos, who would rather play chess than rescue his wife from the infidels; the request to borrow cousin Roldán's sword, which he here refuses to loan to cousin Gaiferos, contrary to the known ballads; the kiss stolen by the Moor from the lips of Melisendra, who spits in disgust and dries her mouth on her sleeve; the clumsy descent from the tower, during which Melisendra's skirt catches on the balcony railing and the princess is left unceremoniously hanging in mid-air by her petticoats.

Like all the narrators mentioned so far, the assistant does not confine himself to narrating events which have first been ordered by someone else. He renders them with commentary. Sometimes his parenthetical remarks are designed to support his claim to historical authenticity either by relating the world of his story to the world of his audience, or by defining the materials of the spectacle, or both: "en la ciudad de Sansueña, que así se llamaba entonces la que hoy se llama Zaragoza," "se presupone que es una de las torres del alcázar de Zaragoza, que ahora llaman la Aljafería . . ." Yet when the assistant points out an innovation in this particular version of the story, he admits to the spectator that an element of *poesis* has crept into the supposedly factual account: "Miren también un nuevo caso que ahora sucede, quizá no visto jamás."

The assistant also indulges in the purely personal aside that allows the spectator to see clearly where the narrator's sympathy lies and to be influenced in his reaction accordingly. His personal commentary twice threatens to turn into long-winded digression and its effect upon the immediate audience can be assessed from the criticism it provokes. I shall consider the criticisms later.

In the assistant, then, Cervantes presents a narrator who is both part of the performance and part of the creative act and is also the ideal spectator. What of the audience in this spectacle? The mute crowd of Tyrians and Trojans finds a voice in Don

Quijote, who is the principal spectator not only by virtue of being the hero of the story, but also because he is the one member of the group who makes his reactions known. Don Quijote is the spectator dramatized, and the effect of the play upon him is what the reader is meant to notice.

Because of his madness, Don Quijote cannot clearly distinguish literature from life. He is convinced that the heroes of romance were once people of flesh and blood and that the account of their deeds given in chivalric novels is history. This conviction is what determines his reaction to the puppet play. Taking the narrator at his word, which requires little or no adjustment, Don Quijote readily accepts the premise that the legend of Gaiferos and Melisendra is history. His remarks show that he prefers to have it treated as such.

When the assistant digresses in order to express his moral indignation against the Moors' dispatch in punishing culprits, Don Quijote breaks into the narrative to remind him: "—Niño, niño . . . seguid vuestra historia línea recta y no os metáis en las curvas o transversales; que para sacar una verdad en limpio menester son muchas pruebas y repruebas."

Later, when the interpreter describes the city of Zaragoza drowned in the pealing of bells, Don Quijote again interrupts the narrative (as well as Maese Pedro's sound effects) to correct the facts. He argues not so much with the narrator as, over the narrator's head, with the playwright himself: "—¡Eso no! . . . En esto de las campanas anda muy impropio maese Pedro, porque entre moros no se usan campanas, sino atabales, y un género de dulzainas que parecen nuestras chirimías; y esto de sonar campanas en Sansueña sin duda que es un gran disparate."

Annoyed by the narrator's digression before, Don Quijote here provides one himself. He apparently supplies historical proof as well. Maese Pedro, from behind the scenes, defends himself and orders his assistant to get on with the story. When the assistant does continue, he repeats the description of Sansueña. But this time he incorporates Don Quijote's correction into his narrative. It begins to seem that the spectator not only experiences the effect of the play but also exerts his effect upon it in turn. The spectator who participates in the telling is an appropriate partner for a narrator who leads the viewing. This is a retable of marvels indeed.

The last time that Don Quijote interrupts the puppet play, it is to make the spectator's effect upon the spectacle felt in a literal way. Having corrected the narrator's style, having altered the narrative, interrupting both action and illusion each time, he now intervenes physically. Aroused by the description of the Moorish cavalcade and by the offstage ringing of bells (for Maese Pedro has not corrected the sound effects), Don Quijote makes his final commitment to the illusion onstage. In his imagination, the puppets have become not only historical beings, but living people whose lives extend forward into a future still to be lived rather than backward into an already determined past. On the pathetic premise that he can alter the course of what he considers history come alive, Don Quijote attacks the Moorish pursuers. He is innocent of the knowledge that the happy escape of Gaiferos and Melisendra is guaranteed not by irreversible history but rather by unalterable legend. In either case, their fate is beyond Don Quijote's power. His noble intentions blindly carried out once more produce contrary results. Luckily, it is only the puppets who suffer. Unable to accept art as art, even in a puppet show where the illusion is minimal, Don Quijote attempts to invade the impenetrable world of fiction. This effort is as vain as his many attempts to impose the world of fiction upon the ordinary lives of men. The disaster that follows is the total destruction of the puppet play and the puppets by the one spectator who demonstrates, in destroying them, how completely he had fallen under their spell. He will realize his mistake too late.

It is now time to take a closer look at Maese Pedro, the itinerant mountebank. His puppets are dehumanized miniatures of human actors, and he himself may be considered a caricature of the *autor* of Spanish Renaissance tradition, the theatrical impresario who both managed his troupe of actors and wrote plays for them to perform. Maese Pedro has created his version of the Liberation of Melisendra by combining a number of scenes from different versions of an old ballad into a continuous story, not without adding a few strokes of his own. He is, in the most literal sense, the prime mover of the puppet play that he animates on his marvelous retable. The strings that lead from his hands to the puppets' limbs (J. E. Varey shows that Cervantes' description is based, to a large extent if not exclusively, on puppets with strings) are the tangible signs of his connection with their movements and with the play's action. The very explicitness of this link between author and puppet must have influenced Cervantes to use in this episode a puppet play rather than a more conventional play with human actors, which Avellaneda treated so unimaginatively in that strikingly similar episode of his spurious second part.

Maese Pedro, serving as his own barker, urges the spectators to take their seats and promises Don Quijote: "Sesenta mil [mara villas] encierra en sí este mi retablo: dígole a vuesa merced, mi señor don Quijote, que es una de las cosas más de ver que hoy tiene el mundo, y *operibus credite, et non verbis,* y manos a labor; que se hace tarde y tenemos mucho que hacer, y que decir, y que mostrar." Do and tell and show. Thus does the creator describe his spectacle. The mechanics of the performance are as important as the story itself. The telling, as we have already seen, is deputed to the assistant. The showing is the function of both the assistant who points out, and Maese Pedro, who figures forth. But the doing will be Maese Pedro's task alone, and on this all else depends. The Latin epigram is not without its irony in this context, where telling stems from showing, words from actions, the whole from Maese Pedro's hands.

After his barker's prologue, Maese Pedro disappears behind the scenes. Most playwrights are content to remain there in silence. Even Pirandello, in that famous case which both Castro and Livingstone have compared to this one, prefers to observe from the wings the struggle of his characters towards an identity, a play and an author. But Maese Pedro is not content to limit himself to so passive a role and to allow his play to speak for itself. He remains hidden, one might say immanent, yet his participation as author in the play is as fully dramatized as the narrator's and spectator's.

Maese Pedro, like his spectator, breaks into the play to offer his commentary on the narrative in progress. When Don Quijote bids the assistant develop the story along a straight line, Maese Pedro seconds the advice: "—Muchacho, no te metas en dibujos, sino haz lo que ese señor te manda, que será lo más acertado; sigue tu canto llano, y no te metas en contrapuntos, que se suelen quebrar de sotiles." It is not often that a playwright is in a position to overhear the spectator, let alone take sides with him, while the play is in progress. In doing so here, he seems to disagree with the assistant's stylistic falsification of his intentions. The assistant, merely a deputy, must obey.

At the point where the assistant harangues the fleeing lovers, "¡Vais en paz, oh par sin par de verdaderos amantes! . . . ," Maese Pedro interrupts the overblown periods to deliver from behind the scenes (as though he were speaking from out of a cloud) a second lesson in the art of storytelling even as the story is being told: "—Llaneza, muchacho: no te encumbres; que toda afectación es mala!" Again he introduces into the performance an element that does not belong there.

Maese Pedro's longest comment occurs when he hears himself criticized for ringing bells in Sansueña. This time he not only intrudes into the sacrosanct precinct of the story but gives himself away besides. The creator controlling the puppets speaks to both spectator and storyteller. He injects into the play a truly gratuitous element, a confession of his own insincerity, his materialistic credo where even an artistic one spoken directly by him would be out of place: "—No mire vuesa merced en niñerías, señor don Quijote, ni quiera llevar las cosas tan por el cabo, que no se le halle. ¿No se representan por ahí, casi de ordinario, mil comedias llenas de mil impropiedades y disparates, y, con todo eso, corren felicísimamente su carrera, y se escuchan no sólo con aplauso, sino con admiración y todo? Prosigue, muchacho y deja decir; que como yo llene mi talego, siquiera represente más impropiedades que tiene átomos el sol." Maese Pedro is again at variance with his deputized narrator. He has just confessed that he does not believe in the kind of historical integrity that his assistant in vain claims for the play. Not does he defend the inaccuracy by dismissing it as the kind of trivial detail that does not matter—in poetry. Who but Don Quijote could remain spellbound after this cynical admission? For though this may well be the truth behind many a creation, to say so in the creation itself is to undermine the illusion at its very source.

With Don Quijote's violent intrusion into the puppet play, the ending of this version of the legend of the liberation of Melisendra is drastically altered. Instead of witnessing the triumphant return to Paris, the audience at the inn sees, rather, the destruction of the paraphernalia of Maese Pedro's production, very nearly of Maese Pedro himself. It is only in what might be called this last act, a finale which neither the legend nor Maese Pedro had envisaged, that the reaction of the rest of the audience is mentioned: "Alborotóse el senado de los oyentes, huyóse el mono por los tejados de la venta, temió el Primo, acobardóse el Paje, y hasta el mesmo Sancho Panza tuvo pavor grandísimo, porque, como él juró después de pasada la borrasca, jamás había visto a su señor con tan desatinada cólera."

The fear of the rest of the audience, which in Sancho's case will give way to pity as well, suggests that for them the history of the Liberation of Melisendra in its unforeseen denouement has turned into something akin to a Senecan tragedy. In this last act of the spectacle, it is the puppeteer on whom the audience focuses its attention. After the violent intrusion of the outside world, the creator stands in the foreground, surrounded by his mutilated creatures and his retable. Maese Pedro is hardly a tragic figure in the Aristotelian mold, yet he is pathetic as he laments the loss of his paraphernalia, of his livelihood. His lament for his lost possessions moves towards the kind of larger context that all elegies seek. It begins as a gloss of the ballad in which King Rodrigo mourns the loss of his kingdom. Maese Pedro, as owner of a puppet theater, was also lord of kings and emperors a moment ago. Yet now he is reduced to nothing. Maese Pedro's figurative language is an echo of the theatrical metaphors that have been commonplace since Antiquity, as Curtius points out. Even Sancho is familiar with them through his preacher. But despite the fact that this language uttered by an impostor is disproportionate to the situation and applied to a mere puppet show, it does evoke serious overtones. The very way that Maese Pedro moves from puppet stage to kingdom recalls the steps described by that other conjurer Prospero, in his enlargement from "the baseless fabric of this vision" through the "cloud-capped towers" to "the great globe itself." For, cynical though his motives are, Maese Pedro is the creator of the puppet play. And even though he does so at the same time that he asks Don Quijote to pay damages, he nevertheless defines his relationship to the creatures, now relics, who enacted *misterios* on his marvelous retable: "Y estas reliquias que están por este duro y estéril suelo, ¿quién las esparció y aniquiló sino la fuerza invencible dese poderoso brazo? Y ¿cúyos eran sus cuerpos sino míos? Y ¿con quién me sustentaba yo sino con ellos?" The maimed puppets, even though for mercenary reasons, are after all so many of Maese Pedro's bodies, other selves that are a little more solid, perhaps, than those spirits of Prospero's who vanish into thin air. They are the creatures used by this greedy demiurge to create his false illusions. Yet Maese Pedro is only a demiurge, a subordinate creator, and his broken little world is contained within the larger one governed by Cide Hamete, who is about to give a more complete account of the puppeteer.

The implied reader, with whom the reader of Cervantes' book is meant to identify, enjoys the advantage of distance and superior knowledge over Maese Pedro's audience as well as over the creator and narrator of the puppet play. He knows that the story of Gaiferos and Melisendra is a fiction and is therefore impervious to the assistant's protestations of historical truth. He sees the fiction in turn as a burlesque of a legend and of chivalric material in general. He watches while the play is cut up into divisions that are travesties of acts not because of any inner necessity but because during this caricature of a dramatic performance a spectator and the playwright keep interrupting the narrator and breaking the continuity. He notes, in a way that the audience seems not to, the creator's destructive admission of insincerity. All of these things amount to what Brecht might call *Verfremdungsefekte* and keep him from falling under the spell of Maese Pedro's illusion. He merely watches others being gulled by a charlatan.

But although the reader experiences the spectacle from this superior vantage point, he is at the same time surpassed in knowledge by the chronicler and the intermediaries, who have one further secret to reveal. While the reader may not succumb to the marvels of Maese Pedro's retable, he unwittingly falls victim to another illusion mounted by Cide Hamete and sustained by the intermediaries.

After witnessing the destruction of Maese Pedro's puppet show and sharing, to some extent, Sancho's sympathy for its creator's loss, the reader looks upon Don Quijote's payment of damages as a fair recompense for the puppeteer's vanished livelihood. It is right that the madman, who could not see the play for what it was, should pay for the equipment he destroyed. Don Quijote himself eventually admits the justice of it. But just after this sympathy is aroused, the reader is told something about Maese Pedro that affects his view. He learns that Maese Pedro is not Maese Pedro at all, but Ginés de Pasamonte, whose acquaintance he had made before. In case he does not remember, the chronicler reminds him that this is the same villainous Ginés who had repaid with a volley of stones Don Quijote's kindness in freeing him from a chain gang. The same Ginés who, after that, had stolen Sancho's donkey and thus wrought an injustice not only upon Sancho but also upon the author of the book, who had to take criticism for the fact that the printer had omitted the passage in part I where the theft is described.

Maese Pedro is an impostor in his own life also and the disguise has been penetrated. The reader has been deceived, then enlightened by the chronicler. The other intermediaries concur in the deception by maintaining Cide Hamete's arrangement of events in their retelling. Theoretically, any one of them might have pointed out the disguise at the beginning and thus spared the reader from squandering his sympathy.

The reader has just been shown how easy it is to be taken in by one illusion at the very moment that he might be satisfied with himself for not having been taken in by another. This knowledge won at his own expense, is not soon forgotten. It is essential for him to be armed with it if he is to understand Cervantes' novel properly. The reader's newly sharpened wariness is immediately applied to the explanation of Maese Pedro's identity itself. The Moorish chronicler is responsible for the unmasking. He swears an oath on it like a true Christian. The second author reports verbatim a literal translation of the oath and passes on the Morisco translator's explanation that "el jurar Cide Hamete como católico cristiano siendo él moro, como sin duda lo era, no quiso decir otra cosa sino que así como el católico cristiano cuando jura, jura o debe jurar verdad y decirla en lo que dijere, así él la decía, como si jurara como cristiano católico . . ." (II, xxvii). But how can the reader trust such a strange oath sworn by a Moor who is suspect and explained by a no less suspect Morisco? That the reader remembers to ask such a question is in itself a protection against the kind of ingenuous belief that Don Quijote has just shown in the puppet show, a necessary protection against the continuing blend of clarification and mystification he finds in *Don Quijote.*

With the final discovery of Maese Pedro's identity, the reader is at last in a position to see the episode of the puppet show from the vantage point of the chronicler, however unreliable that vantage point may be. After he has seen the entire novel, he perceives in addition certain mutually illuminating coincidences between the part and the whole. It is to these that I now turn.

Ginés de Pasamonte is as much a literary man as he is a criminal. He is an author, though an unpublished one. This point is made when he first appears in the chain gang episode of part I, where he and Don Quijote discuss the autobiography he wrote with his own thumbs: *La vida de Ginés de Pasamonte.* The information that he had composed a thick volume describing his crimes is repeated, lest it be overlooked, in the explanation of the Maese Pedro disguise. In the puppet show, Pasamonte works in a different medium. No longer the first-person narrator of an autobiographical narrative which can presumably claim to be historical, he is here the creator of the Liberation of Melisendra which, disguised as Maese Pedro, he animates but which he leaves to a narrator to tell. Ginés de Pasamonte, has, in other words, first assumed a fictitious identity, the Maese Pedro disguise, and then surrendered the actual telling of his hybrid creation to his assistant because that is what this art form demands. When he intervenes in the performance, it is because his narrator or spectator gets out of hand, but he intervenes as Maese Pedro, a character created by him in the living play which is his life now that he is living it as another.

What, if not something very close in principle to this, has Cervantes done in his disposition of the narrative scheme of *Don Quijote*? Cide Hamete once confesses (II, xliv) that speaking "por las bocas de pocas personas" is an unbearable effort for him. So, too, it is for Cervantes, who, rather than narrate the novel in his own person, not only delegates the role of author of the supposed history to Cide Hamete but also adds both a translator and interpreters to interpret and declare—translate and narrate—the story. The relationship that the author-criminal Ginés de Pasamonte bears to the puppeteer Maese Pedro, and he in turn to the assistant is, in its essentials, the same as that which Cervantes bears to the chronicler Cide Hamete and he in turn to his translator and interpreters. Ginés de Pasamonte, the historical self who is the subject of his autobiography, has no place in Maese Pedro's puppet show. Nor has Cervantes left an explicit place for himself as author in *Don Quijote*. His purpose in excluding himself from the novel (except as just another reference in his characters' conversation) was not to elude ultimate authorial responsibility, as many seem still to believe, but rather to render his creation artistically self-sufficient.

Only with reference to this plural *dédoublement*, so intricately constructed, can the reader of *Don Quijote* understand the full implication of the remark that Cervantes utters as author in his own voice in the prologue to part I: "Pero yo, que, aunque parezco padre, soy padrastro de don Quijote. . . ."

The novel as a whole even has its counterparts to Don Quijote who interrupts and corrects Maese Pedro's puppet play and to the assistant who watches both play and audience while he tells the story. These are the intermediaries who are simultaneously dramatized readers and intruding narrators. The discrepancies between puppeteer and assistant, between action and words, are in the novel inaccuracies of translation: "Dicen que en el propio original desta historia se lee que llegando Cide Hamete a escribir este capítulo, no le tradujo su intérprete como él le había escrito" (II, xliv).

There are, finally, other striking similarities between the whole and the part. These have to do with story. The Liberation of Melisendra is a tissue of ballads. So, also, is *Don Quijote* in the early chapters of part I. According to Menéndez Pidal, a short burlesque of ballads is all that Cervantes intended to produce until he discovered the possibilities latent in the material and enlarged his scope to include romances of chivalry. The irreverent treatment of Gaiferos and Melisendra echoes the chronicler's mock-heroic view of Don Quijote and Dulcinea, and certain coincidences of detail seem designed to make the connection explicit. Melisendra captive in the Moorish palace, must be rescued by Gaiferos, just as Dulcinea, prisoner of a wizard's spell, as Don Quijote believes must be rescued from the Cave of Montesinos by Don Quijote— or rather, disenchanted by Sancho, who is just as unwilling to flagellate himself as Gaiferos is to leave his chess game. Melisendra's leap onto the croup of Gaiferos' horse, where she sat "a horcajadas como hombre," invites comparison with the earlier episode in which the country lass (Dulcinea, according to Sancho) falls from her mount and takes a running leap into the saddle, where "quedó a horcajadas, como si fuera hombre" (II, x). All that is made of Melisendra's *faldellín* in the descent from the tower recalls the *faldellín* (and it was this very garment) that the same country lass Dulcinea had already offered Don Quijote as collateral for a loan in the Cave of Montesinos. These similarities are enough to account for Don Quijote's empathy with the fleeing lovers in the puppet show, though only his madness is responsible for transforming empathy into belief and belief into overt action.

Maese Pedro's puppet show is, then, an analogue to the novel as a whole, not merely because the burlesque legend that Maese

Pedro recreates with puppets is a *reductio ad absurdum* of the same chivalric material that Cervantes burlesques through his characters, but also because it reproduces on a miniature scale the same basic relationships among storyteller, story and audience that are discernible in the novel's overall scheme. Yet analogy does not imply absolute identity, and the discrepancies in this case are as meaningful as the correspondences.

Maese Pedro's puppet show is the creation of a charlatan with no purpose but to delude the unwary for money, whereas *Don Quijote* is the creation of a writer who aspires to a higher kind of entertainment aimed at instructing the reader as well as delighting him. Maese Pedro addresses himself to ignorant, superstitious folk and to a benign madman, while *Don Quijote* is directed towards an implied reader who is educable and potentially prudent. In Maese Pedro's show a spectator is carried away by the illusion; but in Cervantes' novel, the constant alienation effects prevent him from remaining spellbound for very long.

It is established from the very beginning of the novel that Don Quijote's madness is caused by an overdose of fiction and shows up most clearly whenever fiction, especially the chivalric romance, comes into play. The novel follows his repeated attempts and failures to revive the chivalric romance in the most literal way: by living it and urging others to follow his example for more than their own amusement at a madman's antics. In the puppet show, Don Quijote comes face to face with fiction presented as history. He reacts predictably, as we have seen, because he is a madman. But Cervantes' reader is prudent, or at least will be when Cervantes has done with him, and the puppet show reminds him of this fact once again, this time in an analogue with implications that concern his reading of the whole novel.

Cervantes' expressed purpose, if not necessarily his only one, in writing *Don Quijote* is to discredit the chivalric romances. He says so several times in a variety of voices. Speaking as author in his own voice in the prologue to part I, he seconds the advice offered by the friend who bursts into his study to deliver the harangue that Cervantes turns into the Prologue itself: "En efecto llevad la mira puesta a derribar la máquina mal fundada destos caballerescos libros, aborrecidos de tantos y alabados de muchos más. . . ." This sentiment is repeated at the end of the novel by another of Cervantes' many second selves. Cide Hamete claims that "no ha sido otro mi deseo que poner en aborrecimiento de los hombres las fingidas y disparatadas historias de los libros de caballerías, que por las de mi verdadero don Quijote van ya tropezando y han de caer del todo, sin duda alguna" (II, lxxiv). The reader has learned to be wary of such "true histories," and Maese Pedro's puppet show has helped make him so.

Yet one must read these statements with caution. *Don Quijote* contains evidence of the delight which the chivalric novel provided for many readers. The Cura and the Barbero spare several romances from the bonfire. Those that escape the holocaust are spared because one or another technical excellence outweighs in the judges eyes the extravagance of the stories they have to tell. The Canónigo de Toledo disapproves of chivalric romances in general, yet confesses that he has enjoyed reading some and has even tried his hand at writing a fragment of one. These characters and others like them are, despite their foibles, people in whom discretion is shown to override whatever human failings they may have. In this, they resemble the reader that Cervantes has molded in the process of telling his story: the discreet reader who learns to be wary through experience and for whom Don Quijote's unrestrained participation in the puppet play stands as an example to be shunned.

In proposing to discredit the chivalric novel, Cervantes does not suggest that we not read chivalric novels, but only that we read them properly for what they are, outlandish and sometimes beautiful lies, fiction rather than history. In order to achieve this end he shows the reader how such fictions masquerading as histories are put together by laying bare their inner workings. Starting with one such invented history written by an unreliable Moorish chronicler, then emphasizing the unreliability by showing how the possibility of error and the impossibility of verification are multiplied with each stage in the transmission of the account to the book, he provides an object lesson in how fiction is created with the very techniques used in the writing of history, itself an ambiguous word in Spanish.

The reader, if he did not know this before, can see the process demonstrated with variations again and again. He witnesses the illusion of lifelike history alternately created and torn down before his eyes. He therefore cannot take the illusion at face value unless he is as mad as Don Quijote. The very presentation ensures his alienation, for Cervantes knows that belief can only interfere with, even destroy, the reader's perception of the bittersweet humor and the rhetorical purpose which it serves. But the techniques of alienation, at the same time that they interfere with identification and belief, direct the reader's attention inevitably towards the artificial nature of the invention itself, soliciting his admiration (as Cervantes through his characters often does in so many words) and above all his appreciation of the fiction as fiction. The friend of the prologue to part I put it this way: "Procurad también que leyendo vuestra historia el melancólico se mueva a risa, el risueño la acreciente, el simple no se enfade, el discreto se admire de la invención, el grave no la desprecie, ni el prudente deje de alabarla." The invention is the handiwork of the novelist. In taking it exactly for what it is, the reader reciprocates the creator's virtuosity with an appropriate aesthetic response.

Notes

This lecture was first delivered on 12 November 1964, for the University of Chicago's Festival of Shakespeare and the Renaissance, and repeated at Bryn Mawr College on 9 March 1965. The material here presented forms part of a longer study in which it will appear in a somewhat revised form. Therefore, no attempt has been made to alter it for the present purpose.

All quotations from the *Quijote* are drawn from Francisco Rodríguez Marín's *Nueva edición crítica* (Madrid: Ediciones Atlas, 1947–1949). Only those passages not found in the prologue or in the Maese Pedro episode itself (II, xxv–xxvi) are identified by part and chapter.

The critical and scholarly works referred to in the text are, in this order: E. C. Riley, *Cervantes's Theory of the Novel* (Oxford: Clarendon Press, 1962), esp. 205–12; José Ortega y Gasset, *Meditaciones del Quijote*, in *Obras completas*, I (Madrid: Revista de Occidente, 1946), 380; J. E. Varey, *Historia de los títeres en España* (Madrid: Revista de Occidente, 1957), esp. 232–37; Américo Castro, "Cervantes y Pirandello," in *Santa Teresa y otros ensayos* (Madrid: Santander, 1929), 219–31; Leon Livingstone, "Interior Duplication and the Problem of Form in the Modern Spanish Novel," *PMLA*, 73 (1958): 397; Ernst Robert Curtius, *European Literature and the Latin Middle Ages*, trans. Willard R. Trask, Bollingen Series, 36 (New York: Pantheon, 1953), 138–44; Ramón Menéndez Pidal, *Un aspecto en la elaboración del "Quijote"* (Madrid: "La Lectura," 1924).

Self-Portraits

Introduced by
Roberto González Echevarría

MIGUEL DE CERVANTES

◆   ◆   ◆

IT IS CUSTOMARY in these casebooks to include an inter-
view with the author in question. Because this is obviously
impossible with Cervantes, I thought that a reasonable substitute
would be the following self-portraits he left in two of his prologues.

Cervantes wrote a great deal about himself not only in the
prologues to his books but also in his fiction, where he incorporates much from his own life. The greatest example of this is
the captive's tale in part I of *Don Quixote*, which is a thinly veiled
autobiographical account of his years as a prisoner in Algiers. I
have no doubt that Cervantes felt that his literary works were a
reflection of his life in many ways, so he had no qualms about
turning episodes of his life into fiction. But by self-portrait I have
something more specific in mind: an overt description of himself
that included physical traits, not just anecdotes or self-evaluations
as an artist. There are plenty of the latter not just in the prologues but also in *Voyage to Parnassus*, where he offers a frank and
harsh assessment of himself as a poet.

Cervantes' self-portraits must be seen in connection to portraiture and self-portraiture in renaissance and baroque painting. The practice of painting portraits began in the Renaissance for two related reasons: the rise of a wealthy class willing and able to pay to have their likeness reproduced and the development of individualism. In his *Oration on the Dignity of Man*, Pico della Mirandola rejects the medieval concepts of humanity as sinful and restricted by predestination to proclaim instead the individual's freedom and capacity for self-cultivation. From a technical point of view, the advent of perspective as a method to represent bodies as three-dimensional in their full measure and weight made possible a degree of realism not available before. Those being painted wanted to be recognizable for their specific features, their portraits a self-celebration and a way to ensure the immortality of their bodies. The glory of renaissance and baroque portraits is the way in which gestures, physical qualities, and clothing define a person. The most important part is, of course, the face, but the body's bearing and mass also serve to capture the uniqueness of the subject. A similar process takes place in literature using different techniques, to be sure, but the emphasis lies in the depiction of details. Who can forget Cervantes' portraits of Don Quijote, Sancho, and Maritornes? In all of them weight, height, and facial features play a significant role.

The first self-portrait by an artist in which the painter appears facing the spectator is Albrecht Dürer's "Self-Portrait with Fur Lined Coat," which is from 1500 and hangs today in Munich's Alte Pinakothek. It is a remarkably individualized picture in which several physical features are highlighted, particularly the eyes, the serene yet penetrating gaze, and a hand, delicate and expressive, as if indicating that it is the instrument of the painter's craft. But the most famous self-portrait is Velázquez's in "Las Meninas." There we see a vigorous man in the act of painting who has usurped the prominent position that should have been the monarchs', who are presumably the subjects of the picture. Velázquez shows himself as a determined individual, full of energy and self-assurance, who is proud of his art and social position. Cervantes offers a more unassuming, characteristically self-deprecating picture of himself in the self-portraits that follow.

In the first, from the prologue to *Exemplary Stories* (1613), he provides the only description that we have of his body, particularly of his face, with details about his nose and hair. What is remarkable in this self-portrait is Cervantes' resigned tone before the ravages of aging: the gray hair, the poor uneven teeth, and the heavy body. It is not an idealized picture. His body appears scarred by time and the wear and tear of life; individualized by them, as it were. In the touching prologue to *The Trials of Persiles and Sigismunda*, Cervantes' farewell, we find again the aging body, this time sickly and on the verge of death. What is most moving in this text is the ironic detachment with which Cervantes deals with his newly acquired fame. His self-image, probably influenced by the infirmity of his body but also by the experiences of a long and hard life, is a humble one. Yet one would like to believe that he knew that his creations would immortalize his spirit if not his frail body; that even if he rebutted the student's celebration of his genius, he nevertheless included it in the prologue because he felt that it was in some way deserved.

From Prologue to *Exemplary Novels* (1613)

I should like, if it were possible, dearest reader, to be excused from writing this prologue—the one I composed for my *Don Quixote* did not turn out so well for me that I should care to follow it here with another. In the present case, a certain friend of mine is to blame, one of the many whom I have acquired in the course of my life, thanks to my disposition rather than to my intellect. He might very well, as the custom is, have made an engraving of me for the frontispiece of this book; for the famous Don Juan de Jáuregui would have provided him with my portrait, and in that way my ambition would have been satisfied, as well as the desire that some have to know what kind of face and figure belong to him who has had the boldness to come out into the market place of the world and exhibit so many stories to the gaze of the peoples. Beneath this portrait my friend might have placed the following inscription:

"This man you see here with the aquiline countenance, the chestnut hair, the smooth, untroubled brow, the bright eyes, the hooked yet well-proportioned nose, the silvery beard that less than a score of years ago was golden, the big mustache, the small mouth, the teeth that are scarcely worth mentioning (there are but half a dozen of them altogether, in bad condition and very badly placed, no two of them corresponding to another pair), the body of medium height, neither tall nor short, the high complexion that is fair rather than dark, the slightly stooping shoulders, and the somewhat heavy build—this, I may tell you, is the author of *La Galatea* and *Don Quixote de la Mancha*; he it was who composed the *Journey to Parnassus*, in imitation of Cesare Caporali of Perusa, as well as other works that are straying about in these parts—without the owner's name, likely as not.

"He is commonly called Miguel de Cervantes Saavedra. He was a soldier for many years and a captive for five and a half, an experience that taught him patience in adversity. In the naval battle of Lepanto he lost his left hand as the result of a harquebus shot, a wound which, however unsightly it may appear, he looks upon as beautiful, for the reason that it was received on the most memorable and sublime occasion that past ages have known or those to come may hope to know; for he was fighting beneath the victorious banner of the son of that thunderbolt of war, Charles V of blessed memory."

And if this friend of mine of whom I am complaining had been unable to think of anything else to say of me, I could have made up and secretly given him a couple of dozen tributes to myself such as would have spread my fame abroad and established my reputation as a genius. For it is foolish to believe that such eulogies are scrupulously truthful, since praise and blame never have precise limits. But the short of it is the opportunity was missed, and I have been left in the lurch and without a portrait.

Prologue to *The Trials of Persiles and Sigismunda* (1616)

As it happened, dearest reader, a couple of friends and I were coming from the famous village of Esquivias—famous for a thousand reasons, one of them being its illustrious families while another is its illustrious wines—when I noticed someone behind us spurring on his mount in great haste with the apparent desire of overtaking us, a desire which he clearly manifested by calling out to us to slacken our pace a little. We waited for him, and a sparrow-like student came riding up on a she-ass; for he was all clad in dark gray, with leggings, round-toed shoes, sword and scabbard, and a Walloon ruff with matching tassels—the truth is, there were but two of them left, since the ruff was continually slipping down on one side, and it was all he could do to straighten it again.

"You gentlemen," he remarked as he reached our side, "must be after some office or benefice in the capital, seeing that His Eminence of Toledo and His Majesty are now there. It surely could be nothing less in view of the speed at which you are traveling; for this donkey of mine, I may tell you, has come out the winner in more than one race."

It was one of my companions who answered him. "Señor Miguel de Cervantes' hack," he said, "must bear the blame; he is somewhat long-paced."

No sooner did he hear the name Cervantes than the student slid down from his mount, letting his saddlebag fall on one side, his portmanteau on the other (for he was carrying all this luggage with him). He ran up to me and threw himself upon me and seized me by the left hand.

"Ah, yes!" he cried, "so this is the maimed one who is whole, the wholly famous and brilliant writer, in short, the darling of the Muses!"

Upon hearing all these compliments lavished upon me in so short a space of time, I felt it would be a lack of courtesy not to show my appreciation; and accordingly I put my arm about his neck, which nearly caused him to lose his Walloon ruff altogether.

"That," I said, "is an error into which many of my ill-informed friends have fallen. I, sir, am Cervantes, but not the Muses' darling nor any of the other foolish things you say I am. Your Grace had best catch your donkey and mount him. We have not much farther to go, and we will have a good talk as we ride along."

The student courteously did as suggested and, reining in somewhat, we continued on our way at a leisurely pace. The conversation happening to turn upon my illness, the worthy student promptly deprived me of all hope by saying, "That sickness of yours is dropsy, and all the water in the ocean cannot cure you, no matter how sweetly you drink it. Señor Cervantes, you should take care to restrain your drinking, but do not forget to eat."

"That," I replied, "is what many have told me; but I might as well resign myself not to drink any more at all, just as if I had been born for no other purpose. My life is drawing to a close, and at the rate my pulse is going it will end its career, at the latest, next Sunday, and that will be the end of me. Your Grace has made my acquaintance at a critical moment, and I have not enough time left to show my gratitude for the good will toward me which you have displayed."

At this point we reached the Toledo bridge, and I proceeded to cross it while he rode off to enter the city by the bridge of Segovia. As to what may be said about all this, my reputation will take care of itself: my friends will take pleasure in repeating such things, which give me an even greater pleasure as I listen to them. We turned to embrace each other once more, and then he spurred his donkey, leaving me as ill-disposed as he was ill-mounted on that she-ass of his.

He had afforded me a fine opportunity to write some charming things about him; but all times are not the same. A time will come, perhaps, when I shall knot this broken thread and say what should be said but which I cannot say here. Good-by, thanks; good-by, compliments; good-by, merry friends. I am dying, and my wish is that I may see you all soon again, happy in the life to come.

Note

Both excerpts are from *The Portable Cervantes*, trans. Samuel Putnam (New York: Viking Press, 1951), 705–6, 800–802.

Bibliography

Annotated Editions

Francisco Rodríguez Marín (Madrid: Ediciones Atlas, 1947), 10 vols.
Luis Andrés Murillo (Madrid: Editorial Castalia, 1978), 3 vols. Volume 3
   has a highly recommended "Bibliografía fundamental."
John Jay Allen (Madrid: Cátedra, 1990), 2 vols.
Francisco Rico, coordinador, edición del Instituto Cervantes, dirigida por
   Francisco Rico (Barcelona: Instituto Cervantes, 1998). Companion
   volume, called *Volumen complementario*, contains notes, commentaries,
   and bibliography.

Translations

The History and Adventures of the Renowned Don Quixote, trans. Tobias Smollett,
   with an introduction by Keith Whitlock. Ware, Herfordshire, U.K.:
   Wordsworth Editions, 1998. /1755/
The Adventures of Don Quixote, trans. J. M. Cohen. London: Penguin Books,
   1950.

273

The Ingenious Hidalgo Don Quixote de la Mancha, trans. John Rutherford, with an introduction by Roberto González Echevarría. New York: Penguin Books, 2001.

Don Quixote. A New Translation, trans. Edith Grossman, with an introduction by Harold Bloom. New York: HarperCollins, 2003.

Biographies

William Byron, *Cervantes: A Biography*. Garden City, N.Y.: Doubleday, 1978.

Jean Canavaggio, *Cervantes*, trans. J. R. Jones. New York: W.W. Norton, 1990.

Malveena McKendrick, *Cervantes*. Boston: Little, Brown, 1980.

Richard Predmore, *Cervantes*. New York: Dodd, Mead, 1973.

Collections of Essays

Harold Bloom, ed. *Miguel de Cervantes*. New York: Chelsea House, 1987.

Ruth El Saffar and Diana de Armas Wilson, eds. *Quixotic Desire: Psychoanalytic Perspectives on Cervantes*. Ithaca, N.Y.: Cornell University Press, 1993.

Angel Flores and M. J. Bernardete, eds. *Cervantes across the Centuries*. New York: Druden Press, 1947.

Lowry Nelson, Jr. ed. *Cervantes: A Collection of Critical Essays*. Englewood Cliffs, N.J.: Prentice Hall, 1969.

Books on Cervantes

John Jay Allen, *Don Quixote: Hero or Fool? A Study in Narrative Technique*. Gainesville: University Presses of Florida, 1969.

Anthony Cascardi, ed. *The Cambridge Companion to Cervantes*. Cambridge: Cambridge University Press, 2002.

Anthony Close, *The Romantic Approach to "Don Quixote": A Critical History of the Romantic Tradition in "Quixote" Criticism*. Cambridge: Cambridge University Press, 1977.

Georgina Dopico Black, *Perfect Wives, Other Women: Adultery and Inquisition in Early Modern Spain*. Durham, N.C.: Duke University Press, 2001.

Edward Dudley, *The Endless Text: Don Quixote and the Hermeneutics of Romance.* Albany: State University of New York Press, 1997.

Manuel Durán, *Cervantes.* New York: Twayne, 1974.

Ruth El Saffar, *Distance and Control in Don Quixote: A Study in Narrative Technique.* Chapel Hill: North Carolina Studies in the Romance Languages and Literatures, 1975.

————. *Beyond Fiction: The Recovery of the Feminine in the Novels of Cervantes.* Berkeley: University of California Press, 1984.

Robert Folger, *Images in Mind: Lovesickness, Spanish Sentimental Fiction and Don Quijote.* Chapel Hill: North Carolina Studies in the Romance Languages and Literatures, 2002.

Alban K. Forcione, *Cervantes, Aristotle and the Persiles.* Princeton: Princeton University Press, 1970.

María Antonia Garcés, *Cervantes in Algiers: A Captive's Tale.* Nashville, Tenn.: Vanderbilt University Press, 2002.

Roberto González Echevarría, *Love and the Law in Cervantes.* New Haven, Conn.: Yale University Press, 2005.

Javier Herrero, *Who was Dulcinea?* New Orleans, La.: The Graduate School of Tulane University, 1985.

David Quint, *Cervantes's Novel of Modern Times: A New Reading of Don Quijote.* Princeton: Princeton University Press, 2003.

E. C. Riley, *Cervantes's Theory of the Novel.* Oxford: Oxford University Press, 1962.

P. E. Russell, *Cervantes.* Oxford: Oxford University Press, 1985.

Journals

Anales cervantinos (Madrid).

Cervantes (Bulletin of the Cervantes Society of America).

Index